Landmarks in the Law

'To every subject in this land, no matter how powerful, I would use Thomas Fuller's words over 300 years ago: "Be you never so high, the law is above you." '

By Lord Denning MR in *Gouriet v Union of Post Office Workers* [1977] 1 QB 729, 761–762.

Landmarks in the Law

by the Rt Hon
LORD DENNING

London
BUTTERWORTHS
1984

Members of the LexisNexis Group worldwide

United Kingdom	LexisNexis UK, a Division of Reed Elsevier (UK) Ltd, Halsbury House,35 Chancery Lane, LONDON WC2A 1EL and 4 Hill Street, EDINBURGH EH2 3JZ
Argentina	LexisNexis Argentina, BUENOS AIRES
Australia	LexisNexis Butterworths, CHATSWOOD, New South Wales
Austria	LexisNexis Verlag ARD Orac GmbH & Co KG, VIENNA
Canada	LexisNexis Butterworths, MARKHAM, Ontario
Chile	LexisNexis Chile Ltda, SANTIAGO DE CHILE
Czech Republic	Nakladatelství Orac sro, PRAGUE
France	Editions du Juris-Classeur SA, PARIS
Germany	LexisNexis Deutschland GmbH, FRANKFURT, MÜNSTER
Hong Kong	LexisNexis Butterworths, HONG KONG
Hungary	HVG-Orac, BUDAPEST
India	LexisNexis Butterworths, NEW DELHI
Ireland	LexisNexis, DUBLIN
Italy	Giuffrè Editore, MILAN
Malaysia	Malayan Law Journal Sdn Bhd, KUALA LUMPUR
New Zealand	LexisNexis Butterworths, WELLINGTON
Poland	Wydawnictwo Prawnicze LexisNexis, WARSAW
Singapore	LexisNexis Butterworths, SINGAPORE
South Africa	LexisNexis Butterworths, DURBAN
Switzerland	Stämpfli Verlag AG, BERNE
USA	LexisNexis, DAYTON, Ohio

© The Rt Hon Lord Denning 1984
Reprinted 2004

A CIP Catalogue record for this book is available from the British Library.

ISBN: 0 406 17614 0

Printed and bound in Great Britain by Antony Rowe Ltd, Chippenham, Wiltshire

Visit LexisNexis UK at www.lexisnexis.co.uk

Preface

Last year I wrote *The Closing Chapter*. I so called it because it was the closing chapter of my judicial life. But it was not the end of my activities. Since my retirement I have done lots of things. My appearances on television have been so frequent that taxi-drivers and passers-by recognise me. They greet me with a friendly word.

Yet I wanted to do more. I wanted to write just one more book. But what about? I would have liked to write a play. But I could not think of a plot. I dallied with a novel. But I could not invent the characters or situations. I prefer fact to fiction. So I turned to the law again.

But what part of the law? No textbooks for me. No treatises on jurisprudence. I was never any good at things of that kind. In the end I decided to tell of some of those great cases of the past which have gone to make our constitution. They are cases of which students of history and of law ought to know much but of which they know little or nothing. At most they have only a nodding acquaintance. They are cases, too, which are full of interest for others. They portray dramatic situations. The characters are real. The scenes are true. The prose is good. The decisions have had lasting consequences. To make them more colourful, I have added sketches and stories of varied kinds.

It is in a way an anthology – a hotchpotch – in which you can dip at will. You can pick it up and read a chapter or two in the train or before you go to sleep: and then put it down. It is not a connected story with a central theme. It is a series of disconnected stories on disconnected themes. Just put together in one volume in the hope that you may be interested.

What should it be called? I tried it out on the family. At last I came to *Landmarks in the Law*. That expresses it neatly.

In old England a landmark was a stone set up to mark the boundary of a man's land. It was used by the translators of the Bible when they recorded the curses in the book of *Deuteronomy* (chap 27 v 17):

Cursed be he that removeth his neighbour's landmark. And all the people shall say, Amen.

At sea the sailors set their course by landmarks – such as the Boston Stump off the coast of Lincolnshire or Chanctonbury Ring up the Channel.

So here these stories tell you of landmarks in the law. They are like stones which mark the boundaries of principles. They are like lighthouses from which our forefathers have taken their bearings. They have set the course of the law for future generations. That is why I have collected them for you.

Some of the stories are of cases long past. Some are of cases very recent. I have tried to keep them up to date, right up to the middle of August 1984. That is even after writing the Epilogue. The law never stands still. It goes on apace. You have to run fast to keep up with it. I hope you will manage it.

Denning

August 1984

Contents

Contents

Part Three   The Chancellor's Foot

Contents

Contents

Table of cases

Part One

High Treason

Introduction

High treason is still punishable by death. It is the only offence now left which is so punishable. If a man is convicted and found guilty, the judge has no option. He must sentence the man to be hanged by the neck until he is dead. It is therefore the most heinous offence known to English law.

It is not governed by any modern statute. It is governed only by a statute passed over 600 years ago in the year 1351. The Parliament Roll is in Norman French. It is that language which has to be interpreted by our judges. But there is an authorised translation into English. You can find it set out (page 21) in the account of the trial of Roger Casement.[1]

I will tell the story of three men who were executed for it: Sir Walter Ralegh, Sir Roger Casement and William Joyce.

---

[1] *R v Casement* [1917] 1 KB 98, 98-99.

1 The trial of Ralegh

1 Sir Walter Ralegh himself

i *A constitutional landmark*

Very few lawyers know anything about the trial of Sir
Walter Ralegh. Yet they should do. No trial has ever been
marked by so much unfairness. *The Dictionary of National
Biography* tells us:

> The trial is a landmark in English constitutional history. The harsh
> principles then in repute among lawyers were enunciated by the judges
> with unprecedented distinctness, and as a consequence a reaction steadily
> set in from that moment in favour of the rights of individuals against the
> state (Gardiner, i. 138).

ii *His new plush cloak*

But before I tell of the trial itself, I would tell you something
of the ventures of this remarkable man. He was born in
Devon and retained a broad Devon accent all his life. There is
a charming painting by Sir John Millais of 'The Boyhood of
Ralegh'. It shows him sitting on the seashore at Budleigh
Salterton, listening to a sunburnt sailor who is telling of his
adventures.

He was handsome, with dark eyes and bright complexion,
full of life, always dressed in fine clothes. As a young man he
was sent with a message to the Queen at Greenwich. He took
off his new plush cloak and spread it on a muddy road for the
Queen to walk on. That brought him with a sudden bound

into the royal favour. She showered appointments and gifts upon him. He responded by being the courtier *par excellence*.

iii *The maid of honour*

He fell into disfavour, however, by falling in love with one of her maids of honour, Elizabeth Throgmorton. He seduced her and they were both sent to the Tower. John Aubrey tells a naughty and untrue story but tells it so prettily that I cannot help repeating it:

He loved a wench well; and one time getting one of the Maids of Honour up against a tree in a wood ('twas his first lady) who seemed at first boarding to be something fearful of her honour, and modest, she cried, 'Sweet Sir Walter, what do you me ask? Will you undo me? Nay, sweet Sir Walter! Sweet Sir Walter! Sir Walter!' At last, as the danger and the pleasure at the same time grew higher, she cried in the ecstasy, 'Swisser Swatter, Swisser Swatter!' She proved with child, and I doubt not but this hero took care of them both, as also that the product was more than an ordinary mortal.[1]

Sir Walter redeemed his character, however, by marrying the lady and they lived in true love ever after, though with many griefs and sorrows. The 'product' was a son who was said by Ben Jonson to be 'knavishly inclined'.

iv '*The little* Revenge'

Sir Walter wrote prose of quality. This is shown by his *Report of the Fight about the Isle of Azores betwixt the Revenge and an Armada of the King of Spain*.[2] It was put into verse by Tennyson in his ballad of *The Revenge*.

All the powder of the *Revenge* to the last barrel was now spent, all her pikes broken, forty of her best men slain, and the most part of the rest hurt. In the beginning of the fight she had but one hundred free from sickness, and fourscore and ten sick, laid in hold upon the ballast. A small troop to man such a ship, and a weak garrison to resist so mighty an army. By those hundred all was sustained, the volleys, boardings, and enterings of fifteen ships of war, besides those which beat her at large. . . . Sir Richard finding himself in this distress, and unable any

[1] *Oxford Book of Literary Anecdotes*, No. 10.
[2] *Oxford Book of English Prose*, No. 87.

5

longer to make resistance . . . commanded the master Gunner, whom he knew to be a most resolute man, to split and sink the ship; that thereby nothing might remain of glory or victory to the Spaniards. . . .

Tennyson gives the finishing touch:

> And the little *Revenge* herself went down by the island crags
> To be lost evermore in the main.

v '*Come live with me*'

As a poet, Sir Walter was one of the galaxy of his age. When Christopher Marlowe write the lines of *The Passionate Shepherd to His Love*:

> Come live with me and be my Love,
> And we will all the pleasures prove
> That hills and valleys, dales and fields,
> Or woods or steepy mountain yields. . . .

Sir Walter Ralegh wrote *Her Reply*:

> If all the world and love were young,
> And truth in every shepherd's tongue,
> These pretty pleasures might me move
> To live with thee and be thy Love. . . .

vi *He founds Virginia*

But Sir Walter is chiefly to be remembered as an explorer. He fitted out expeditions which led to the foundation of the colony of Virginia. It was so named after Elizabeth, the Virgin Queen of England. He brought back tobacco plants and potato roots. Potatoes became and are a staple food. Smoking spread rapidly among all classes until our present time, when it is known to be a prime cause of cancer.

vii *His study in the Strand*

The Queen so favoured Ralegh that she gave him Durham House in the Strand. It is described by John Aubrey:[1]

Durham-house was a noble palace; after he came to his greatness he lived there, or in some apartment of it. I well remember his study, which was

[1] *Lives of Eminent Men.*

on a little turret, that looked into and over the Thames, and had the prospect, which is as pleasant, perhaps, as any in the world, and which not only refreshes the eie-sight, but cheers the spirits, and (to speake my mind) I believe enlarges an ingeniose man's thoughts.

viii 'He was damnably proud'

You would have thought that on all this Sir Walter was equal to the knight who rode with Chaucer to Canterbury:

> He loved chivalrye,
> Trouthe and honour, freedom and curteisye . . .
> He was a verray parfit gentil knight.[1]

But not a bit of it. Sir Walter Ralegh had many faults. He was inordinately proud and vain. John Aubrey says:

> He was a tall, handsome, and bold man; but his undoing was, that he was damnably proud.

ix A pointed rebuke

Just as he owed all to the favouritism of Queen Elizabeth the First, her death saw the end of his ascendancy. During the discussions about the succession, he was much opposed to James Stuart whom he regarded as a Scottish interloper. This was reported to James who made a pointed rebuke to Ralegh (which was pronounced Rawley). John Aubrey tells us:

> . . . At a consultation at Whitehall after Queen Elizabeth's death, how matters were to be ordered, and what ought to be donne, Sir W. R. declared his opinion, 'twas the wisest way for them to keep the government in their owne hands, and sett up a commonwealth, and not be subject to a needy naggarly nation (Scotland); it seems there were some of this caball (small consultative body) who kept not this secret, but that it came to King James's eare, who when the English Noblesse mett and received him, being told, upon their presentment to his Majesty, their names; when Sir W. R.'s name was told; 'Ralegh,' said the King, 'O my soule, mon, I have heard *rawly* of thee.'

x He is humiliated

As soon as James Stuart ascended the throne of England, he

[1] *The Canterbury Tales*, Prologue.

7

did everything he could to humiliate Ralegh. He got him evicted from Durham House. Ralegh resented this greatly. He wrote to Lord Keeper Egerton:[1]

To cast out my hay and oates into the streats at an hours warninge, and to remove my family and stuff in 14 days after, is such a severe expultion as hath not been offred to any man before this daye.

Added to this indignity, James deprived Ralegh of his office of captain of the guard and put a Scotsman in his place.

xi *He is cast into the Tower*

Everyone knew about it. What is more, rumours spread that Ralegh was plotting to remove James Stuart from the throne and replace him by Arabella Stuart, who was a direct descendant of Henry VII. She had been born in England and was therefore an Englishwoman and not Scotch. The rumours told of others who were involved in the plot. One of the principals was Lord Cobham who was a close friend of Ralegh.

These rumours so affected King James that Ralegh and Cobham were both arrested and taken to the Tower. Each was interrogated by the Lords of the Council. Their statements were taken down in writing. No torture was used but they were hard pressed. Cobham in his statement made a confession of his own guilt: but he said that it was Ralegh who instigated it and was the prime mover. Ralegh made no confession: he asserted his own innocence: but said that he knew that Cobham was going to see a Spanish agent.

2 The trial itself

i *The Great Hall at Winchester*

The best account of the trial of Sir Walter Ralegh is to be found in *Criminal Trials* written by David Jardine in 1832. In the autumn of 1603 a plague was raging with great violence

[1] Bowen *The Lion and the Throne*, p 159.

in London. So the trial was held at Winchester in the Great Hall of the Castle. The King was at Wilton, near Salisbury. The trial was held by a special commission of oyer and terminer. It was an impressive sight. On the bench there were the commissioners, six noblemen and four judges. In the jury-box there were twelve jurors of Middlesex, four knights and eight others. They had been selected by the Sheriff as being men 'who could be depended upon'. In modern words, it was a packed jury. The Attorney-General, Sir Edward Coke, led for the prosecution. Sir Walter appeared in person. He was not allowed counsel to speak for him. The indictment charged Sir Walter Ralegh with treason. The overt acts alleged were that on 9 June 1603 Sir Walter Ralegh had conferred with Lord Cobham about advancing Arabella Stuart to the Crown of England and dispossessing the King; and that it was then arranged that Lord Cobham should go to the King of Spain and the Archduke of Austria to obtain 600,000 crowns for the purpose of supporting Arabella's title.

To this indictment Sir Walter Ralegh pleaded not guilty and put himself upon the country.

ii *Coke opens the case*

Sir Edward Coke opened the case. He relied on Cobham's confession and emphasised that it was obtained, '*not rigorously, because no torture hath been used*'. When Sir Walter courteously interrupted him, Sir Edward said:

I will prove you to be the most notorious traitor that ever came to the bar. . . . Thou art a monster; thou hast an English face, but a Spanish heart.'

When Sir Walter said:

If my Lord Cobham be a traitor, what is that to me?

Sir Edward Coke said:

All that he did was by thy instigation, thou viper, for I *thou* thee, thou traitor! I will prove thee the rankest traitor in all England.

iii *Cobham accuses Sir Walter*

After these exchanges, the Clerk of the Crown read out the statement made by Lord Cobham at his examinations by the Lords of the Council. It contained a confession of his own guilt but throwing the blame on Ralegh. First, Cobham said that he had conferred with the Count Aremberg about procuring 500,000 or 600,000 crowns from the King of Spain and that the money was to be handed to Sir Walter for distribution to those that were discontented in England. He said that he would never have entered into these conversations but by Ralegh's instigation and that he (Ralegh) would never let him (Cobham) alone. Here Sir Edward called the Clerk of the Crown to read these last words again: 'He would never let him alone.'

iv *'Lady Arabella doth protest'*

At one point Lord Nottingham, being in court with the Lady Arabella, said:

The Lady doth here protest, upon her salvation, that she never dealt in any of these things; and so she willed me to tell the Court.

Apart from Cobham's confession, there was no evidence to implicate Ralegh. Sir Walter admitted his meetings with Cobham and some of the things that were said: but he gave good explanations. He behaved with a calm dignity. He made an eloquent speech. Very much in contrast to the Attorney-General.

v *A letter in an apple*

The climax came towards the end of the trial. Four days before leaving the Tower for Winchester, Sir Walter Ralegh wrote a letter to Lord Cobham, put it in an apple, and got it thrown up to the chamber-window of Lord Cobham. In it, he asked Cobham to write a letter exonerating him (Ralegh). Cobham did so. He wrote this letter and sent it to Ralegh:

vi *Cobham clears Sir Walter*

Now that the arraignment draws near, not knowing which should be first, I or you, to clear my conscience, satisfy the world with truth, and free myself from the cry of blood, I protest upon my soul and before God and his angels, I never had conference with you in any treason, nor was ever moved by you to the things I heretofore accused you of; and for any thing I know, you are as innocent and as clear from any treasons against the King as is any subject living. Therefore I wash my hands, and pronounce with Daniel, *Purus sum à sanguine hujus;*[1] and God so deal with me and have mercy on my soul, as this is true!

vii *Coke's trump card*

That letter bears the stamp of truth. But afterwards at Winchester, the day before the trial, Cobham wrote in his own hand a letter withdrawing that letter to Ralegh and accusing him of treason once again. As I briefly told you in *What Next in the Law*, at the last moment of the trial Coke produced it. It was his trump card. Sir Edward Coke had it in his hand.

Attorney-General   Thou art the most vile and execrable traitor that ever lived.

Sir Walter Ralegh   You speak indiscreetly, uncivilly, and barbarously.

Attorney-General   Thou art an odious fellow; thy name is hateful to all the realm of England for thy pride.

Sir Walter Ralegh   It will go near to prove a measuring cast between you and me, Mr Attorney.

Attorney-General   Well, I will now lay you open for the greatest traitor that ever was.

Then, waving the letter in his hand, he said:

See, my Lords, what it hath pleased God to work in the heart of my Lord Cobham, even since his coming hither to Winchester; he could not sleep quietly till he had revealed the truth to the Lords, and therefore voluntarily wrote the whole matter to them, with his own hand, but yesterday.

---

[1] Cobham made a mistake. The correct quotation is from *St Matthew* 27:24 saying that Pilate 'washed his hands before the multitude, saying, "I am innocent of the blood of this just person: see ye to it." '

viii *Cobham's final confession*

He read the letter in full. In it, Cobham repeated his original
confession accusing Ralegh (adding more about a pension of
£1,500 from Spain) and craving pardon for his 'double
dealing.' The reporter tells us that this confession of the Lord
Cobham seemed to give great satisfaction, and cleared all the
former evidence, which stood very doubtful.

It turned the scale. Was any inducement held out to
Cobham to make him write it? We shall never know. The
Chief Justice asked two of the Commissioners. They said:
'Not to our knowledge.' But Sir Walter Ralegh suggested
that Cobham had done it so as to save his own life.

During the trial, Ralegh had repeatedly asked for
Cobham to be called in person to give evidence, so as to
confront him. But this request was denied. His confession
was taken as true by Sir Edward Coke. He had played his
trump card and won the rubber.

ix *Guilty of treason*

The jury went out. They stayed not a quarter of an hour,
when they returned, bringing in their verdict of Guilty of
Treason.

The Lord Chief Justice then delivered the judgment of the
court in the usual form in cases of high treason.

3 Execution delayed

i *A moving letter*

After the trial, Sir Walter Ralegh wrote a moving letter to
his wife, which runs:

You shall now receive, my dear wife, my last words in these my last
lines. My love I send you, that you may keep it when I am dead,
and my counsel that you may remember it when I am no more . . .

My dear wife, farewell! Bless my poor boy; pray for me and let
my good God hold you both in his arms! Written with the dying
hand of sometime thy husband, but now, alas! overthrown.

Walter Ralegh

ii *His life is spared*

But Ralegh was not executed at that time. The King spared his life. He was committed to the Tower, there to remain during pleasure. He was well treated. He had apartments in the upper storey of the Bloody Tower where he had his wife and son with him, and their personal attendants. He had the use of a garden. The young Prince Henry was most friendly and visited him there. He wrote a *History of the World* and did experiments in chemistry.

iii *Adventure to Guiana*

After 13 years there, he proposed to the King that he should equip an adventure to Guiana to explore for gold. A commission was issued by the King, authorising the expedition. His proposal was accepted. He went there. His elder son (of whom I have told you) was killed in battle. He wrote a griefful letter to his wife:[1]

I was loth to write, because I know not how to comfort you; And God knows I never knew what sorrow meant till now . . . You shall hear from me if I live, from new Found Land, where I mean to Clean my ship and revictual, for I have Tobacco enough to pay for it. The Lord bless you and Comfort you, that you may bear patiently the death of your most valiant son.

Your Wal. Ralegh

March the 22th from the Isle of St Christophers

iv *Execution ordered*

His expedition was a failure. On his return home to Plymouth the Spanish ambassador demanded his blood. The King complied. He required the judges to proceed to execution against Ralegh on his sentence in November 1603. Ralegh claimed that he had been discharged from the judgment by the commission to go overseas. The judges decided against him. They held that the death sentence of 1603 was still in force. In 1618 they granted execution.

[1] *Oxford Book of English Prose*, No. 89.

4 Death on the scaffold

i *'I will now take my leave'*

On 29 October 1618 he was executed. The event is described in a striking passage of English prose:

Upon Thursday, the 29th of October, 1618, Sir Walter Ralegh was conveyed by the Sheriffs of London to a scaffold, in Old Palace Yard, at Westminster, about eight in the morning . . . When Sir Walter came upon the scaffold, he saluted, with a cheerful countenance, the Lords, Knights, and Gentlemen who were there present. . . .

Then a proclamation being made that all men should depart the scaffold, he prepared himself for death, giving away his hat, his cap, with some money, to such as he knew that stood near him. And then taking his leave . . .: 'I will now take my leave; for I have a long journey to go, and an assured hope to be quickly there.' And then putting off his doublet and gown, desired the executioner to show him the axe; which not being suddenly granted unto him, he said, 'I prithee let me see it; dost thou think that I am afraid of it?' So it being given unto him, he poised it in his hand, and felt along upon the edge of it with his thumb, to see if it was keen; and smiling, spake unto Mr Sheriff, saying, 'This is a sharp medicine, but it will cure all diseases.' And then he kneeled down to prayer, and entreated the people to pray for him. After that, he called for the executioner, who, kneeling down and asking his forgiveness, he laid both hands upon his shoulders, and said he heartily forgave him. And there being some dispute that his face should be towards the east, he made answer and said, 'So the heart be straight, it is no matter which way the head lieth.' As he was laying his head on the block, the executioner would have blindfolded him; upon which he rebuked him, saying, 'Think you I fear the shadow of the axe, when I fear not the axe itself?' He gave the headman a sign when he should strike, by lifting up his hands; and the executioner struck off his head at two blows, his body never shrinking nor moving. His head was showed on each side of the scaffold, and then put into a red leather bag, and his wrought velvet gown thrown over it, which was afterwards conveyed away in a mourning coach of his Lady's. The body was interred in the chancel, near the altar, of St Margaret, Westminster.

ii *A travesty of justice*

According to the law of evidence, as we know it, the trial of Sir Walter Ralegh was outrageous. It was a travesty of justice. The conduct of the Attorney-General, Sir Edward Coke, was monstrous. Every bit of the evidence against Ralegh was inadmissible. It was all hearsay, rumour and conjecture. Much of it was the evidence of a self-confessed accomplice. It was not corroborated in any respect. None of it was taken in the presence of Ralegh. It was all done in his absence. He had no opportunity of cross-examining or seeing any of the witnesses. His request that Cobham be brought to confront him was refused. One of the judges said afterwards that 'the justice of England has never been so degraded and injured as by the condemnation of Sir Walter Ralegh.' If he had been given a fair trial, he should have been found Not Guilty.

It was a monstrous injustice, too, that after 15 years the judges should have granted execution of the death sentence. He had a commission from the King to go and explore for gold in South America. He was set free to do it. That was as complete a pardon as any formal document.

iii *But he was guilty*

But notwithstanding all this, there is the outstanding question: Did Sir Walter Ralegh engage in a plot to overthrow James Stuart as King of England? There is, to my mind, every likelihood of it. James Stuart was a bad king, one of the worst we have ever had. In the first few weeks of his reign, he had humiliated Ralegh beyond endurance. It would have been much better for England if he had been replaced by Arabella Stuart – a lady who would rule with the aid of a Council of State – and not by the divine right of kings. Ralegh had the brains to devise a scheme to that end. He probably did, and used Cobham as the tool to execute it. The conclusion by David Jardine is that it 'is exactly what might have been expected from a man of his character, and is precisely the conclusion which was generally drawn by contemporaries from the intimacy which subsisted between them.'

15

5 Legal points

i *The conduct of counsel for the prosecution*

There was universal condemnation of the conduct of Sir
Edward Coke, the Attorney-General. Those present were so
taken aback that they wrote down his very words. There was
such a revulsion to it that there has grown up a great
tradition that counsel for the prosecution must be frank in
his presentation of the case and, above all, he should be fair to
the accused. He must not stress the case against him. He must
only tell the jury the facts which he hopes to prove by
evidence. He must not say anything which he cannot prove.
He must call any credible witness who can give material
evidence, no matter whether for the prosecution or the
defence: or at any rate he must give his name to the defence
so that the defence can call him.[1]

ii *Confessions*

In Ralegh's time, confessions were extracted by all sorts of
means: torture by the rack, or threats of it, was commonplace. Guy Fawkes was put on the rack. So was Edmund
Peacham. Other means were used also: such as no food day
after day, and so forth.

Ralegh's case exposed the evil. Fifty years later under the
beneficial influence of Sir Matthew Hale the law was
transformed. All confessions were excluded unless they were
shown to have been made *voluntarily* by the accused. In 1914
this principle was affirmed by Lord Sumner in the classic case
of *Ibrahim v R:*[2]

It has long been established as a positive rule of English criminal law, that
no statement by an accused is admissible in evidence against him unless it
is shewn by the prosecution to have been a voluntary statement, in the
sense that it has not been obtained from him either by fear of prejudice or
hope of advantage exercised or held out by a person in authority. The
principle is as old as Lord Hale.

But that principle has since been found to be inadequate.

[1] *Dallison v Caffery* [1965] 1 QB 348, 369.
[2] [1914] AC 599, 609.

16

So in 1972 the Criminal Law Revision Committee suggested a change.[1] Instead of asking whether a confession was *voluntary*, the court should ask whether it was *reliable*. There are many circumstances which might make it unreliable. Such as oppression by keeping a man for long hours in close confinement and harassing him with many questions. The change is given effect in the Police and Criminal Evidence Bill now going through Parliament. It says that a confession is to be excluded if it was or may have been obtained

(a) by *oppression* of the person who made it: or
(b) in consequence of anything said or done which was likely, in the circumstances existing at the time, to render *unreliable* any confession which might be made by him in consequence thereof.

iii *Evidence unlawfully obtained*

It sometimes happens that the police extort a confession unlawfully, but nevertheless get most valuable evidence from it. Thus under improper questioning, a murderer may describe the place where he buried the corpse. The police find the body there. Can they give that fact in evidence? Take another case. The police wish to search a house for drugs. They know they should get a search warrant, but there is no magistrate available for 24 hours. So – without a warrant – they search the house and find large quantities of drugs. Can they give that fact in evidence?

In England it has long been held that the police can give evidence of their finding of the corpse or the drugs, without reference to the unlawfulness which preceded it, see *R v Sang*.[2] In the United States, until recently it was held that the police could not give evidence of any fact that was unlawfully obtained. It was the 'fruit of the poisonous tree' and fell with the tree itself. But all is now changed. The Chief Justice of the United States, Warren Burger, was over here this July. He told me of dramatic developments in the Supreme Court a few weeks earlier. They have held, in the cases I have put, that the police can give evidence of the

[1] Cmnd 4991, para 65.
[2] [1980] AC 402.

finding of the corpse and the drugs, see *Nix v Williams*[1] and *Segura v United States*.[2]

The matter was debated in the House of Lords in the course of the Police and Criminal Evidence Bill. By an amendment moved by Lord Scarman, if evidence is improperly obtained it is to be excluded unless the judge is satisfied that the public interest requires it to be given. But I would keep to the common law.

iv *Against whom*

In Ralegh's time, confessions were not only admissible against the person who made them (Cobham) but also against other persons who were not present and had no opportunity of contradicting them or cross-examining (Ralegh). Now, of course, they are not admissible against other persons.

v *Examination before trial*

In Ralegh's time, it was common practice for witnesses to be examined before trial and their statements taken down in writing. They were not called at the trial. Their statements were read. There was no opportunity for the accused to see them or to cross-examine them.

Nowadays, there is a preliminary examination at which depositions are taken. Each witness gives his evidence before the magistrates. This is in the presence of the accused who is entitled to cross-examine. It is taken down in writing and transmitted to the court of trial. It is not itself admissible in evidence except in cases within section 1 of the Criminal Justice Act 1967. This is a useful procedure which saves the attendance of witnesses on points which are not in controversy – these written statements are admissible without the witnesses attending. It saves a lot of time and money.

vi *Conclusion*

All these modern rules of evidence have come into being since the trial of Walter Ralegh. The abuses there evident were a powerful factor in making the changes.

[1] Decided 11 June 1984, not yet reported.   [2] Decided 5 July 1984, not yet reported.

2 The trial of Casement

Introduction

The trial of Sir Roger Casement took place in 1917 during the First World War. It raised a new point. The guilty act had been committed – not in England – but by Casement in Germany. Was that High Treason?

1 Sir Roger Casement himself

i *He is knighted*

Roger Casement was born in County Dublin in Ireland in 1864. It was then part of the United Kingdom. So he was British. He was brought up by his uncle, an Ulster Protestant. He never married. He was, it is said, a homosexual. He entered the British Consular Service and served all over the world. He made expeditions after the fashion of Sir Walter Ralegh. He revealed atrocious cruelty in the Congo and in Peru. The white traders treated native labour abominably. Casement's reports made him famous. He was knighted for his services in 1911. In 1912 he retired to Ireland.

ii *He goes to Germany*

He was always a strong Irish nationalist. So strong that at the outbreak of war in 1914 he thought he could obtain help from Germany to secure Irish independence. He went from

Ireland to the United States and from there to Germany. He then visited the camps where there were British prisoners of war.

iii *The Irish Brigade*

He tried to form an Irish Brigade. He issued leaflets to the Irish prisoners in these words:[1]

IRISHMEN! Here is a chance for you to fight for Ireland! You have fought for England, your country's hereditary enemy. You have fought for Belgium in England's interest, though it was no more to you than the Fiji Islands! Are you willing to fight FOR YOUR OWN COUNTRY with a view to securing the national freedom of Ireland?

With the moral and material assistance of the German Government an IRISH BRIGADE is being formed. The object of the Irish Brigade shall be to fight solely for THE CAUSE OF IRELAND and under NO CIRCUMSTANCES shall it be directed to any GERMAN end. The Irish Brigade shall be formed and shall fight under the Irish flag alone. The men shall wear a special distinctively Irish uniform, and have Irish officers. The Irish Brigade shall be clothed, fed, and efficiently equipped with arms and ammunition by the German Government. It will be stationed near Berlin and be treated as guests of the German Government. At the end of the war the German Government undertakes to send each member of the brigade who may so desire it to the United States of America with necessary means to land. . . .

iv *Its failure*

By that leaflet he managed to get about 50 Irish prisoners to join him. They forsook their allegiance, and joined the armed forces of Germany: but most of the Irish prisoners rejected his proposals indignantly. So his attempt failed.

v *He is captured*

In 1916 there was an Easter rising in Ireland. Casement persuaded the Germans to get him over to Ireland to join the rebels. They took him in a submarine, accompanied by a surface ship loaded with arms. Our ships captured her and seized the arms. The submarine landed Casement in County

[1] *R v Casement* [1917] 1 KB 98, 100.

Kerry. He was captured. He was taken to London. He was indicted for High Treason.

2 The trial itself

i *Trial at bar*

The trial was a 'trial at bar.' That was the practice in former times when the case was of exceptional importance. It meant that the trial was by three judges of the King's Bench and a jury. (Such was the trial in the *Tichborne case.*[1]) The facts in *Casement's case* were hardly in dispute. The argument was on the law.

ii *Words in Norman French*

It depended on a few words in the Treason Act 1351. They were in Norman French.

The words are these: may commit treason by levying war against the King, and so on, 'Ou soit aherdant as enemys nre Seign[r] le Roi en le Roialme donant a eux eid ou confort en son Roialme ou par aillours,' and that has been translated 'or be adherent to the King's enemies in his realm, giving to them aid and comfort in the realm, or elsewhere.'[2]

iii *The learned Serjeant*

The case for Casement was argued by Serjeant Sullivan, a member of the Irish Bar and the English Bar. I remember him well. He was a most eloquent, learned and able advocate, very well liked by Bench and Bar. He had a remarkable memory. His clerk used to come into court, place the brief, tied up with red tape, on the front row. Serjeant Sullivan would not trouble to untie the tape. He knew the facts so well that he would tell them to the court without untying the tape. It was, of course, a piece of showmanship. But it was very effective.

[1] *R v Orton alias Castro* (1873) (not reported).
[2] *R v Casement* [1917] 1 KB 98, 134.

iv *His argument*

His argument for Casement won him high praise from the
Court of King's Bench and the Court of Criminal Appeal.
He submitted that

> . . . this statute had neither created nor declared that it was an offence to
> be adherent to the King's enemies beyond the realm of the King, and that
> the words meant that the giving of aid and comfort *par aillours* – that is
> outside the realm – did not constitute a treason which could be tried in
> this country unless the person who gave the aid and comfort outside the
> realm – in this case within the Empire of Germany – was himself within
> the realm at the time he gave the aid and comfort. This argument was
> founded upon the difficulties which must arise owing to the doctrine of
> venue, that people were only triable within certain districts where the
> venue could be laid.[1]

v *Found Guilty and hanged*

The Serjeant argued with much skill and learning. But the
Court decided against him. Casement was found Guilty.
The Lord Chief Justice pronounced sentence of death.

Strong efforts were made for a reprieve but these failed.
On 3 August 1916 Casement was hanged at Pentonville
prison. Nearly 50 years later his remains were returned to
Ireland and given a state funeral.

vi *His diaries*

In July 1959 his diaries were made available for inspection by
scholars at the Public Record Office. They contained
detailed descriptions of homosexual practices in Casement's
handwriting. I do not suppose the jury were influenced by
them. His guilt was plain to an English jury.

---

[1] Ibid at 135.

3 The trial of Joyce

Introduction

The trial of William Joyce took place in 1945 after the end of the Second World War. It raised another new point. He was an American citizen. As such he owed no allegiance to the King. But he held a British passport. Could he be convicted of High Treason?

1 William Joyce himself

i *His affected voice*

In 1939 Joyce's voice became familiar to hundreds of thousands in England. It was known as the voice of 'Lord Haw-Haw,' because of his affected style. He broadcasted propaganda for the enemy. He did it in educated English and sought to frighten us. It did not do so. We just thought he was a foul traitor.

ii *An American citizen*

He was born in the United States of America in 1906. So he was an American citizen. When he was three years of age, his parents brought him, with the rest of their family, to Ireland. When he was 15, they all came to England and made their home here. In 1933, at age 27, he applied for a British passport for a holiday in France and Switzerland. In his application he described himself as a British subject. It was granted for five years. In September 1938, when he was 32, he applied for renewal for a year. In it he declared that he was a British subject and had not lost that national status. It was granted.

iii *War – His passport renewed*

The war, you will remember, started on 3 September 1939. The week before, on 24 August 1939, William Joyce applied for his passport to be renewed for a further year. It was granted – till 1 July 1940. As soon as he got it he left his home: his parents, his brothers and his sister remaining in England.

iv *He broadcasts for Germany*

He went to Germany. When he arrived there he entered into an agreement with the German radio company of Berlin as an announcer of English news. Between 3 September 1939 and 10 December 1939[1] he broadcasted propaganda on behalf of the enemy. All this must have been pre-arranged before he left England.

2 The trial itself

i *The charge*

In 1945, when we had won the war, he was arrested in Germany and brought back to England. He was charged in these words, which I take from the report in *Joyce v DPP:*[2]

Statement of offence

High Treason by adhering to the King's enemies elsewhere than in the King's Realm, to wit, in the German Realm, contrary to the Treason Act, 1351.

Particulars of offence

William Joyce, on September 18, 1939, and on divers other days thereafter and between that day and July 2, 1940, being then – to wit on

---

[1] The dates in the charge quoted below are different.
[2] [1946] AC 347, 348.

the several days – a person owing allegiance to our Lord the King, and whilst on the said several days an open and public war was being prosecuted and carried on by the German Realm and its subjects against our Lord the King and his subjects, then and on the said several days traitorously contriving and intending to aid and assist the said enemies of our Lord the King against our Lord the King and his subjects did traitorously adhere to and aid and comfort the said enemies in parts beyond the seas without the Realm of England, to wit, in the Realm of Germany by broadcasting to the subjects of our Lord the King propaganda on behalf of the said enemies of our Lord the King.

ii *Found Guilty and sentenced*

He was tried by Mr Justice Tucker and a jury at the Old Bailey. The crucial point was whether William Joyce was 'a person owing allegiance to our Lord the King.' The judge directed the jury that he was. He was found Guilty and sentenced to death.

He appealed to the Court of Appeal, who dismissed his appeal, but certified it as a point of exceptional public importance. He appealed to the House of Lords, who dismissed it by a majority of four to one.

iii *Did he owe allegiance?*

It was conceded on all hands that a man cannot be guilty of treason unless he owes allegiance to the King. The argument for William Joyce was that he was an alien: and that, although he owed allegiance whilst he was resident in England, he did not owe any allegiance when he left and went to Germany.

iv *The effect of his British passport*

To this argument the House held that his possession of a British passport made all the difference. Lord Jowitt LC said:[1]

By its terms it requests and requires in the name of His Majesty all those whom it may concern to allow the bearer to pass freely without let or

[1] Ibid at 369–370.

hindrance and to afford him every assistance and protection of which he may stand in need. It is, I think, true that the possession of a passport by a British subject does not increase the sovereign's duty of protection, though it will make his path easier. For him it serves as a voucher and means of identification. But the possession of a passport by one who is not a British subject gives him rights and imposes upon the sovereign obligations which would otherwise not be given or imposed. It is immaterial that he has obtained it by misrepresentation and that he is not in law a British subject. By the possession of that document he is enabled to obtain in a foreign country the protection extended to British subjects. By his own act he has maintained the bond which while he was within the realm bound him to his sovereign.

v *Can he withdraw allegiance?*

The Lord Chancellor acknowledged that there was nothing to prevent the alien from withdrawing from his allegiance when he left the realm. But in this case there was nothing to show that he had withdrawn it, at any rate by the time he started broadcasting in September 1939. So he was under a duty of allegiance to the King at the time he broadcasted for the enemy. Three other Law Lords agreed.

vi *A dissenting opinion*

Lord Porter dissented. He thought that Joyce might have used the passport to gain admittance to Germany but then discarded it as of no further use to him. Then he would have withdrawn his allegiance. And that point had not been left to the jury.

On 18 December 1945 the House dismissed his appeal.

So the sentence of death stood. He was hanged at Wandsworth prison on 3 January 1946.

4 Capital punishment

Times out of number, I have been asked: What do you think about capital punishment?

i *The Royal Commission*

In 1953 I gave evidence before the Royal Commission. In their Report they quoted my view:

As Lord Justice Denning put it:
'The punishment inflicted for grave crimes should adequately reflect the revulsion felt by the great majority of citizens for them. It is a mistake to consider the objects of punishment as being deterrent or reformative or preventive and nothing else ... The ultimate justification of any punishment is not that it is a deterrent, but that it is the emphatic denunciation by the community of a crime: and from this point of view, there are some murders which, in the present state of public opinion, demand the most emphatic denunciation of all, namely the death penalty.'
The Archbishop of Canterbury, while expressing no opinion about the ethics of capital punishment, agreed with Lord Justice Denning's view about the ultimate justification of any punishment.

ii *A rhetorical question*

After the debates in Parliament I altered my view. I asked the rhetorical question: Is it right for us, as a society, to do a thing – hang a man – which none of us individually would be prepared to do or even to witness? The answer is 'No, not in a civilised society.'

iii *An instinctive feeling*

Yet even today when I read of 'murders most foul,' I feel
instinctively, like many of my countrymen, 'They ought to
be hanged.'

Seeing that capital punishment has been abolished for
murder, some may suggest that it be abolished for High
Treason. Take the bombs which were planted in
Birmingham and Regent's Park and outside Harrods. Some
of them were planted by terrorists from Northern Ireland
who owed allegiance to the Queen. In Northern Ireland
terrorists deliberately shoot to kill the soldiers of the Queen.
Are they not waging war against the Queen in her realm?
Are they not guilty of High Treason? Yet none of them has
been been charged with it. They have only been charged
with murder. This is probably sufficient to meet the case.
The death penalty has not been abolished in Northern
Ireland but I believe it has not actually been carried out. If it
were, it might lead the terrorists to retort by further killings.

Part Two

Torture and Bribery

Introduction

Torture and bribery are, I hope, extinct in England today. But they are still alive and active in some parts of the world. So let me tell you about them.

Torture and bribery were once regarded as normal practice in England. Torture was used so as to get a man to confess his guilt. Also to make him give the names of his confederates. Bribery was used so as to influence a judge to decide in favour of the briber. Thomas Wolsey and Thomas More were accused of it, but it was not proved. Francis Bacon was accused of it and found Guilty.

1 Bacon's use of torture

1 Francis Bacon himself

i *His feet of clay*

Francis Bacon was a character like the one portrayed by Robert Louis Stevenson in *The Strange Case of Dr Jekyll and Mr Hyde*. Jekyll is the one who 'would do good.' Hyde is the 'evil that is present.'

So with Francis Bacon. He had an intellect of the first quality. He had superb command of language. He laid down moral principles of high worth. But he failed miserably to keep them himself. His mind was golden but he had feet of clay. His fame was broken in pieces and carried away with the wind like the image in Nebuchadnezzar's dream:

This image's head was of fine gold, his breast and his arms of silver, his belly and his thighs of brass, his legs of iron, his feet part of iron and part of clay.[1]

In the dream a stone smote the image upon the feet and brake them in pieces, bringing down the whole image. The pieces became 'like the chaff of the summer threshing floors: and the wind carried them away.'

ii *He did not pay his debts*

Francis Bacon was born in 1560 with every advantage open to him. His father was Sir Nicholas Bacon, the Lord Keeper to Queen Elizabeth I – a most accomplished statesman and

[1] *Daniel* 2:32–33 (Authorised version).

judge – whose portrait looks down on me in my library as I write these words. Francis had the best of educations. He joined Gray's Inn and became a successful barrister. Yet he did not pay his debts. He was perpetually insolvent.

He was not at all happy in his domestic affairs. He wanted to marry a wealthy widow, Lady Hatton, but was outdone by the widower, Sir Edward Coke, who married her himself. Bacon did not marry until he was aged 45. Then he married an alderman's elderly ugly daughter for money. They had no children and after 15 years they separated.

iii *His* Essays

Before I tell you of his wicked doings, I would remind you of some of the sayings in his *Essays* which have come down the centuries. He was fond of striking phrases which captured the attention of his readers. You will know them:

Essay I Of Truth

What is truth? said jesting Pilate, and would not stay for an answer . . . These winding and crooked courses are the goings of the serpent; which goeth basely upon the belly, and not upon the feet. There is no vice that doth so cover a man with shame as to be found false and perfidious.

Yet he had that vice himself!

Essay II Of Death

Men fear death as children fear to go in the dark; and as that natural fear in children is increased with tales, so is the other . . . But above all, believe it, the sweetest canticle is *Nunc dimittis*; when a man hath obtained worthy ends and expectations.

The *Nunc dimittis* says, 'Lord, now lettest thou thy servant depart in peace.' Francis Bacon departed in disgrace and misery.

Essay LVI Of Judicature

Speaking of judges, he said:

. . . Above all things, integrity is their portion and proper virtue. *Cursed* (saith the law) *is he that removeth the land-mark.* The mislayer of a meere stone is to blame. But it is the unjust judge that is the capital remover of land-marks, when he defineth amiss of lands and property. One foul sentence doth more hurt than many foul examples. For these do but corrupt the stream; the other corrupteth the fountain.

Yet Bacon himself was an unjust judge, lacking in integrity and proper virtue.

Essay L Of Studies

Studies serve for delight, for ornament, and for ability. Their chief use for delight is in privateness and retiring; for ornament, is in discourse; and for ability, is in the judgement and disposition of business . . . Some books are to be tasted, others to be swallowed, and some few to be chewed and digested.

This is all excellent. Bacon's books, in his day, were to be chewed and digested.

iv *His subservience to the King*

In the year 1614 Francis Bacon was Attorney-General, the highest law officer of the Crown. But he was a time-server and place-seeker. He would do everything he could to please the King (James I) and thereby gain advancement for himself. And as for the King, he was a Scotsman who did not understand the English. He believed in the 'divine right of kings,' that is, in the notion that kings reign by direct ordinance of God, quite apart from the will of the people. As Alexander Pope put it: 'The right divine of kings to govern wrong.'[1] James I had an extreme idea of the royal prerogative. He held that, by virtue of it, he could do what he liked: and that his conduct could not be called in question by the courts. Some of the judges supported his extended view of the prerogative. The historian, J R Green, puts it thus:

The lawyers had been subservient beyond all other classes to the Crown. In the narrow pedantry with which they bent before precedents, without admitting any distinction between precedents drawn from a time of freedom and precedents drawn from the worst times of tyranny, the judges had supported James in his claims to impose Customs duties, and even to levy benevolences.[2]

[1] *Dunciad*, iv, 188.
[2] *A Short History of the English People*, vol 2, chap VIII, sect 2.

2 Edmund Peacham is tortured

i *His draft sermon*

But the great mass of people were appalled by the wickedness of the King and his favourites. There was a ground-swell of revolt amongst the strong Puritan element in the country. One of the Puritan clergy was Edmund Peacham. He was a clergyman well advanced in years – in his middle sixties. He was much disturbed by what was going on. So were many of his friends. One of them suggested that he should give a sermon exposing the misdeeds of the King and his officers. So Edmund Peacham sat down in his study and drafted something out. But he never delivered it and never intended to deliver it. He thought that it was too strong and that he ought to soften it down a lot. So he put the draft in a 'lidless cask' in his room. (That was the description given by the King himself in a letter.) But before Peacham had time to make his amendments, some officers came and searched his house. (They had come at the instance of the Bishop of Bath and Wells who had taken proceedings against him for slander.) These officers found the draft and took it off to the Bishop who took it off to the King.

ii *Words of ill omen*

The draft contained these words of ill omen for the King:[1]

The King might be striken with death on the sudden, or within eight days, as Ananias or Nabal . . . I make doubt whether the people will rise against the King for taxes and oppressions . . . If the Prince should get the crown-land again it would cost blood, and bring men to say, 'This is the heir, let us kill him' . . . All the King's officers ought to be put to the sword. . . .

When the King read those words, he was frightened. He thought that there was a conspiracy against him by men of whom Edmund Peacham was just the tool. He was anxious

---

[1] For this and following extracts, see Cobbett's (afterwards called Howell's) *State Trials*, vol II, 869, *The Case of Edmund Peacham, for Treason*.

to know who were the conspirators. Peacham would say nothing. So the King consulted Bacon. Could not this Peacham be put on the rack? Now Bacon knew that torture was forbidden by the common law: but he told the King that it was within the royal prerogative.

iii *Bacon prepares interrogatories*

So he got the Privy Council to allow it. James himself signed the warrant authorising the torture of Edmund Peacham. Bacon prepared the interrogatories to be administered. These were the first two of the questions in general:

1. Who procured you, moved you, or advised you, to put in writing these traiterous slanders which you have set down against his majesty's person and government, or any of them?

2. Who gave you any advertisement or intelligence touching those particulars which are contained in your writings . . .?

iv *Before, in, between, and after torture*

Francis Bacon and several officers of state went to the Tower to administer the interrogatories. This is the note made by the Secretary of State in his own handwriting:

Upon these Interrogatories, Peacham this day was examined before torture, in torture, between torture, and after torture; notwithstanding, nothing could be drawn from him, he still persisting in his obstinate and insensible denials, and former answers.

That note was signed by these officers (I have added their ranks):

Ralphe Winwood	(Secretary of State)
Jul Caesar	(Master of the Rolls)
Fr Bacon	(Attorney-General)
H Montague	(King's Serjeant)
Gervase Helwysse	
Ran Crewe	(King's Serjeant)
Henry Yelverton	(Solicitor-General)
Fr Cottington	
	Jan the 19th 1614

v *The rack*

We do not know what 'torture' was inflicted on Edmund Peacham. But the usual instrument was the 'rack.' It was a frame having a roller at each end. The victim was fastened to these by the wrists and ankles and had the joints of his limbs stretched by their rotation. Another instrument was Skevington's irons. He was the lieutenant of the Tower in the reign of Henry VIII. The machine compressed the body by bringing the head to the knees, and so forced blood out of the nose and ears.

vi *'A dumb devil'*

Five days later Francis Bacon wrote a letter to the King, full of venom against Peacham. He described him as a 'raging devil' who had become a 'dumb devil':

It may please your excellent majesty; It grieveth me exceedingly that your majesty should be so much troubled with this matter of Peacham, whose raging devil seemeth to be turned into a dumb devil. But although we are driven to make our way through questions, which I wish were otherwise, yet, I hope well, the end will be good. But then every man must put to his helping hand; for else I must say to your majesty, in this and the like cases, as St Paul said to the centurion, when some of the mariners had an eye to the cock-boat, 'Except these stay in the ship ye cannot be safe.'[1]

A month later Bacon proposed to the King that he and his fellows should go to the Tower and threaten Peacham with torture by burning:

I think also it were not amiss to make a false fire, as if all things were ready for his going down to his trial, and that he were upon the very point of being carried down, to see what this will work with him.

3 Was it treason?

i *Bacon consults the judges*

All this torture did not quell Peacham's spirit. So Bacon, as

[1] Bacon was there quoting from *The Acts of the Apostles* 27:31. Some of the shipmen had let down the small boat (towed behind) so as to flee out of the ship: but it was cut loose to stop them escaping.

Attorney-General, decided that Peacham should himself be charged with treason. But there was a great difficulty. What was the law about treason? Was Peacham guilty of treason when all he had done was to draft a sermon which was never delivered?

Francis Bacon hit on a plan. He decided to approach each of the judges of the King's Bench singly – one after the other – so as to get each to say that it was treason. But he did not see them all himself. He got the Solicitor-General (Henry Yelverton) to see Mr Justice Dodderidge; Mr Serjeant Montague to see Mr Justice Croke; and Mr Serjeant Crewe to see Mr Justice Houghton. Each of those judges was pliable enough. Each would say it was treason.

ii *Coke says 'No'*

But there was more difficulty with the Chief Justice, Sir Edward Coke. Bacon decided to see him himself. Sir Edward had made it clear that he did not agree with this 'auricular taking of opinions' ('auricular' means 'privately by the ear'). He said that it was contrary to the custom of the realm. Bacon did all he could to persuade Coke to give his opinion. Coke said he wanted time to consider it.

On 14 February 1614 Coke came to Bacon. He handed him his written opinion. Bacon read it. Coke's view was that Peacham was Not Guilty of treason. Bacon then reported to the King:

I send your majesty inclosed my lord Coke's answers; I will not call them rescripts, much less oracles. They are of his own hand, and offered to me as they are in writing. . . .

iii *The King's opinion*

On receiving this report King James in his own handwriting gave his own opinion on 'The true State of the Question, whether Peacham's Case be Treason or not.' He said that there was 'plain proof that he intended to compass or imagine, by this means, the King's destruction.'

4 Peacham indicted for High Treason

i *Found Guilty*

Thereupon Peacham was indicted for High Treason. It was at Taunton in his own county of Somerset. He was tried before the Chief Baron of the Exchequer and King's Serjeant Mountague. The prosecution was conducted by King's Serjeant Crewe and Henry Yelverton, the Solicitor-General. (Three of them had been present at the torture.) Peacham was found Guilty and sentenced to death. But the sentence was never executed. The poor old man died of illness in the gaol at Taunton.

ii *Not in the law report*

The case was not reported by any lawyer for many years and then the report contained no word about the torture. It merely said:

Edmund Peacham was indicted of Treason for divers treasonable passages in a Sermon which was never preached, nor intended to be preached, but only set down in writings, and found in his study: he was tried and found guilty, but not executed. – Note, That many of the Judges were of opinion, that it was not Treason.

That report was by Sir George Croke, the son of Mr Justice Croke, who was one of the judges consulted.

iii *The last instance*

That was the last instance of torture in England that I know of. James I's son, Charles I, wanted to use it in 1628 but failed. John Felton, a lieutenant in the Army, stabbed the King's favourite, the 1st Duke of Buckingham, in the heart. The common people of England applauded Felton. They drank his health in all the taverns. But the King, in the Privy Council, proposed that Felton should be put on the rack so as to discover his accomplices. Blackstone says in his *Commentaries* (IV, 326):

The judges, being consulted, declared unanimously, to their own honour

39

and the honour of the English law, that no such proceeding was allowable by the laws of England.

But although John Felton did not undergo the rack, he was convicted and hanged at Tyburn.

5 The legal side

i *Torture in England*

Torture was used in the Middle Ages to exact confessions or to get names of accomplices. It is now proscribed by the United Nations in its Declaration of Human Rights. In England it is gone forever.

ii *Torture in Zimbabwe*

But torture loomed large in the recent case in Zimbabwe when six Zimbabwe Air Force officers (all white) were charged with assisting in the sabotage of a dozen fighter aircraft. It was alleged that they assisted unknown persons from South Africa. They were said to have made confessions but their defence was that these had been extracted from them by torture. The investigating officers were all black. The trial took 44 days. The judge was Mr Justice Dumbutshena, Zimbabwe's first black High Court judge, and a much-respected figure, courageous and independent as a judge should be. He acquitted them. *The Times* reported his judgment on 1 September 1983. He

dealt at length with the officers' allegations that they had been intimidated, assaulted and in four cases subjected to electric shock torture to get them to make confessions ... Although the police denied mistreatment, the officers' stories corroborated each other and had the ring of truth, he added. 'The psychological effects of lengthy interrogation, incommunicado incarceration and torture suffered at the hands of the police drive an accused person to hopelessness,' he said.

But soon after their release the six were re-arrested under detention orders. It was, said *The Times* on 2 September 1983, ' a disgraceful demonstration of contempt for human rights.' Since that time three of them have been released and have returned to England. And now the remaining three also.

iii *Grass and supergrass*

It is common slang now to speak of a 'grass,' that is, a criminal who tells the police about his colleagues in crime: and of a 'supergrass' who gives evidence against them. Is it lawful for the police, not only to promise they will not be prosecuted, but also to protect them from vengeance, and even to pay them money as a reward? It is a debatable question but I should have thought it was lawful, so long as the tribunal – be it judge or jury – are warned of the dangers of acting on the evidence unless it is corroborated.

iv *'Auricular' opinions*

Bacon in his Essay *Of Judicature* sought to justify his seeking the opinions of the judges. He said:

> It is an happy thing in a state when kings and states do often consult with judges; and again, when judges do often consult with the king and state: the one, when there is matter of law intervenient in business of state; the other, when there is some consideration of state intervenient in matter of law.

That doctrine is to be condemned. It is cardinal in our Constitution that judges are independent of the executive government. They do not give advice to the government on points of law or of fact; nor do they receive it. It would be highly improper for the Crown or anyone else in authority to seek the opinion of a judge on a pending case which he may be called upon to try: or on any point of fact or law which he may be required to decide. It would also, of course, be highly improper for a judge himself to give an 'auricular' opinion on it.

v *Plea bargaining*

A few years back there grew up a practice of 'plea-bargaining' – by which counsel for an accused would ask to see the judge before the trial. He would suggest that, if the accused pleaded Guilty, instead of Not Guilty, the judge should give a light sentence or only bind him over to be of good behaviour. That is highly improper, see *R v Turner.*[1] It may however, sometimes, be proper for counsel to discuss preliminary matters with the judge (eg 'that the accused has not long to live, is suffering maybe from cancer, of which he is and should remain ignorant'[2]); but this must only be in the presence of both counsel for the defence and counsel for the prosecution. The judge must never be asked to indicate – and must never indicate – what sentence he is minded to impose: save that he can indicate in an appropriate case '. . . that, whatever happens, whether the accused pleads guilty or not guilty, the sentence will or will not take a particular form, eg a probation order or a fine, or a custodial sentence.'[3]

[1] [1970] 2 QB 321.
[2] Ibid at 326.
[3] Ibid at 327.

2 Bacon guilty of bribery

1 At the pinnacle of fame

i *His grand banquet*

In the year 1618 Francis Bacon became Lord Chancellor. Two years later, in 1620, he was at the pinnacle of his fame. He had a great mansion and gardens in the country at Gorhambury near St Albans. He had his magnificent York House in the Strand near the river. He had inherited it from his father, Sir Nicholas Bacon. To celebrate his 59th birthday, he gave a grand banquet there. Ben Jonson praised 'the fare, the wine, the men' and wrote these verses to commemorate the occasion:

> England's high Chancellor, the destin'd heir
> In his soft cradle, to his father's chair,
> Whose even thread the Fates spin round and full
> Out of their choicest and their whitest wool.

ii *His most learned work*

In that same year Francis Bacon published his most learned work, the *Novum Organum*. He gave a presentation copy of it to Sir Edward Coke, the former Chief Justice of the King's Bench. But Coke had no love for Bacon. He thought nothing of him or his works. In this presentation copy Coke wrote in his own hand these caustic lines in Latin to which I add my translation:

> *Edw. C. ex dono auctoris.*
> Auctori Consilium.
> Instaurare paras veterum documenta sophorum,
> Instaura Leges Justitiamque prius.

> (A gift to Edward C. from the author.
> Advice to the author.
> You presume to build upon the learning of the wise men of old,
> But you should first build up the laws and justice.)

On the book there was a drawing of a ship, against which Sir Edward had made this cutting criticism, also in his own hand:

> It deserves not to be read in schooles,
> But to be freighted in the *ship of Fools*.

iii *A keg of gunpowder*

Unbeknown to Bacon, at this very time there was a mine being dug out beneath him. It was full of gunpowder. The fuse was laid. It was about to be lit. Before long there would be an explosion. It would bring him down. In three months.

The gunpowder was a keg of money and presents from litigants. They had given them to the Lord Chancellor whilst their cases were pending before him.

2 *Awbrey's case*

i *£100 might help*

The first to come up was Mr *Awbrey's case*.[1] He brought proceedings in Chancery against Sir William Brooker. The case never seemed to come on for hearing. When Mr Awbrey complained of the delay, he was advised by some 'that are near my lord' that £100 might help.

The poor gentleman, not able by any means to come to his wished-for port, struck sail at this, and made a shift to get an £100 from the usurer.

Having got the £100, Mr Awbrey went with Sir George Hastings and Mr Jenkins to the Lord Chancellor's house in

.[1] (1620) 2 State Tr 1087.

Gray's Inn. Those two took the £100 into the Lord Chancellor and gave it to him, saying:

This is to help Awbrey in his Cause.

The Lord Chancellor accepted it:

Tell him I am thankful and that I assure him of good success in his business.

ii *'I will lay you by the heels'*

But still the case did not come on. So Awbrey wrote letters to the Lord Chancellor. He got no reply until the last letter when the Lord Chancellor told him:

If you importune me any more, I will lay you by the heels.

Not long afterwards the case did come on. At the hearing, 'a very prejudicial and murdering order was made against Awbrey in his cause.' Sir George Hastings remonstrated with the Lord Chancellor. He asked him to rectify the order and to do the poor man justice. The Lord Chancellor promised to do so but did not.

Sir George Hastings then told the Lord Chancellor he would have to make it known. The Lord Chancellor said:

You are not to do so. If you do, George, I must deny it upon my honour.

3 *Egerton's case*

i *£400 in gold sovereigns*

The next to complain was Edward Egerton who was suing his brother Sir Rowland Egerton. He presented the Lord Chancellor with a basin and ewer of the value of £50 and upwards: and afterwards a bag full of £400 in gold sovereigns. The Lord Chancellor started at first at the sight of it. He said:

It is too much. I will not take it.

ii *He could not resist temptation*

But he could not resist temptation. He took the gold sovereigns, saying:

Mr Egerton has not only enriched me. He has laid a tye upon me to do him favour in all his just causes.

Yet when the case came on, he decided against Edward Egerton and in favour of Sir Rowland.

In those two instances Bacon had accepted the bribes and afterwards decided *against* the bribers. They were so aggrieved that they complained. We do not know whether the successful parties also bribed him. They may have done. They would not complain.

4 A Committee of Inquiry

i *Charged with corruption*

Those two complaints led the House of Commons to set up a committee to inquire into abuses in the Courts of Justice. They made a report on 15 March 1620:

1. The Person against whom it is alledged, is no less than the Lord Chancellor, [Francis lord Verulam, viscount St Albans], a man so endued with all parts, both of nature and art as that I will say no more of him; being not able to say enough.

2. The Matter alledged, is Corruption.

3. The Persons by whom this is presented to us, are two, viz. Awbrey and Egerton. . . .

ii *A fair lady's purse*

Soon afterwards, the Commons' committee were told of cases where bribes were paid and the decision was given in favour of the bribers. Lady Wharton sought a decree in Chancery. She went in her coach and took £100 to York House. She carried it in a purse.

The Lord Chancellor asked her:

What do you have in your hand?

She replied:

A purse of my own making

and handed it to him. He accepted it, saying:

What lord could refuse a purse of so fair a lady's working?

After this a decree was made in her favour but it was not
perfected. She gave £200 more and her decree 'had life.'

iii *Gold and diamonds*

Thenceforward day after day complaints poured in about
more bribes. Many gifts of £100 in gold, and more. But
presents too. Gold buttons to the value of £50. A cabinet
worth £800. A diamond ring worth £500 or £600.

5 The trial itself

i *A written confession*

All these complaints were reported by the Commons to the
Lords, together with supporting ev.dence. The Lords
appointed a Select Committee of their House who examined
witnesses. They formulated 28 separate Articles of Charge
against the Lord Chancellor, each charging a separate
bribery and corruption. The Lords invited the Lord
Chancellor to appear before them to answer the charge. But
he never appeared. He said he was sick. He wanted to take
exception to the witnesses, and so forth. But at length on
Monday 30 April 1620 he sent this written confession:

To the right honourable the Lords Spiritual and Temporal, in the High
Court of Parliament assembled:

The humble Confession and Submission of Me the Lord Chancellor.

Upon advised consideration of the Charge, descending into my own
conscience, and calling my memory to account so far as I am able, I do
plainly and ingenuously confess, that I am guilty of Corruption, and do
renounce all Defence, and put myself upon the grace and mercy of your
lordships.

He then went through all the 28 Articles and asked for
leniency, that

47

your Sentence may not be heavy to my ruin, but gracious and mixed with mercy.

He added:

After this example, it is like that judges will fly from any thing that is in the likeness of Corruption (though it were at a great distance) as from a serpent.

The Lords sent some of their member' to see if the confession was genuine. Bacon said:

My lords, it is my act, my hand, my heart; I beseech your lordships to be merciful to a broken reed.

ii *Sentence upon him*

The Lords then summoned the Lord Chancellor to appear before them in the House. The Serjeant at Arms went with his mace and handed him the summons. He was in bed. He said:

I am sick. I am not feigning. If I had been well I would willingly have come.

The Lords nevertheless resolved to proceed. They sent a message to the Commons inviting them to attend. On 3 May 1620 the Speaker went with them to the bar. He made three low obeisances and said:

. . . I, their Speaker, in their name do humbly demand, and pray Judgment against him the said Lord Chancellor. . . .

The Lord Chief Justice gave judgment:

. . . This high Court hath thereby, and by his own Confession, found him Guilty of the Crimes and Corruptions complained of by the Commons, and of sundry other Crimes and Corruptions of like nature. And therefore this high Court having first summoned him to attend, and having his excuse of not attending, by reason of infirmity and sickness, which he protested was not feigned, or else he would most willingly have attended, doth nevertheless think fit to proceed to Judgment: and therefore this high Court doth adjudge:
'That the lord Viscount St Albans, Lord Chancellor of England, shall undergo a fine and ransom of £40,000. – That he shall be imprisoned in the Tower during the King's pleasure. – That he shall for ever be

incapable of any office, place, or employment, in the state or commonwealth. – That he shall never sit in parliament, nor come within the verge of the Court.' – This is the Judgment and Resolution of this High Court.

iii *His end*

On the last day of May 1620 he was carried a prisoner to the Tower. A barge came to the stairs of York House. He was taken to the Traitor's Gate. He was soon released, however, and went to Gorhambury. But he had to sell York House and reduce his establishment at Gorhambury. He spent most of his time in his chambers in Gray's Inn. In the *State Trials* it is said:[1]

He was in great want to the very last, living obscurely in his chambers at Gray's Inn, where his lonely and desolate condition so wrought upon his melancholy temper, that he pined away; and after all his height of abundance was reduced to so low an ebb, as to be denied beer to quench his thirst.

An old story tells that he caught his 'death of cold' whilst experimenting with a chicken. But I expect it was what is now called influenza. He died on 9 April 1626.

iv *His own verdict*

His own verdict on himself was:

I was the justest judge that was in England these fifty years. But it was the justest censure in Parliament that was these two hundred years.

v *Latimer's condemnation*

Long before Bacon's time judges had been taking bribes. Seventy years before it had been condemned by the brave old Bishop Hugh Latimer:

Omnes diligunt munera. They all love bribes. Bribery is a princely kind of thieving. They will be waged by the rich, either to give sentence against the poor, or to put off the poor man's cause. This is the noble theft of princes and magistrates. They are bribe-takers. Nowadays they call them gentle rewards. Let them leave their colouring, and call them by their Christian name – bribes.

[1] (1620) 2 State Tr 1114.

3 Later cases

Many years ago in *The Road to Justice*, I described two later cases, but as that book is out of print I would repeat them now:

1 Lord Macclesfield

i *Demands an honorarium*

Another Lord Chancellor to show us what not to do was Lord Macclesfield, who was appointed Lord Chancellor in 1718 and proved himself a very able judge, his decisions being regarded with much respect. (One of the most famous of his cases was *Mitchel v Reynolds*,[1] the leading case on covenants in restraint of trade.) Yet he fell into the prevalent vice of 'selling offices.' He did not take bribes as Bacon did, but whenever he appointed a new Master in Chancery he demanded an honorarium just as his predecessors had done. The trouble about Lord Macclesfield was that he increased the price for offices so enormously that the new Masters had to get it back somehow and they got it back out of the parties in Chancery. The Masters used to delay the cases and then extract money from the parties for expediting them: and they sometimes used for their own purposes the actual cash which they held for the parties. One of these Masters speculated in the South Sea Bubble and when it burst, the whole sorry story came out. The Lord Chancellor was

[1] (1711) 1 P Wms 181.

50

impeached, found guilty and fined £30,000. That was the end of him.

ii 'Guineas are handsomer'

One of the Masters who gave evidence told how he became a Master. The Lord Chancellor saw him and said he believed that he would make a good officer but added that 'you and I must not make bargains, but just consider of it.' The applicant did consider of it and proposed £5,000 to one of the Lord Chancellor's followers. The immediate reply he got was 'Guineas are handsomer.' So the applicant got 5,000 guineas in gold and bank notes, and as they were very heavy, he took them in a basket to the Lord Chancellor. He went in a sedan chair and took the basket with him in the chair.

iii An empty basket

He was duly appointed a Master and the Lord Chancellor invited him to dinner and swore him in. Some months afterwards he saw one of the Lord Chancellor's officers and desired him, if he saw such a basket, he should give it back. He did so, but no money was returned in it.

The strange thing is that, with his illicit gains, the Lord Chancellor was extremely liberal, dispensing with an almost extravagant hand large sums in the promotion of learning and in aid of the poor. He prayed this in aid at his trial, but it did him no good.

iv 'Give it to the poor'

Since that time we have had no Lord Chancellor – and no judge for that matter – who has accepted a bribe. But this is not to say that they have not been tempted. In 1747 the Mayor of Yarmouth, one Martin, attempted to bribe Lord Hardwicke, the then Lord Chancellor. The mayor knew that an action was being brought against him in the Court of Chancery. So he sent £20 in bank notes to the Lord Chancellor and asked him to accept them. Instead of accepting them, the Lord Chancellor held it to be a great contempt: the mayor very wisely made a humble apology and asked for pardon, so he was excused on payment of costs, but he did not get his £20 back. The Lord Chancellor ordered that it should be applied to the relief of poor persons in the Fleet prison.[1]

2 Lord Cottenham

i *Bricks in the canal*

It is yet another Lord Chancellor who teaches us the next lesson – that a judge must not have the slightest interest in any case depending before him. Over a hundred years ago the Lord Chancellor of the day, Lord Cottenham, was a shareholder in the Grand Junction Canal Company. He had 92 shares in it. The company had a dispute with a Mr Davies who claimed that the canal was his property. He placed a bar across it and threw bricks into it. The company applied for an injunction against the man. It was granted by the Vice-Chancellor and on appeal to Lord Cottenham the Lord Chancellor affirmed the decree. Lord Cottenham did not disclose that he was a shareholder in the company.

ii *'A salutary influence'*

The House of Lords, after consulting the judges, held that the decree must be set aside. In the course of his speech Lord Campbell said:[2]

No one can suppose that Lord Cottenham would be, in the remotest degree, influenced by the interest that he had in this concern, but it is of the last importance that the maxim that no man is to be a judge in his own cause should be held sacred . . . It will have a most salutary influence when it is known that, in a case in which the Lord Chancellor of England had an interest, his decree was set aside.

---

[1] *Martin's case* (1747) 2 Russ & M 674.
[2] *Dimes v Grand Junction Canal* (1852) 3 HLC 759, 793.

52

3 Well-settled principles

Underlying all these cases, there are well-settled principles. There have been very many cases of bribery of an agent or of persons in a fiduciary position. No person must have an interest in conflict with his duty. No agent of one party must accept a secret commission from the other party. I gave these instances in *Reading v R:*[1]

Take the case of the master who tells his servant to exercise his horses, and whilst the master is away, the servant lets them out, and makes a profit by so doing. There is no loss to the master, the horses have been exercised, but the servant must account for the profits he makes. The Attorney-General for the Crown put in argument the case of a uniformed policeman who at the request of thieves in return for a bribe, directs traffic away from the site of the crime. Is he to be allowed to keep the money? So also here the use of the facilities provided by the Crown in the shape of the uniform, and the use of his position in the Army were the sole reason why the suppliant was able to get this money. It was solely on that account that he was able to sit in the front of these lorries, and give them a safe conduct through Cairo. There was no loss of profit to the Crown. The Crown would have been violating its duty if it had undertaken the task. But the soldier was certainly violating his duty, and it is money which he ought not to be allowed to keep. The law says in those circumstances it must be paid over to the master, in this case, the Crown.

[1] [1948] 2 KB 268, 275–276.

Part Three

The Chancellor's Foot

Introduction

How many of you know the phrase, 'the Chancellor's foot'?
It was first used by the very learned John Selden who was a
little younger than Francis Bacon. He wrote in 1617 a brief
discourse touching the office of Lord Chancellor in England.
In it he said:

Equity is a roguish thing; for law we have a measure to know what to
trust to. Equity is according to the conscience of him who is Chancellor:
as it is larger or narrower so is equity. Tis all one as if they should make
the standard for the measure we call a foot to be the Chancellor's foot.

It is a charming metaphor. The standard measure of a
'foot' is certain. It is 12 inches. But the 'Chancellor's foot'
may be anything from 9 inches to 11 inches. So equity
(which is administered by the Lord Chancellor) is very
personal to him. It varies as much as the foot of one Lord
Chancellor varies from that of his successor.

I will now tell you of two Lord Chancellors who gave
decisions shortly before Selden's time. It was their decisions
which gave rise to his comment about the length of the
Chancellor's foot. You must remember, however, that we
have no reports of their decisions. The reporting of cases in
Chancery did not start until 1557.

I will also tell you of a later Lord Chancellor who
repudiated the notion of the 'Chancellor's foot.'

But first of all, Thomas Wolsey and Thomas More. What
a pair! Beyond doubt the two greatest of our Lord
Chancellors. Each raised up by King Henry VIII. Each felled

by him because of his wives. But their judicial achievements are little known. They should be. Each was an exponent of the new equity. Each stepped in to mitigate the rigours of the old law. Each of them granted injunctions whenever it was just and convenient so to do. Just as I sought to do when I was Master of the Rolls.

1 Thomas Wolsey

1 Thomas Wolsey himself

i *A butcher's son*

We know a good deal about Thomas Wolsey. He lived 500 years ago. He had a gentleman usher named George Cavendish who wrote an account of his life. He tells us that Wolsey was an 'honest poor man's son.' He was born in 1471, the son of a butcher at Ipswich. By his book-learning and accomplishments he came to excel the greatest in the land. So much so that Shakespeare put this description in the mouth of his noble enemy, the Duke of Buckingham:

> This butcher's cur is venom-mouth'd, and I
> Have not the power to muzzle him: therefore best
> Not wake him in his slumber. A beggar's book[1]
> Out-worths a noble's blood.[2]

ii *'Wolsey's Tower'*

He went at an early age to my own college, Magdalen College, Oxford. It had only recently been founded by William of Waynflete. He took his degree so young that they called him 'the boy Bachelor.' He became a Fellow and Master of the College School. He was for a time the Bursar and in 1492 designed and commissioned the Great Tower which was known as 'Wolsey's Tower.' Recently restored, its grace and elegance charm all beholders.

[1] Book-learning, scholarship.
[2] *King Henry VIII*, Act I, sc 1.

iii '*An unbounded stomach*'

Wolsey was remarkably handsome, except for a blemish in
his right eye. He was so self-conscious of this that in all the
pictures of him he is shown in profile, showing only the left
side. He was exceptionally able and intelligent. He used
every stratagem to gain advancement. He became the most
powerful in the land. In Shakespeare's words:

> He was a man
> Of an unbounded stomach, ever ranking
> Himself with princes.[1]

He was proud, vain and dissolute. He had three illegitimate
children, one of whom he made the Dean of Wells.
Shakespeare wrote of him:

> Of his own body he was ill, and gave
> The clergy ill example.[1]

He became a cardinal of the Church of Rome. He founded
Christ Church College, Oxford. At every turn there you still
see the red of his cardinal's hat.

2 As Lord Chancellor

i *His grand procession*

But here I tell of his exploits as Lord Chancellor. He had a
palace in York House which was in the street now called
Whitehall. He slept there, rose at daybreak, heard mass, had
breakfast, got dressed in all his finery, and then went into the
Great Hall of York House where gentlemen were awaiting
him. Then he went in procession to Westminster Hall to try
the cases in Chancery. The pomp is almost unbelievable, but
it is vouched for in this delightful piece by George
Cavendish. I quote from his *Life of Cardinal Wolsey*:[2]

. . . He would issue out into them (the public rooms), appareled all in red,
in the habit of a cardinal; which was either of fine scarlet, or else of

[1] *King Henry VIII*, Act IV, sc 2.
[2] Vol I, pp 42–45.

crimson satin, taffety, damask, or caffa, the best that he could get for money: and upon his head a round pillion, with a noble of black velvet set to the same in the inner side; he had also a tippet of fine sables about his neck; holding in his hand a very fair orange, whereof the meat or substance within was taken out, and filled up again with the part of a sponge, wherein was vinegar, and other confections against the pestilent airs; the which he most commonly smelt unto, passing among the press, or else when he was pestered with many suitors. There was also borne before him first, the great seal of England, and then his cardinal's hat, by a nobleman or some worthy gentleman, right solemnly, bareheaded. And as soon as he was entered into his chamber of presence, where there was attending his coming to await upon him to Westminster Hall, as well noblemen and other worthy gentlemen, as noblemen and gentlemen of his own family; thus passing forth with two great crosses of silver borne before him; with also two great pillars of silver, and his pursuivant at arms with a great mace of silver gilt. Then his gentlemen ushers cried, and said: 'On, my lords and masters, on before; make way for my Lord's Grace!'

ii *His entry into Westminster Hall*

He rode upon a mule. It was the only sign of humility.

Thus passed he down from his chamber through the hall; and when he came to the hall door, there was attendant for him his mule, trapped all together in crimson velvet, and gilt stirrups. When he was mounted, with his cross bearers, and pillar bearers, also upon great horses trapped with [fine] scarlet. Then marched he forward, with his train and furniture in manner as I have declared, having about him four footmen, with gilt pollaxes in their hands; and thus he went until he came to Westminster Hall door. And there alighted, and went after this manner, up through the hall into the chancery; howbeit he would most commonly stay awhile at a bar, made for him, a little beneath the chancery [on the right hand], and there commune some time with the judges, and sometime with other persons. And that done he would repair into the chancery, sitting there till eleven of the clock, hearing suitors, and determining of divers matters. And from thence, he would divers times, go into the star chamber, as occasion did serve; where he spared neither high nor low, but judged every estate according to their merits and deserts.

iii *Into the Star Chamber*

You will notice that he went on occasion to the Star Chamber. That was a chamber nearby in the Palace of Westminster. Stow in his *Survey of London* (1598) tells us:

This place is called the Star Chamber, because the roof thereof is decked with the likeness of stars gilt: there be plaints heard of riots, routs, and other misdemeanors.

iv *He does justice*

There are no reports of any actual decisions that Wolsey gave: but there are statistics from which much can be learnt. They show that the work of the Courts of Star Chamber and Chancery multiplied a hundredfold whilst the work of the old courts of common law fell off to a trickle. Professor Guy puts it clearly:[1]

In origin the court's (Star Chamber's) development arose from Wolsey's basic desire to hear complaints about crime and wrongdoing from private individuals. It was axiomatic under his scheme that men with grievances who were eager to obtain justice . . . should be allowed to file bills in Star Chamber 'where the complainants shall not dread to show the truth of their grief.' Such bills were sometimes received in Chancery too, but most went to Star Chamber.

And Professor Chambers tells us:[2]

The abuses of the common law (and they were many) were controlled by Wolsey as Chancellor: 'He did a good deal in detail by means of injunctions staying the execution of what the judges called law in the interests of what Wolsey called equity.'[3]

v *The doctor and student*

In this approach Wolsey was supported by a most influential book by Christopher St German, a barrister of the Inner Temple. It is called *Doctor and Student: or Dialogues Between A Doctor of Divinity and A Student in the Laws of England.* The doctor expounds the fundamental principles of justice and the student tells how they fit in with the laws of England. On reading it now, I am astonished to find that, written in 1523, it states the principles in a manner very relevant today:[4]

---

[1] *The Public Career of Sir Thomas More*, p 38.
[2] *Thomas More*, p 271.
[3] Pollard *Wolsey*, p. 95.
[4] Christopher St German *Doctor and Student*, Chapter XVI, p 45.

Wherefore in some cases it is necessary to leave the words of the law, (ie the strict meaning) and to follow that (which) reason and justice requireth, and to that intent equity is ordained; that is to say, to temper and mitigate the rigor of the law.

And I find that the statutory interpretation is recommended in much the same way as I would recommend it today. Thus he says that the judges should not go by the letter but by the intendment – doing what the makers of the statute would have done if they had thought of it; and filling in gaps accordingly. He gives this illustration:[1]

vi *The valiant beggar*

Also notwithstanding the statute of *Edw 3* made the 14th year of his reign, whereby it is ordained, that no man, upon pain of imprisonment, should give any alms to any valiant beggar, that is well able to labour; yet if a man meet with a valiant beggar in so cold a weather, and so light apparel, that if he have no clothes he shall not be able to come to any town for succour, but is likely rather to die by the way, and he therefore giveth him apparel to save his life, he shall be excused by (from the operation of) the said statute, by such an exception of the law of reason as I have spoken of . . .

. . . it shall be taken that it was the intent of the makers of the statute to except such cases. And the judges may many times judge after the mind of the makers so far as the letter may suffer (ie allow), and so it seemeth they may in this case.

vii *The Vale of the White Horse*

But this approach was roundly condemned by the old common lawyers. One of them, a learned Serjeant of Gray's Inn, points out that the Lord Chancellor was not trained as a lawyer and says that, if he had been, he would not have attempted these reforms. The passage is most entertaining, but to my mind it proves the opposite of what the Serjeant intended. He takes the figure in the Vale of the White Horse on our chalk downs: and says that you see it best at a distance. When you are close to it, then, as the modern saying is: 'You cannot see the wood for the trees.'

[1] Ibid pp 46–47.

... In my conceite in this case I may liken my lord Chaunceler, which is not learned in the lawes of the realme, to him, that stands in the Vale of Whitehorse farre from the horse and holdeth (ie beholdeth) the horse; and the horse seemeth and appeereth to him a goodly horse and well proportioned in every poincte, and that if he come neere to the place wher the horse is, he can perceave no horse nor proportion of any horse. Even so it fareth by my lord chauncelor that is not learned in the lawes of the realme; for whan such a bill is put unto him, it appeereth to him to be a matter of great conscience and requireth reformation: and the matter in the bill appeereth so to him, because he is farre from the understandinge and the knowledge of the lawe of the realme and the goodness thereof; but if he drawe neere to the knowledge and understandinge of the common law of the realme, soe that he maie come to the perfecte knowledge and goodnes of it, he shall well perceive that the matter contayned in the bill put to him in the chauncerie is no matter to be refourmed there. ...[1]

viii *His judicial work*

Despite this criticism by the old common lawyers, Wolsey proceeded vigorously with his reforms. He presided in the Court of Chancery for 14 years. His attendance was regular and punctual. His decisions are acknowledged to have been equitable and just. His reputation for his judicial work stands high.

3 'Those twins of learning'

His good points are recorded by Shakespeare in the scene between Catherine, the Dowager Queen, and Griffith, her Gentleman-usher.[2] Shakespeare tells of Wolsey's support for the University of Oxford on which rests his enduring fame: and of his failure to found a university at Ipswich.

> This cardinal,
> Though from an humble stock, undoubtedly
> Was fashion'd to much honour from his cradle.
> He was a scholar, and a ripe and good one;
> Exceeding wise, fair-spoken, and persuading:
> Lofty and sour to them that lov'd him not,

[1] See (1960) 76 LQR 502.
[2] *King Henry VIII*, Act IV, sc 2.

But to those men that sought him, sweet as summer.
And though he were unsatisfied in getting,
Which was a sin, yet in bestowing, madam,
He was most princely: ever witness for him
Those twins of learning, that he raised in you,
Ipswich and Oxford! one of which fell with him,
Unwilling to outlive the good that did it;
The other, though unfinish'd, yet so famous,
So excellent in art, and still so rising,
That Christendom shall ever speak his virtue.

Those were his virtues in encouraging learning. I add the virtue in doing what was just and equitable.

4 His fall from power

i 'A night Crow'

His fall from power was due to the charms of Anne Boleyn. She wanted to marry King Henry VIII: but she thought that Wolsey was opposed to her influence with him. According to Wolsey, she was

a night Crow, which possessed the royal ear, and misrepresented the most harmless of his (Wolsey's) actions.

The uxorious King wanted a divorce from Queen Catherine, the mother of Mary Tudor. She had been previously married to the King's deceased brother. On account of it, her marriage to the King was said to be bad. Two Cardinals, Wolsey and Campeggio, were appointed by the Pope as commissioners to examine the validity of the King's marriage to Catherine. The proceedings were greatly delayed. Anne blamed the delay on Wolsey. She got the King to dismiss Wolsey from his office as Lord Chancellor. The Attorney-General filed an information against him. He was accused of offending against the Statute of Premunire of Richard II 1393. He was charged with receiving instructions from Rome and acting on them without the King's consent. It was a 'put-up job.' That statute had been repeatedly broken with impunity before. But that argument would not have helped Wolsey. He knew it. He allowed judgment to go against him. He surrendered the Great Seal. It was almost immediately placed in the hands of Sir Thomas More. The King took possession of Wolsey's palace at York House and changed its name to Whitehall.

ii 'Fling away ambition'

You will remember the advice which Wolsey gave to his secretary, Thomas Cromwell, as recorded by Shakespeare.[1] I have often quoted it:

> Mark but my fall, and that that ruin'd me.
> Cromwell, I charge thee, fling away ambition:
> By that sin fell the angels; . . .
>   Be just, and fear not.
> Let all the ends thou aim'st at be thy country's,
> Thy God's, and truth's; . . .
>   O Cromwell, Cromwell,
> Had I but serv'd my God with half the zeal
> I serv'd my king, he would not in mine age
> Have left me naked to mine enemies.

5 His last days

i *The abbey of Leicester*

Wolsey retired to his Bishopric of York. But six months later he was arrested on a charge of high treason, and started for London. He got as far as Leicester. Cavendish describes what happened:

. . . By the way he waxed so sick that he was divers times likely to have fallen from his mule; and being night before we came to the abbey of Leicester, where at his coming in at the gates the abbot of the place with all his convent met him with the light of many torches; whom they right honourably received with great reverence. To whom my lord said, 'Father Abbot, I am come hither to leave my bones among you.' . . . As soon as he was in his chamber, he went incontinent to his bed, very sick. . . .

As he lay sick in bed there, he was visited by the Lieutenant of the Tower and said to him:

[1] *King Henry VIII*, Act III, sc 2.

And, Master Knygton, had I but served God as diligently as I have served the King, He would not have given me over in my grey hairs.

ii *The clock struck eight*

Then Cavendish goes on:

Upon Monday in the morning, as I stood by his bed side, about eight of the clock, the windows being close shut, having wax lights burning upon the cupboard, I beheld him, as me seemed, drawing fast to his end. He perceiving my shadow upon the wall by his bed side, asked who was there? 'Sir, I am here,' quoth I; 'How do you?' quoth he to me. 'Very well, sir,' quoth I, 'if I might see your grace well.' 'What is it of the clock?' said he to me. 'Forsooth, sir,' said I, 'it is past eight of the clock in the morning.' 'Eight of the clock?' quoth he, 'that cannot be,' rehearsing divers times, 'eight of the clock, eight of the clock, nay, nay,' quoth he at the last, 'it cannot be eight of the clock: for by eight of the clock ye shall lose your master: for my time draweth near that I must depart out of this world.'

iii *'Farewell'*

Next day, Wolsey said:

'Farewell. I can no more, but wish all things to have good success. My time draweth on fast. I may not tarry with you. And forget not, I pray you, what I have said and charged you withal: for when I am dead, ye shall peradventure remember my words much better.' And even with these words he began to draw his speech at length . . . The clock struck eight, at which time he gave up the ghost, and thus departed he this present life. And calling to our remembrance his words, the day before, how he said that at eight of the clock we should lose our master, one of us looking upon an other, supposing that he prophesied of his departure.

It was 29 November 1530.

It should be noticed that the King's divorce from Queen Catherine, and his marriage with Anne Boleyn, the cause of Wolsey's fall, were not completed until two years and a half after his death.

2 Thomas More

1 Thomas More himself

i *A son of Lincoln's Inn*

We know a good deal too about Thomas More. He was only
seven years younger than Thomas Wolsey. According to his
epitaph, which he wrote himself, he came of a *'familiâ non
celebri sed honestâ natus'* which may be translated as an
'honourable though not distinguished family.' He was very
much a son of Lincoln's Inn. His grandfather was the butler
of the Inn – an office very similar to the Under-Treasurer
today (that is, the head of the servants). His father, John, was
also the butler of the Inn, but he was afterwards admitted to
the Bar and became a judge. There is a famous painting by
Holbein of the father (John the judge) and the son (Thomas
the Lord Chancellor) and all the family. It hangs now in
Nostell Priory in Yorkshire, the home of Lord St Oswald.
Thomas has fine features, but is pale and thin-lipped. His
father is rotund and red-faced. Thomas praised the good
meals at Lincoln's Inn:[1]

... We will begin with Lincoln's Inn diet, where many right worshipful
and of good years do live full well.

It is the same today.

ii *Kisses in England*

Soon after Thomas joined the Inn, Erasmus, the great Dutch

[1] Chambers *Thomas More*, p 67.

humanist, came to England. They became firm friends. Much of our knowledge of Thomas More is gleaned from the letters of Erasmus. Erasmus delighted in the attractions of England. He writes to a friend in Paris:[1]

To mention only one attraction out of many; there are girls here with divine features, gentle and kind . . . And, moreover, there is a custom which cannot be sufficiently praised. Wherever you go, you are received with kisses from everybody; when you leave you are dismissed with kisses. You go back, and your kisses are returned to you. People arrive: kisses; they depart: kisses; wherever people foregather, there are lots of kisses; in fact, whatever way you turn, everything is full of kisses.

We are getting back to that custom now!

iii *His family*

Whilst still making his way at the Bar, More married his first wife in 1505. She was a girl of 17. After a rebellious start, the marriage was very happy. They had three daughters and one son. But his wife died six years later. Soon afterwards, More married a widow. It was to provide a mother for his children. She was 'neither a pearl nor a girl.' They had no children. But she was a 'vigilant housewife.'

Here I am concerned with his time as a judge. After Wolsey was dismissed, Henry VIII appointed Thomas More to be Lord Chancellor. He was the first layman to be appointed to that office. But his pre-eminence as a lawyer made him most suitable. His tenure only lasted two-and-a-half years as against Wolsey's 14 years. But there are many fascinating stories about his time there. They are told for the most part by his son-in-law, William Roper. I give them here in the original spelling. You must remember that there were no dictionaries in those days. Everyone spelt words as he thought best.

2 As Lord Chancellor

i *His regard for his father*

At the time of his appointment, his father, Sir John More,

[1] Ibid p 71.

was still a judge at the age of 75. In Westminster Hall the
Court of King's Bench was adjacent to the Chancery Court.
Roper tells us of the respect which Thomas paid to his
father, John:[1]

Whensoever he passed through 'Westm: Hall to his place in the
Chauncerie by the Court of the King's Bench, if his father, one of the
Judges there, had beene satt e're he came, he would goe into the same
Court, and there reverently kneelinge downe in the sight of them all
duely aske his Father's blessinge. . . .

ii *Readings in Lincoln's Inn*

Roper also tells us of the discussions held in Lincoln's Inn. He
would always invite his father to speak first, but the father
never did so. This is how Roper puts it:[1]

And if it fortuned that his Father and he at readinges in Lincolne's Inn
mett to gither (as they sometyme did) notwithstandinge his heigh office
he would offer in argument of the preheminence to his Father, though he
for his office sake would refuse to take it.

iii *The judges come to dinner*

I find much interest in the way in which Thomas More, as
Lord Chancellor, granted injunctions – just as Thomas
Wolsey had done – whenever it was just and convenient to
do so. The common law judges objected to it. So Thomas
had a docket prepared of all the cases in which he had granted
injunctions, and called the judges together to explain what
he had done. Roper tells us that he convinced them of the
rightness of his decisions:[1]

He invited all the Judges to dinner with him in the Councell Chamber at
Westminster, where after dinner when he had broken with them what
complaints he hard hard (had heard) of his Injunctions, and moreover
shewed them both the number and causes of every of them in order soe
plainely, that, upon full debatinge of those matters, they were all
inforced to confess, that they, in like case, could have done no otherwise
themselves, . . .

Then he told them to do likewise and mitigate the rigour of
the law by doing equity themselves:

[1] *The Life of Sir Thomas More.*

. . . then offered he this unto them, that if the Justices of every Court, unto whome the reformation of rigor of the Law, by reason of there office, most specially appertained, would, upon reasonable considerations, by there owne discretions (as they were, as he thought, in conscience bound) mittigate and reforme the rigor of the Law themselves, there should from thenceforth by him no more Injunctions be graunted.

(If they would do equity themselves, he would grant no more injunctions.)

iv *He continues to grant injunctions*

But the judges refused to follow his advice, so he told them he must continue to grant injunctions:

Whereupon when they refused to condiscend (comply), then sayd he unto them: 'Forasmuch as your selves, my Lords, drive me to that necessitie for awardinge out Injunctions to relive (relieve) the peopl's injurie, you cannot here after any more justly blame me.

v *A pun on 'More'*

Thomas More was expeditious. He disposed of his lists so well one day that there was no more work for the court. This gave rise to the pun:[1]

> When MORE some time had Chancellor been
> No *more* suits did remain:
> The same shall *never* more be seen,
> Till MORE be there again.

vi *The little dog*

There is no reported judgment of Sir Thomas More, except a story which is probably apocryphal. It reads too much like the judgment of Solomon.

It happened on a time that a beggar-woman's little dog, which she had lost, was presented for a jewel to Lady More, and she had kept it some se'nnight very carefully; but at last the beggar had notice where her dog was, and presently she came to complain to Sir Thomas, as he was sitting in his hall, that his lady withheld her dog from her. Presently my Lady

---

[1] Campbell *Lives of the Lord Chancellors*, Vol I, p 544.

was sent for, and the dog brought with her; which Sir Thomas taking in his hands, caused his wife, because she was the worthier person, to stand at the upper end of the hall, and the beggar at the lower end, and saying that he sat there to do every one justice, he bade each of them call the dog; which, when they did, the dog went presently to the beggar, forsaking my Lady. When he saw this, he bade my Lady be contented, for it was none of hers; yet she, repining at the sentence of my Lord Chancellor, agreed with the beggar, and gave her a piece of gold, which would well have bought three dogs, and so all parties were agreed; every one smiling to see his manner of inquiring out the truth.[1]

3 Gifts to him

i *A great gilt cup*

But Thomas More was not without fault. He was accused of taking bribes. It was brought up against him at his attainder. One case arose out of litigation between two merchants in the City of London. Parnell agreed to sell 1,000 kerseys (coarse woollen cloths) to Vaughan for cash on delivery. Vaughan agreed to re-sell them to merchants in Antwerp for delivery there. Vaughan did not pay the cash. So Parnell did not deliver. Vaughan sued Parnell for non-delivery. It was a complicated case, but in the end More gave judgment for Vaughan.

Vaughan was so grateful that he sent his wife to Thomas More with a gilt cup. This is how Roper describes it:[2]

This Parnell to the Kinge's Highnes had greevously complayned, that Sir Tho. Moore for making the decree had of the same Vaughaun (unable for the goute to travell abroad himselfe) by the handes of his wif taken a faire great gilte Cupp for a bribe. . . .

More was charged before the council. Roper tells us that he

. . . forthwith confessed, that for asmuch as that Cupp was longe after the aforesaid decree brought unto him for a new yeare's gift, he upon her importunat pressinge upon him, therfore of courtesie refused not to take it. Then the Lord of Wilshire . . . with much rejoycinge said unto the

---

[1] Ibid pp 545–546.
[2] *The Life of Sir Thomas More.*

Lords, 'Loe my Lords, loe, did not I tell you that you should find this matter true?'

ii *A mountain out of a molehill*

I must say that thus far I would agree with Lord Wiltshire. But More obtained an adjournment and then came forward with a defence which he had not put forward before. He said that he had not really accepted the cup. He had returned it straightaway. This is how Roper puts it:

> He further declared unto them, that albeit indeed (he) had with much worke received that Cupp, yet immediatly thereupon he caused his butler to fill that with wine, and of that Cupp drunke to her, and that when she had pledged him, then as freely as her husband had given it unto him, even soe freely gave he the same unto her againe, to give unto her husband for his new yeare's gift, which at his instant Request, though much against her will, yet at length she was faine to receave, as her self and certaine other there presently deposed before them (the council). Thus was the grete mountaine turned scarse unto a moale hill.

It does not appear whether the council accepted this explanation.

iii *Another gilt cup*

Another case of bribery is mentioned by Roper in which More's conduct seems to me to be open to criticism:

> And one Mr Gresham likewise having a cause dependinge in the Chauncery against him, sent him for a new yeare's gifte a faire gilted Cupp, the fashione wherof he very well likinge, and caused one of his owne (though not in his fantisie of soe good a fashion) yet better in valew, to be brought out of his Chamber, which he willed the messenger to deliver to his Mrs in recompence, and under other conditions would he in no wise receave it.

4 He whips heretics

i *At 'the tree of Troth'*

In More's garden in Chelsea, he had a tree called 'the tree of truth.' He was so devout a Roman Catholic that he caused some unbelievers to be whipped against the tree. John Foxe in his *Book of Martyrs* tells us that

Burnham, a reformer, was carried out of the Middle Temple to the Chancellor's house at Chelsea, where he continued in free prison awhile, till the time that Sir Thomas More saw that he could not prevail in perverting of (converting) him to his sect (Roman Catholicism). Then he cast him into prison in his own house, and whipped him at the tree in his garden called '*the tree of Troth*,' and after sent him to the Tower to be racked.

ii '*Till he waxed weary*'

More admitted that he kept heretics in prison. In his own apology, he denied the whipping except in two cases:

. . . Except their sure keeping, I never else did cause any such thing to be done unto any of the heretics in all my life, except only twain: one was a child . . . which heresy this child, in my house, began to teach another child . . . I caused a servant of mine to strip (whip) him, like a child, before mine household . . . Another was one who . . . (had) old frensies . . . Being informed of his relapse, I caused him to be taken by the constables, and bounden to a tree in the street, before the whole town, and there striped (whipped) him till he waxed weary.

By modern standards, More was not such a saint as he is said to have been.

5 He hands over the Great Seal

i *A plea of ill-health*

The stumbling-block for More – as for Wolsey – was the divorce of Queen Catherine. The King wanted his marriage to her to be annulled because she was his brother's widow – so that he could be free to marry Anne Boleyn and have a legitimate son. More knew there was no chance of a divorce being granted by the Church of Rome: and that nevertheless the King would marry Anne Boleyn. This made his position untenable. So on 10 May 1532 he resigned the Great Seal on the plea of ill-health. Such a plea is familiar to us still.

ii *He refuses to take the oath of supremacy*

After a year, controversy broke out. The King married Anne
Boleyn and she was declared Queen of England. More was
invited to the Coronation but refused to attend. An Act of
Parliament was passed so as to give succession to their child
and to make the King supreme head of the Church. It also
required his subjects to take an oath in these words:

To bear faith and true obedience to the King, and the issue of his present
marriage with Queen Anne, *to acknowledge him the Head of the Church of
England, and to renounce all obedience to the Bishop of Rome, as having no more
power than any other bishop.*

Commissioners were appointed to administer the oath.
More was taken first. He was prepared to subscribe to the
succession to the throne, because Parliament could so enact.
But he was not prepared to swear to the rest (which I have
shown in italics). He would not allow the King to be the
supreme head of the Church of England. Because of his
refusal he was kept a close prisoner in the Tower of London.

6 In the Tower of London

i *His visitors*

Whilst there, he was visited by his beloved daughter Meg,
and also by his second wife Alice. She was a plain, outspoken
woman. She upbraided him roundly. She told him how silly
he was to refuse to take the oath. The story is told by Roper,
his son-in-law, in homely words.[1] I hope you will have the
patience to read it carefully, despite the difficult spelling. It is
so charming.

ii *'Why play the fool here?'*

When Sir Thomas Moore had continued a good while in the Tower, my
Ladye his wife obtayned license to see him, who at her first comminge
like a simple woman, and somewhat worldlie too, with this matter of
salutations bluntly saluted him,
   'What the good yeare, Mr. Moore,' quoth shee, 'I marvell that you,
that have beene allwayes hitherunto taken for soe wise a man, will now

---

[1] *The Life of Sir Thomas More.*

soe playe the foole to lye here in this close, filthie prison, and be content thus to be shutt upp amonge myse and rattes, when you might be a broad at your libertie, and with the favour and good will both of the King and his Councell, if you would but doe as all the Bushopps and best learned of this Realme have done.

And seeinge you have at Chelsey a right fayre house, your librarie, your books, your gallerie, your garden, your orchards, and all other necessaries soe handsomely about you, where you might, in the companie of me your wife, your children, and househould be merrie, I muse what a God's name you meane her still thus fondlye to tarry.'

After he had a while quietly hard her, with a chearefull countenaunce he sayd unto her, 'I pray thee good Mrs. Alice, tell me, tell me one thinge.' 'What is that?' (quoth shee.) 'Is not this house as nighe heaven as myne owne?' (quoth he.)

iii 'Tille valle, Tille valle'

To whome shee, after her accustomed fashion, not likeinge such talke, answeared, 'Tille valle, Tille valle.'*

'How say you, Mrs. Alice, is it not soe,' quoth he? *Bone Deus, bone Deus*, man, will this geere never be left?' quoth shee. 'Well then, Mrs. Alice, if it be soe, it is verie well. For I see noe great cause whie I should much joye of my gaie house, or of any thinge belonginge thereunto, when, if I should but seaven yeares lye buried under the ground, and then arise and come thither againe, I should not fayle to finde some therin that would bidd me gett me out of the doores, and tell mee that we are none of myne. What cause have I then to like such an house as would soe soone forgett his master?' Soe her perswasions moved him but a little.

I must say I agree with Mrs Alice and not with Thomas More.

7 His trial

i Sentenced to death

When he was in the Tower, he was visited by the new Lord Chancellor (Lord Audley) and other Privy Councillors. They asked him to withdraw his opposition to the Act of

---

* 'Tille valle, Tille valle' is now obsolete. It meant 'rubbish,' 'fiddlesticks.' It was used by Mistress Quickly in Shakespeare's *King Henry IV*, Part II, Act II, sc 4:
Mistress Quickly Pray ye, pacify yourself, Sir John: there comes no swaggerers here.
Falstaff Dost thou hear? it is mine ancient.
Mistress Quickly Tilly-fally, Sir John, ne'er tell me: your ancient swaggerer comes not in my doors.

Parliament making the King supreme head of the Church. He refused. He was then indicted for high treason. The indictment was of enormous length. The only tenable count was that he had positively denied the King's supremacy and thereby attempted to deprive the King of his dignity and title. He was tried in the Court of King's Bench in Westminster Hall. The only evidence against him was given by the Solicitor General. He told about a private conversation in the Tower. The jury found More guilty. The Lord Chancellor pronounced sentence of death in the frightful form that he should be disembowelled and his four quarters should be set over four gates of the City and his head upon London Bridge. It was changed afterwards to beheading.

ii *The Winchester man*

Six days later, he was executed. On his way, a Winchester man pushed through the crowd. The story is set out by Professor R W Chambers. He says it is one of the great stories of the world:[1]

Afterwards, as he passed, there came to him a citizen of Winchester, who had been once with Sir Thomas before, and it was upon this occasion.

This poor man was grievously vexed with very vehement and grievous tentations of desperation, and could never be rid of it, either by counsel or prayer of his own or of his friends. At last a good friend of his brought him to Sir Thomas, then Chancellor. Who, taking compassion of the poor man's misery, gave him the best counsel and advice he could. But it would not serve. Then fell he to his prayers for him, earnestly beseeching Almighty God to rid the poor man of his trouble of mind. He obtained it; for, after that, the Hampshire man was never troubled with it any more, so long as he would come to Sir Thomas More; but after he was imprisoned and could have no access unto him, his tentation began again more vehement and troublesome than ever before. So he spent his days with a heavy heart, and without all hope of remedy.

But when he heard that Sir Thomas was condemned, he posted from Winchester, hoping at least to see him as he should go to execution, and so determined to speak with him, come what would of it. And for that cause he placed himself in the way. And at his coming by, he thrust through the throng, and with a loud voice said, 'Mr. More, do you know

[1] *Thomas More*, pp 40–41.

me? I pray you for our Lord's sake, help me: I am as ill troubled as ever I was.' Sir Thomas answered, 'I remember thee full well. Go thy ways in peace, and pray for me: and I will not fail to pray for thee.'

And from that time after, so long as he lived, he was never troubled with that manner of tentation.

iii *His end*

More went on to the scaffold. It seemed unsafe. He turned to the officer and said to him:

Pray, master lieutenant, pray see me safe up, and as to my coming down I will shift for myself.'

When there, he turned and said to those standing by:

Pray for me in this world. I will pray for you elsewhere. I die the King's good servant, but God's first.

Then he knelt down on the scaffold and said (from *Psalm* 51):

Have mercy upon me, O God, after thy great goodness: according to the multitude of thy mercies do away mine offences.

One blow was enough. His head was stuck on a pole and placed on London Bridge. He has been canonised by the Church of Rome which he supported against the Church of England.

8 Legal points

i *The granting of injunctions*

There is a catch-phrase which says that 'History repeats itself.' It goes back to Thucydides who wrote a history of the great war between Athens and Sparta about 2,400 years ago. He said the usefulness of his history was that events were very likely, in accordance with human nature, to repeat themselves at some future time.

This is well shown by the repeated occasions where lawyers have insisted on the strict letter of the law and it has needed equity to intervene to mitigate the rigour of it. It was so in Rome when the praetors intervened. It has been so in England when the Chancellor intervened. Wolsey and More were the first and greatest exponents of it. They used injunctions with great effect. I like to think that we followed their good example when we introduced the *Mareva* injunction of which I have told you in *The Due Process of Law* and in *The Closing Chapter*.

ii *Statutory interpretation*

It is interesting also to see that statutory interpretation was as much an issue in those days as now. Christopher St German in 1539 stated the law much as I stated it in 1949 in *Seaford Court Estates Ltd v Asher:*[1]

> Put into homely metaphor it is this: A judge should ask himself the question: If the makers of the Act had themselves come across this ruck in the texture of it, how would they have straightened it out? He must then do as they would have done. A judge must not alter the material of which it is woven, but he can and should iron out the creases.

iii *A judge accepting gifts*

In the days of Wolsey and More, people used to give New Year gifts to their friends. They did not give Christmas presents as we do now. It was, I am sorry to say, the practice of litigants to give New Year gifts to judges – sometimes before the case was heard – sometimes afterwards if the decision was favourable to them. It was also the practice to make substantial payments to their clerks and attendants. Roper tell us:[2]

> When Cardinall Wolsey was Lord Chauncellor, not onely divers of his privie chamber, but such also as were his doer keepers gott greate gaine.

Nowadays there is no such practice. No judge in modern times, as far as I know, has ever been offered a present from a litigant before or after a case. If it were he would certainly refuse it. He would not try the case himself, lest he be prejudiced. He would send it to another judge. He would draw it to the attention of the Attorney-General with a view

---

[1] [1949] 2 KB 481, 499.
[2] *The Life of Sir Thomas More.*

to proceedings for contempt of court. There is the humorous story of the man who asked his friend whether he should send a present to the judge. 'Of course not,' was the reply. He won the case. Afterwards the friend said: 'I hope you took my advice.' Answer: 'No. I did send a present to the judge, but I sent it in the other man's name.'

3 John Scott

Introduction

In 1617 when John Selden told of the 'Chancellor's foot,' equity was variable and flexible. But 200 years later in 1818 it had become rigid and technical. It had lost its flexibility. This was largely due to John Scott, later Lord Eldon. He was Lord Chancellor for over 25 years. In *Gee v Pritchard* he scorned the phrase. He said:[1]

> The doctrines of this Court ought to be as well settled and made as uniform almost as those of the common law, laying down fixed principles, but taking care that they are to be applied according to the circumstances of each case . . . Nothing would inflict on me greater pain, in quitting this place, than the recollection that I had done any thing to justify the reproach that the equity of this Court varies like the Chancellor's foot.

1 John Scott himself

i *Like me*

He was born in 1751 in Newcastle-upon-Tyne. Like me, he was one of a large family. Like me, his father was a tradesman. Like me, he went to the grammar school. Like me, he went to Oxford. Like me, he fell in love with a girl in his home town. Like me, he courted her with devotion.

---

[1] (1818) 2 Swan 402, 414.

ii *He elopes with Bessy*

Unlike me, he eloped with her. He got a ladder and placed it against her window on the first floor. Campbell tells us:[1]

Down it Bessy Surtees, 'with an unthrift love,' descended into the arms of John Scott.

He had a post-chaise in waiting. They drove 'over the border and away.' Not to Gretna Green – but to Blackshiels near Edinburgh, where they were married according to the rites of the Church of England. They came back to Newcastle. His parents welcomed the couple, but hers did not.

iii *'The poor lad is undone!'*

Everyone thought it was the ruin of him. His old schoolmaster beat his breast, saying:

Jack Scott has run off with Bessy Surtees! The poor lad is undone! the poor lad is undone!

As it turned out, it was the greatest blessing that he ever had. He had been destined for the Church – as I was for teaching – but he turned it down.

iv *'The world was all before them'*

In his *Anecdote Book* he wrote:

I quitted my Fellowship upon my Marriage with Miss Surtees – and, having then the world before us, and, as it proved, a most kind providence my Guide, I gave up the purpose of taking Orders, and entered as a Student in the middle Temple in January 1773.

He was there quoting from the last lines of Milton's *Paradise Lost*:

> The world was all before them, where to choose
> Their place of rest, and Providence their guide:
> They hand in hand with wandering steps and slow
> Through Eden took their solitary way.

[1] *Lives of the Lord Chancellors*, Vol VII, 26.

v *'Not one shilling'*

Like me, he got no work for a time. In his first year he made
half a guinea. I made three guineas. Later on he told this story
about it:[1]

When I was called to the bar, Bessy and I thought all our troubles were
over; business was to pour in, and we were to be almost rich
immediately. So I made a bargain with her, that during the following
year all the money I should receive in the first eleven months should be
mine, and whatever I should get in the twelfth month should be hers.
That was our agreement, and how do you think that it turned out? In the
twelfth month I received half a guinea; eighteen pence went for charity,
and Bessy got nine shillings. In the other eleven months I got not one
shilling.'

vi *He joins the Chancery Bar*

Their marriage was one of great happiness and devotion on
both sides. It lasted nearly 60 years till Bessy died in 1831. He
died in 1838 aged 87. They had six children.

At first he attended the Common Law Courts. He went
the Northern Circuit. But not getting much work, he joined
the Chancery Bar which only numbered 15. There he
succeeded.

vii *A brief for one guinea*

His success at the Bar all flowed from a brief for one guinea in
Ackroyd v Smithson.[2] It was tried in Lincoln's Inn Old Hall in
1780. He was aged 28. It was on a question of succession.
How should a testator's estate be distributed? He was
instructed to consent to the application, but instead he
opposed it. He submitted an argument on a point of law
which succeeded. His argument is reported (page 505) and
the reporter adds a note:

This most able argument confirmed the increasing reputation of Mr
Scott, which quickly led him, under the well-merited high estimation of

---

[1] Campbell *Lives of the Lord Chancellors*, Vol VII, 45.
[2] (1780) 1 Bro CC 503.

Lord Thurlow and his contemporaries, through successive honours, to the most elevated station in his country.

Campbell also tells us:[1]

Mr Scott's argument in *Ackroyd v Smithson* made a great sensation in Westminster Hall, and, in the words of Lord Byron, 'next day he awoke and found himself famous.'

2 As Lord Chancellor

i *Longer than any other*

He got more briefs. He entered Parliament. He became successively Solicitor-General, Attorney-General, Chief Justice of the Common Pleas, and then in 1801 Lord Chancellor. Apart from a short interval, he was Lord Chancellor until 1827. Longer than any Lord Chancellor before or since. He resigned at the age of 76.

ii *The most Die-hard Tory*

He was the most Die-hard Tory who ever lived. He opposed every reform in the law. He resisted the great Reform Act 1832, Catholic Emancipation, the Great Western Railway and many other measures. He opposed any change of any kind. But he was a kind and courteous judge. He listened patiently to everything everybody had to say, relevant or irrelevant.

iii *His delays*

He was not a great judge. His delays caused great injustice. Campbell tells us (page 625):

... Yet he not unfrequently expressed doubts – reserved to himself the opportunity for further consideration – took home the papers – never read them – promised judgment again and again – and for years never gave it – all the facts and the law connected with it having escaped from his memory.

[1] *Lives of the Lord Chancellors*, Vol VII, 56.

iv *He excuses himself*

In his *Anecdote Book* he sought to excuse himself:

During my Chancellorship I was much, very much blamed, for not giving Judgement at the close of the Arguments. I persevered in this, as some thought from obstinacy, but, in Truth, from principle – from adherence to a Rule of Conduct, formed, after much consideration what Course of proceeding was most consonant with my Duty . . . I always thought it better to allow myself to doubt before I decided, than to expose myself to the Misery, after I had decided, of doubting whether I had decided rightly and justly.

That is no excuse at all. The duty of a judge is to decide the case at once, at most a few days' delay, whilst it is still in his mind. That was always my practice.

v *His style was appalling*

Next, his style was appalling. Campbell tells us (pages 641, 636):

His manner was so diffuse, his arrangement so immethodical, and his style so repulsive, that I have in vain searched for specimens of his judgments which might be perused with pleasure. Not even when he is discoursing on the management of theatres, or on copyright in libellous publications, or on taking the custody of children from an immoral parent, is he readable without a fee . . .

. . . Very few of his judgments can be perused without a most painful effort . . . His statement of facts to be found in them is desultory and slovenly, and is often mixed up with propositions of law; he is occasionally very illogical, and you cannot tell from what premises he draws his conclusion.

I quite agree. So much so that I do not remember myself quoting any of his judgments.

4 Equity today

A great change was made by the Judicature Act 1873 when Lord Selborne was Lord Chancellor. The rules of law and of equity were fused together. Whenever there was any conflict between them, the rules of equity were to prevail. For a long time they were still kept separate by the practitioners who had been used to the old ways. But now, after 100 years, the fusion is complete. Every court now applies equitable considerations. I have told you the story of it in *The Family Story* (pages 176–177).

I said in a lecture in 1952:

We stand at the threshold of a new Elizabethan era. Let us play a worthy part in it.

Now, thirty years later in 1984, I can say that in my time the courts have discovered the new equity. It is fair and just and flexible, but not as variable as the 'Chancellor's foot.' It is a great achievement.

If I were setting an examination paper for students, I would ask them to give examples of the truth of that statement. They would find them in the doctrines of promissory estoppel, proprietary estoppel, constructive trusts, licences of land, granting of injunctions, and so forth.

Part Four

Martyrdom

Introduction

We look with scorn upon anyone who seeks to 'make a martyr of himself.' He is ready to suffer death or grievous pain in order to gain credit for himself for doing it. Such a man is not entitled to the credit which he seeks.

A true martyr is one who does not seek credit for himself. He suffers death or grievous pain because of the faith in which he believes. He is called upon to renounce it, but refuses to do so: and is punished for his refusal. Those who are of the same faith call him a martyr. Those who are of a different faith call him a heretic or misguided.

Martyrdom does enhance the credit of the cause for which he dies or suffers pain. Judges should be careful not to pass a sentence so severe as to make the offender a martyr.

This lesson is taught by the cases of Hugh Latimer and the Tolpuddle Martyrs.

1 Hugh Latimer

1 Hugh Latimer himself

i *The Martyrs' Memorial*

Every student at Oxford knows the Martyrs' Memorial. It is at the fork of the road where St Giles goes into the Cornmarket on one side and past Balliol on the other. Thousands pass it every day. Students in high spirits rag there. They climb it. They place rude ornaments at the top. But how many know who were the Martyrs? How many could give their names? How many know how they met their deaths? And for what cause they died? I confess that I, as a student, did not know. But I do now. Their names were Nicholas Ridley and Hugh Latimer. They were burnt alive. They were condemned for heresy. Because they would not accept the doctrine of transubstantiation. What is that doctrine? You may well ask. Go to one of the theological colleges. They may be able to tell you. Or you may find it out by the story I have to tell of their trial. But I will keep it mostly to Hugh Latimer.

ii *One of the greatest preachers*

He was born in Leicestershire in 1491. He was one of the greatest preachers that England ever had. We have samples of his preaching in the sermons which he preached before King Edward VI in the year 1549. He wrote them out himself in his own spelling which I hope you will follow. In the first of these he gave a vivid account of his own boyhood:

iii *His own boyhood*

My father was a Yoman, and had no landes of hys own, only he had a farme of iii. or iiii. pound by yere at the uttermooste, and here upon he tilled so much as kept half a dosen men. He had walke for a hundred shepe, and my mother milked xxx. kyne. He was able and did finde the kyng a harnesse, with himselfe, and his horse, whyle he came to the place that he shoulde receive the kynges wages. I can remembre, that I buckled hys harnesse, when he wente unto Blacke heathe felde. He kept me to schole, or els I hadde not bene able to have preached before the kinges majesty now. He maryed my systers wyth v. pounde, or xx. nobles a piece, so that he brought them up in godlinesse, and fear of God. He kepte hospitality for his pore neighboures. And some almesse he gave to the pore, and al thys dyd he of the said farm.

He also told of his soldierly training. It is good advice for those who practice archery now:

My father was delighted to teach me to shoot with the bow. He taught me how to draw, how to lay my body to the bow, not to draw with strength of arm as other nations do but with the strength of the body.

iv *'Til his tong be worn to the stomps'*

Then he goes on to commend good education for the sons of yeomen:

But let the precher preach till his tong be worn to the stomps, nothing is amended. We have good statutes made for the common wealth as touching commeners, enclosers, many metings and sessions, but in the end of the matter, there commeth nothing forthe. Well, well, thys is one thing I wil say unto you, from whence it commeth I know, even from the devil. I know his intent in it. For if ye bring it to passe, that the yomanry be not able to put their sonnes to schole (as in dede universities do wondrously decay al redy) and that they be not able to marrye theyr daughters to the avoidynge of whoredome I say ye plucke salvation from the people, and utterly destroye the realme. For by yomans sonnes, the faith of Christe is, and hath bene maintayned chieflye. Is this realme taughte by rich mens sonnes? No, no, read the chronicles, ye shall finde somtime noble mennes sonnes, whych have bene unpreaching bishops and prelates, but ye shal fynde none of them learned men.

2 Mary's reign of terror

i *300 Protestants burnt*

Hugh Latimer was then Court Preacher. But the young

King Edward VI died in 1553. He was succeeded by Mary Tudor. She insisted on marrying Philip of Spain in flat disregard of her subjects' wishes. She married him, too, I am sorry to say, in our cathedral at Winchester. She revived the Pope's jurisdiction over England. She got Parliament to bring back the laws against heresy. She entrusted their enforcement to the ecclesiastical courts. They condemned 300 Protestants in four years. They were burnt at the stake. This reign of terror bred in England a hatred of Roman Catholics and all they stood for. The story was told in simple, homely style by John Foxe in his *Book of Martyrs*. He was a Fellow of my own College, Magdalen. For the next 200 years and more his book was placed beside the Bible in parish churches. I will tell of the trial of Ridley and Latimer as set down by Foxe.

ii *Three Bishops sit*

The Pope's representative in England at the time was Cardinal Pole. He issued a Commission to the Bishops of Lincoln, Gloucester and Bristol. They sat as an ecclesiastical court to try Nicholas Ridley, Bishop of London, and Hugh Latimer, previously Bishop of Worcester. The prosecution charged them with heresy from April to July 1554 in the University of Oxford. The first two Articles alleged that they had denied the doctrine of transubstantiation.

iii *What transubstantiation means*

Now I can tell you what 'transubstantiation' means. It means the transfer of the actual substance of bread and wine into the actual body and blood of Christ. It is described in the *Shorter Oxford Dictionary* as:

The conversion in the Eucharist of the whole substance of the bread into the body and of the wine into the blood of Christ, only the appearances of bread and wine remaining: according to the doctrine of the Roman Catholic Church 1533.

It was not the doctrine of the Church of England. In 1562 (after Latimer's death) the 28th of the Articles of Religion of the Church of England (in the *Book of Common Prayer*) said and still says:

Transubstantiation (or the change of the substance of Bread and Wine) in the Supper of the Lord, cannot be proved by holy Writ; but is repugnant to the plain words of Scripture, overthroweth the nature of a Sacrament, and hath given occasion to many superstitions.

In short, Latimer was held right – after his death.

iv *The charge is formulated*

The charge against Ridley and Latimer was that they affirmed, and openly defended and maintained,

(1) that the true and natural Body of Christ, after the Consecration of the Priest, is not really present in the Sacrament of the Altar, and
(2) that in the Sacrament of the Altar remaineth still the substance of Bread and Wine.

3 The trial – First day

i *He has to wait outside*

Foxe describes the trial at length in his book.[1] The three Bishops – of Lincoln, Gloucester and Bristol – sat in the Divinity School. It is one of the loveliest rooms in Oxford. (I was examined in it when I first went up.) The trial began on 30 September 1554. Nicholas Ridley was tried first. Hugh Latimer had to wait outside. When he was called in, Foxe describes the scene in graphic language:

Lat. My Lords, if I appear again I pray you not to send for me until you be ready. For I am an old man, and it is great hurt to mine old age to tarry so long gazing upon the cold walls.

Then the Bishop of Lincoln.

Linc. Mr Latimer, I am sorry you are brought so soon, although it is the Bayliffs fault, and not mine; but it shall be amended.

ii *His simple dress*

Then Mr Latimer bowed his knee down to the ground, holding his hat in his hand, having a Kerchief on his head and upon it a night-Cap or two,

[1] *Book of Martyrs*, vol III, pp 419–431.

and a great Cap (such as Towns-men use, with two broad flaps to butten under the Chin) wearing an old thred-bare *Bristow* Frize gown girded to his Body with a penny leather Girdle, at the which hanged by a long string of leather his Testament, and his spectacles without case, depending about his neck upon his brest.

iii *He is invited to recant*

The Bishop of Lincoln then invited Hugh Latimer to recant and to subscribe to the doctrine of transubstantiation, in which case he would go free.

. . . If you shall now recant, revoke, and disannul these your Errors, and together with all this Realm, yea all the world confess the Truth, we upon due repentance of you part shall receive you, reconcile you, acknowledge you no longer a strayed sheep, but adjoyn you again to the unity of Christ Church, from the which you in the time of Schism fell. So that it is no new place to the which I exhort you; I desire you to return thither from whence you went.

Hugh Latimer did not accept the invitation. Foxe tells us that:

Mr Latimer, which before leaned his head to his hand, began somewhat to remove his Cap and Kerchief from his ears.

iv 'A rotten member of the Church'

The Bishop then went on:

. . . If you shall stubbornly persevere in your blindness, if you will not acknowledge your Errors, . . . then must we proceed to . . . (do that) which we would be loth to do, that is, not to condemn you, for that we cannot do (that the temporal Sword of the Realm, and not we, will do) but to separate you from us, acknowledge you to be none of us, to renounce you as no member of the Church, to declare that you are *filius perditionis*, a lost Child, and as you are a rotten member of the Church, so to cut you off from the Church, and so to commit you to the temporal Judges, permitting them to proceed against you, according to the tenor of their Laws.

v *The Bishop of Rome has no authority*

Then this polite exchange took place:

Lat. Then will your Lordship give me leave to speak a word or two?

Linc. Yes, Mr Latimer, so that you use a modest kind of talk, without railing or taunts.

Lat. I beseech your Lordship, licence me to sit down.

Linc. At your pleasure, Mr Latimer, take as much ease as you will.

Lat. Your Lordship gently exhorted me in many words to come to the unity of the Church. . . . (I summarise his words) But the only Church which I acknowledge is a Catholick Church spread throughout all the world: not the Church which has its foundation in Rome only. Those Bishops in Rome ought to rule according to the Word of God: but they have turned it so that they rule according to their own pleasures and as it pleases them best.

Hugh Latimer also took exception to the jurisdiction of the Commissioners. They had been appointed by the Bishop of Rome. He could not acknowledge any authority of the Bishop of Rome.

4 The trial – Next day

i '*A very evil Back*'

The hearing was adjourned and continued the next day. There was such a crowd of people at the entrance that Mr Latimer asked their Lordships to see there was better order.

Lat. . . . I am an Old man, and have a very evil Back, so that the press of the multitude doth me much harm.

Linc. I am sorry, Mr Latimer, for your hurt. At your departure we will see to better order.

With that Mr Latimer thanked his Lordship, making a very low courtesie.

ii *He denies transubstantiation*

There was a discussion again on theology. Latimer gave his answer about transubstantiation in these words:

Lat. . . . In the Sacrament the worthy receiver receiveth the very Body of Christ, and drinketh his Blood by (as a token of) the Spirit and Grace. But after (as to it being) a corporal (physical) being (presence) which the

Romish Church prescribeth, (I say that) Christs Body and Blood is not in the Sacrament under the forms of Bread and Wine.

This was a denial of the doctrine of transubstantiation.

iii *Condemned as a heretic*

Once more the Bishop of Lincoln exhorted Mr Latimer to recant. Once more Mr Latimer refused.

Then the Bishop of Lincoln, speaking for all three Bishops, said:

We judge and condemn Hugh Latimer to be a Heretick. We declare him to be no member of the Church. We commit him to the Secular Powers, of them to receive due punishment according to the tenor of the temporal Laws.

iv *Handed over for execution*

You will notice that the Commissioners did not pass sentence of death. They only condemned Ridley and Latimer as heretics. That being done, the Queen herself in Council issued a writ *de haeretico comburendo*. It was issued to the Mayor of the City or Sheriff of the County, commanding him to take the body of the offender and burn him. Blackstone tells us:[1]

... the Romish ecclesiastics determining, without appeal, whatever they pleased to be heresy, and shifting off to the secular arm the odium and drudgery of executions; with which they themselves were too tender and delicate to intermeddle. Nay they pretended to intercede and pray, on behalf of the convicted heretic: well knowing at the same time that they were delivering the unhappy victim to certain death.

5 Preparations for the burning

i *Next Balliol College*

As I have said Queen Mary in Council issued a writ *de haeretico comburendo* for the burning of Ridley and Latimer. I propose now to describe that last scene by taking the very words of John Foxe but shortening them.

[1] *Commentaries* IV, pp 45–46.

Upon the North-side of the Town, in the Ditch over against Baily-Colledge, the place of Execution was appointed: . . . and when every thing was in a readiness, the Prisoners were brought forth by the Mayor and the Bayliffs.

ii *Dressed for the occasion*

Mr Ridley had a fair black Gown furred, and faced with Foins,[2] such as he was wont to wear being Bishop, and a Tippet of Velvet furred likewise about his neck, a Velvet Night-cap upon his head, and a Corner-cap upon the same, going in a pair of Slippers to the Stake, and going between the Mayor and an Alderman, &c.

After him came Mr Latimer in a poor *Bristow* freez Frock all worn, with his buttoned Cap, and a Kerchief on his head, all ready to the Fire, a new long Shroud hanging over his Hose down to the feet: which at the first light stirred mens hearts to rue upon them, beholding on the one side, the honour they sometime had, and on the other, the calamity whereunto they were fallen.

iii *An exhortation to recant*

A Dr Smith (who had previously himself recanted) preached a sermon.

'. . . He ended with a very short exhortation to them to recant and come home again to the Church, and save their lives and Souls, which else were condemned. His Sermon was scant in all a quarter of an hour.'

They did not recant.

iv *Stripped ready*

. . . Incontinently they were commanded to make them ready, which they with all meekness obeyed. Mr Ridley took his gown and his tippet, and gave it to his Brother in Law . . . Some other of his apparel that was little worth, he gave away, other the Bayliffs took.

He gave away besides, divers other small things to Gentlemen standing by . . .

Master Latimer gave nothing, but very quietly suffered his Keeper to pull off his hose, and his other array, which to look unto was very simple: and being stripped into his shrowd, he seemed as comely a person to them that were there present, as one should lightly see; and whereas in his clothes he appeared a withered and crooked silly old man, he now stood bolt upright, as comely a father as one might lightly behold . . .

---

[2] The fur of a beech-marten.

v *Gunpowder is brought*

Then the Smith took a chain of Iron, and brought the same about both Doctor Ridleys, and Mr Latimers middles: and as he was knocking in a staple, Doctor Ridley took the chain in his hand, and shaked the same, for it did gird in his belly, and looking aside to the Smith, said; Good fellow, knock it in hard, for the flesh will have his course. Then his Brother did bring him gun-powder in a bag, and would have tied the same about his neck, Master Ridley asked what it was. His Brother, said, Gun-powder. Then said he, I will take it to be sent of God, therefore I will receive it as sent of him. And have you any said he, for my Brother, meaning Master Latimer? Yea Sir, that I have (quoth his Brother:) Then give it unto him (said he) betime, lest ye come too late. So his Brother went, and carried of the same Gun-powder unto Master Latimer . . .

vi *'Light such a candle'*

Then they brought a Faggot, kindled with fire, and laid the same down at D. Ridleys feet. To whom Mr Latimer spake in this manner; Be of good comfort, Mr Ridley, and play the man, we shall this day light such a candle by Gods grace in England, as I trust shall never be put out.

6 The fire is lit

i *Latimer soon dies*

And so the fire being given unto them, when Doctor Ridley saw the fire flaming up towards him, he cried with a wonderful lowd voyce; *In manus tuas, Domine, commendo Spiritum meum: Domine recipe Spiritum meum*, and after repeated this later part often in English, Lord, Lord, receive my Spirit: Master Latimer crying as vehemently on the other side, O Father of Heaven receive my Soul: who received the flame as it were imbracing of it. After that he had stroaked his face with his hands, and as it were bathed them a little in the fire, he soon died (as it appeareth) with very little pain or none. And thus much concerning the end of this old and blessed Servant of God, Master Latimer, for whose laborious travels, fruitful life, and constant death, the whole Realm hath cause to give great thanks to Almighty God.

ii *Ridley in torment*

But Master Ridley by reason of the evil making of the fire unto him, because the wooden faggots were laid about the goss,[1] and over high

[1] Gorse.

built, the fire burned first beneath, being kept down by the wood . . .
Yet in all this torment he forgot not to call unto God still, having in his
mouth, Lord have mercy upon me . . . And when the flame touched the
Gun-powder, he was seen stirr no more, but burned on the other side,
falling down at Master Latimers feet . . .

Some said that before he was like to fall from the stake, he desired
them to hold him to it with their bills. However it was, surely it moved
hundreds to tears, in beholding the horrible sight. For I think there was
none, that had not clean exiled all humanity and mercy, which would not
have lamented to behold the fury of the fire so to rage upon their
bodies. . . .

iii *The verdict of history*

I cannot do better than quote to you the words of G M
Trevelyan in his *History of England:*[1]

In the hands of able propagandists like John Foxe, the memory of the
martyrs bred a hatred of the Church of Rome, which proved the one
constant element in English opinion during the coming centuries of civil
and religious faction. For the next two hundred years and more Foxe's
Book of Martyrs was often placed beside the Bible in the parish churches,
and was read in manor-house and cottage, by Anglican and Puritan, in an
epoch when there was relatively little else to read and when interest in
religion was profound and widespread.

Most of the victims were inhabitants of London or the Home
Counties, and most of them were humble folk. But Latimer died as he
might have desired, lighting the candle of his own clear certainty to
illuminate the more complex and hesitating opinion of others. In an age
of mixed measures, confused counsels and compromise, he had held a
straight course which the English of the new era could understand and
imitate.

7 Ecclesiastical law

i *An ecclesiastical judge*

I was once an ecclesiastical judge. The appointment is in the
hands of the bishop of the diocese. In 1937, our friend George
Cockin (afterwards Bishop of Bristol) mentioned me (still a
junior at the Bar) to the Bishop of Southwark. He appointed
me Chancellor of the Diocese. Afterwards Geoffrey Fisher,

[1] Book III, chapter IV.

when Bishop of London, appointed me Chancellor of the Diocese of London. I gave up each office on becoming a judge of the High Court in March 1944. Then soon afterwards, the House of Lords had a question of ecclesiastical law. It was whether the rector was liable to repair the chancel of a church (*Representative Body of the Church in Wales v Tithe Redemption Commission*[1]). The Lord Chancellor, Lord Simon (after the hearing and before the decision) asked me – a very young judge – to look into it. I did so and told him. I wrote an article for the *Law Quarterly Review* on 'The Meaning of Ecclesiastical Law.'[2]

ii *Importance in old days*

Nowadays, people do not realise how important ecclesiastical law was in the old days. Lord Coke made a great study of it in *Caudrey's case*.[3] He says (page 9):

As in temporal causes the King by the mouth of the judges in his Courts of Justice doth judge and determine the same by the temporal laws of England: so in causes ecclesiastical and spiritual, as namely, blasphemy, apostasy from Christianity, heresies, schisms, . . . rights of matrimony, divorces, . . . reparation of churches, probate of testaments, administration and accounts upon the same, . . . adulteries, solicitation of chastity . . . and others (*the conusance whereof belongs not to the common laws of England*) the same are to be determined and decided by Ecclesiastical Judges, according to the King's Ecclesiastical Laws of this Realm.

iii *Powers of enforcement*

The great difference between the temporal law and the ecclesiastical law was in the powers of the judges. Ecclesiastical law had no power of sentencing a man to imprisonment or ordering him to pay damages. That was left to the temporal courts. The remedies provided by ecclesiastical law, against both clergy and laity, were monition (an order telling the man to do his duty), penance (an order to show contrition in a specified way for

---

[1] [1944] AC 228.
[2] [1944] 60 LQR 235.
[3] (1591) 5 Co Rep 1.

wrongdoing), suspension *ab ingressu ecclesiae* (forbidding admission to church), and excommunication ('which if it was effectual here and hereafter, was a very terrible sentence, and at the time when the ecclesiastical law was framed and adopted in England, it was believed to be effectual in this life and the next': *per* Lord Blackburn in *Mackonochie v Penzance*[1]). The only means of enforcing any of the lesser sentences was by excommunication.

iv *Little left now*

Most of the ecclesiastical jurisdiction has since been transferred by Parliament to the temporal courts. The matrimonial causes are dealt with by the Family Division. The probate cases are dealt with by the Chancery Division. All that is left to the ecclesiastical courts is the discipline of clergy and the grant of faculties and marriage licences.

All the old ecclesiastical offences such as heresy, apostasy, adultery, and immorality are gone altogether. They are not punishable by the ecclesiastical courts. They are not offences either by ecclesiastical law or by temporal law. The ecclesiastical law upon them is now obsolete. So said the Court of Appeal in *Blunt v Park Lane Hotel*.[2]

v *A modern revival*

But we have very recently seen a revival of a branch of ecclesiastical law. It appears that a curate's wife and a country solicitor had associated with one another. They were barred from Holy Communion. The decision was announced publicly in two churches. And then spread in headlines in all the newspapers of the country.

The public announcement was justified by reference to the canon law. The rubric in the *Book of Common Prayer of 1662* says:

And if any of those be an open and notorious evil liver, or have done any wrong to his neighbours by word or deed, so that the Congregation be

[1] [1881] 6 App Cas 424, 448.
[2] [1942] 2 KB 253.

thereby offended; the Curate, having knowledge thereof, shall call him and advertise him, that in any wise he presume not to come to the Lord's Table, until he have openly declared himself to have truly repented and amended his former naughty life, that the Congregation may thereby be satisfied, which before were offended; and that he have recompensed the parties, to whom he hath done wrong; or at least declare himself to be in full purpose so to do, as soon as he conveniently may.'

I should have thought myself that that too was obsolete. A private intimation to the two would have sufficed without crying 'scandal' publicly.

vi *The new rubric*

Such was the old rubric in the 1662 *Book of Common Prayer*. The Church authorities have now made a new rubric. It is not in the 1980 *Alternative Service Book* and the ordinary reader has no access to it. It is too complicated to set out in full. The effect of it is that Holy Communion can only be refused when a person has been guilty of 'grave and open sin without repentance.' Even in such a case, however, the clergyman must not refuse it on his own initiative. He must first tell the Bishop of the Diocese. The Bishop must hear what the offender has to say and then direct the clergyman what to do.

If a clergyman should refuse Holy Communion without the approval of the Bishop he is guilty of an ecclesiastical offence and can be punished by the Consistory Court. He may also be liable to a civil action. If a person should present himself at the altar rail – and the clergyman should openly pass him by – that would convey the imputation that he was a notorious sinner. He might in some circumstances have a civil action for damages for slander.

If the sin is very grave and scandalous, and there is no time to consult the Bishop, the clergyman can refuse at once so long as he tells the Bishop within seven days: and then obeys the directions of the Bishop.

2 The Tolpuddle Martyrs[1]

1 George Loveless himself

i *On the Piddle*

You will have heard tell of the Tolpuddle Martyrs: but do you know the story? Do you even know where Tolpuddle is? It is a little village in Dorset. It gets its name, Tolpuddle, because it is on a stream there called, if you please, the Piddle. It came into the news in 1834, 150 years ago. The men in Tolpuddle worked on the farms roundabout. Their wages were at starvation level. Only nine shillings a week. In other parts of Dorset farm labourers were getting 10 shillings. The Tolpuddle men got together and asked for a rise. The Vicar went with them to see the farmers. No good came of it. They went to the magistrates. They could do nothing. So one of the men, George Loveless, said to the others, 'Let us form a trade union.'

ii *A 'village-Hampden'*

You should know about George Loveless. He turned out to be, in the words of the poet:

> Some village-Hampden, that with dauntless breast
> The little tyrant of his fields withstood.[2]

---

[1] Ref *The Martyrs of Tolpuddle*, published by the Trades Union Congress General Council, London (1934).
[2] Thomas Gray *Elegy Written in a Country Churchyard.*

George Loveless was aged 37. He was living with his wife and three children in a thatched cottage in Tolpuddle. It was a 'tied' cottage. It went with his job. He worked on the farm six days a week. On Sundays he went round preaching in the villages: for he was a religious man and had the gift of speech. He knew his Bible well. He was a Methodist, following the teaching of John Wesley. So were others in Tolpuddle. John Wesley had been there 50 years before, giving his simple message:

> Do all the good you can,
> By all the means you can,
> In all the ways you can,
> In all the places you can,
> At all the times you can,
> To all the people you can,
> As long as ever you can.[1]

iii *He read about trade unions*

George Loveless read other books too besides the Bible. He got to know much about trade unions. They were sweeping the country. They were combining together to form one general union. Sidney Webb tells us that:

Within a few weeks the Union appears to have been joined by at least half a million members, including tens of thousands of farm labourers and women . . . Numerous missionary delegates, duly equipped with all the paraphernalia required for the mystic initiation rites, perambulated the country; and a positive mania for Trade Unionism set in.[2]

2 The six Tolpuddle men

i *A family affair*

In October 1833 two of these missionary delegates came to Tolpuddle. They helped George Loveless form a trade union. They called it the 'Friendly Society of Agricultural Labourers.' Six Tolpuddle men became founder members. It

[1] *Letters* (1915), *Rule of Conduct.*
[2] Webb *Trade Unionism*, pp 120–122.

was very much a family affair. They were George Loveless, aged 37; his younger brother, James (25); their brother-in-law, Thomas Standfield (44), who had married their sister; their nephew, John Standfield (21); James Hammett (22); and James Brine (20). Once the Society was founded, they held regular meetings in an upper room in Thomas Standfield's cottage.

ii *The five Affpuddle men*

A mile downstream from Tolpuddle there is another village on the Piddle. It is called Affpuddle. In December 1833 the Tolpuddle men sought to get the Affpuddle men to join them. Two of them called on five men at Affpuddle. They got them to go with them to Thomas Standfield's cottage at Tolpuddle. There they agreed to join the newly-formed trade union. The object of it was perfectly lawful. It was to get a rise in their wages. They were to pay an entrance fee of one shilling and a penny a week thereafter. But, in order to become members, they had to go through a mystic initiation ceremony and take an oath. Just as Freemasons had done for the previous 200 years.

iii *Solemn ritual*

All over the country at that time these initiation ceremonies were taking place. It was a solemn ritual which followed much the same pattern in towns and villages. It was a survival from the time when trade unions were illegal. (They had been liberated by the statutes of 1824 and 1825.) Its essence was a pledge of loyalty and secrecy. At Tolpuddle the ceremony was held in that upper room of Thomas Standfield's cottage. On one side of the room there was a full-size picture of a skeleton. It represented 'Death.' On a table there was a large Bible. In front of it stood James Loveless – the brother of George – wearing a surplice. Before entering the room, the five Affpuddle men had been blindfolded. They were led into the room and told to kneel down. They heard a voice say:

> Strangers, within our secret walls we have admitted you,
> Hoping you will prove honest, faithful, just and true . . .
> When you have our mystic rights gone through,
> Our secrets all will be disclosed to you . . .
> Woe, woe and dishonour attend the faithless and unjust.

More was said. Then the bandages were removed from their eyes. They stood up. Immediately in front of them was the skeleton. James Loveless pointed to it and said:

. . . Shouldst thou ever prove deceitful, remember thy end, remember. . . .

Again they were blindfolded. Again they were required to kneel down. A voice told them to repeat words after him. It was an oath, pledging support and loyalty. Each of the Affpuddle men took the oath, ending with the words:

. . . If ever I reveal either part or parts of this my most solemn obligation . . . may what is now before me [pointing to the skeleton] plunge my soul into the everlasting pit of misery. Amen.

They were then asked to kiss the book. Each did so. The bandages were removed from their eyes. They stood up and saw the six Tolpuddle men all there. That was the end of the ceremony.

3 The Dorset magistrates

i *One turns informer*

One of the Affpuddle men was John Lock. He told his father he had joined the union and a little about the initiation ceremony. Now his father was gardener to Mr Frampton, a wealthy Dorset squire and a leading magistrate. And his father passed it on to Mr Frampton who took a serious view of it. He wrote to the Home Secretary, Lord Melbourne, telling him that

Societies are forming . . . in which the labourers are induced to enter into combinations of a dangerous and alarming kind to which they are bound by oaths administered clandestinely.

He added that the magistrates were in communication with 'Trusty persons' to obtain information. In reply the Home Office wrote:

Lord Melbourne thinks the Magistrates have acted wisely in employing trusty persons to endeavour to obtain information regarding the unlawful combinations which they believe to be forming among the labourers.

ii *The magistrates are told*

Mr Frampton did get hold of the information. He got it from his gardener's son, John Lock, and another Affpuddle man, Edward Legg. Edward Legg risked eternal damnation. He broke his oath. He gave Mr Frampton a statement telling all that he could remember about the initiation ceremony. Mr Frampton sent it to Lord Melbourne who turned to the lawyers for advice.

iii *A caution is given*

The Home Office in London looked into the law. Could the farm labourers be prosecuted? and for what offence? It was very difficult to say. It was not unlawful to combine into a trade union to raise wages. That was enacted by statutes in 1824 and 1825. So what were they guilty of? It was so difficult that Lord Melbourne asked the Law Officers for their opinion. They advised him to concentrate upon the taking of an oath and to use the Mutiny Act 1797. It had been used in a case in 1802 against the clothworkers of Trowbridge.[1] That Act of 1797 made it an offence in certain circumstances to administer an oath. This advice was passed on to the Dorset magistrates. They put up posters giving this caution to all the people of Dorset:

CAUTION

WHEREAS it has been represented to us from several quarters, that mischievous and designing Persons have been for some time past, endeavouring to induce, and have induced, many Labourers in various

---

[1] *R v Marks* (1802) 3 East 157.

Parishes in this County, to attend Meetings, and to enter into Illegal Societies or Unions, to which they bind themselves by unlawful oaths, administered secretly by Persons concealed, who artfully deceive the ignorant and unwary, – WE, the undersigned Justices think it our duty to give this PUBLIC NOTICE and CAUTION, that all Persons may know the danger they incur by entering into such Societies.

. . .

Any Person who shall administer . . . any Unlawful Oath . . .

WILL BECOME

GUILTY OF FELONY,

AND BE LIABLE TO BE

TRANSPORTED FOR SEVEN YEARS

That was on Saturday 22 February 1834. George Loveless read it, made a copy and put it in his pocket. He was most concerned. He had never thought before that he had done anything unlawful.

iv *The six are arrested*

Only a Sunday came in between. On the morning of Monday 24 February 1834 George Loveless at daylight left his cottage to go to work. He closed the door quietly so as not to awaken the children. As he walked down the street the village constable (then called the tithing-man), a friend of his, met him:

I have a warrant from the magistrates for your arrest, Mr Loveless.

For me?

Yes, and for others beside you, James Hammett, Thomas Standfield, and his son John, young Brine, and for your brother, James.

What is the warrant for? What have we done?

You'd best take it and read it for yourself.

George Loveless read it. He went with the constable to the cottages of the other men. Then all six peacefully and without any resistance went with the constable. He took them on foot the seven miles to Dorchester. They were

108

taken before two magistrates, who committed them to prison. Afterwards the magistrates held a hearing in the prison at which Mr Frampton presided. They took the depositions of Edward Legg and others. The six were committed for trial at the next Assizes at Dorchester.

4 The trial itself

i *The judges come to Dorchester*

Two judges went the Western Circuit that spring. Mr Justice Bosanquet and Mr Baron Williams. They had been to Salisbury. Their next place was Dorchester. Travelling day was Friday 14 March 1834. When they came to the county boundary they were met by the High Sheriff of Dorset in his carriage, with his trumpeters and javelin men, all on horseback. The judges, in their full robes, were in their coach and four. The postilions were so skilled that they drew up the coach so that the judges could step across to the High Sheriff's carriage without putting foot to the ground. The judges' marshals went ahead in the judges' coach. The High Sheriff and the judges rode in state with their cavalcade into Dorchester.

Already the town was full of many who had come for the Assizes from a distance and had to stay the night. The High Sheriff and judges went to the County Hall where the Commission was opened and read. They went to the Church for the Assize Sermon. Then to the judges' lodgings.

It was Mr Baron Williams who was to try the crime. He had only been appointed a judge a fortnight before. Yet here he was to try one of the most momentous cases in our history. On Saturday he charged the Grand Jury. They returned a true bill against the six Tolpuddle men.

ii *The indictment is massive*

On Monday 17 March 1834 the six men were put up to plead. Their hair had been close cropped whilst they were in prison. Yet they bore themselves with dignity. The Clerk of Assize read out the indictment to them. It was a massive document of many pages. It had been prepared by the best lawyers of the day on behalf of the Government. It contained 12 counts putting the charge in 12 different ways. All to the effect of administering an unlawful oath to Edward Legg, prohibiting him from disclosing what had been done. Each count was put to each of the six.

George Loveless, how say you? Are you Guilty or Not Guilty?

Not Guilty.

Each one pleaded Not Guilty to each count.

iii *The judge takes up the running*

The jury were sworn. Counsel for the prosecution opened the case. He called two of the Affpuddle men, John Lock and Edward Legg. They turned out to be most reluctant witnesses. They did their best to help the six men in the dock. When counsel for the prosecution asked them about the initiation ceremony, time and again they said they could not remember. It was the judge who took up the running. He had the depositions in front of him. Using them, he cross–examined the witnesses himself:

You said before the magistrates that whilst you were blindfolded, you were given a book which you kissed. Was that the truth? Be careful what you say.

Witness I suppose so, if it is there.

The judge wrote it down as his evidence.

This was the account given by a gentleman at the Bar who was present at the trial:

The counsel for the prosecution in vain endeavoured to elicit such answers as would have supported the indictment, and such answers as were drawn from them, with great difficulty, were suggested to them in the form of leading questions by the judge reading from the depositions.

iv *'All hard-working men'*

Edward Legg did manage to say one thing in favour of the six. Answering their counsel, he said:

I know all the prisoners; they are all hard-working men, and I never heard a word against any of them.

None of the six gave evidence himself. A prisoner was not allowed to give evidence at that time in our history. But they were represented by counsel who addressed the jury on their behalf. After their speeches, the judge looked at the six men in the dock.

Have you anything to say on your own behalf?

v *George Loveless puts their defence*

George Loveless handed up a paper on which he had written:

My Lord, if we have violated any law, it was not done intentionally; we have injured no man's reputation, character, person, or property: we were uniting together to preserve ourselves, our wives and our children, from utter degradation and starvation. We challenge any man, or number of men, to prove that we have acted, or intended to act, different from the above statement.

Do you wish this to be read in court?

Yes.

The judge read it out but it was hardly audible to the jury.

vi *Verdict of guilty*

The judge then summed up to the jury. He told them that they must be satisfied of two things: first, that an oath was administered to Edward Legg; second, that it was to prohibit him from disclosing what had been done. The judge read the evidence to them. He told them to consider their verdict. In about 20 minutes the jury returned a verdict of guilty. In addition to their verdict the jury made a finding at the instance of the judge:

The prisoners at the time of administering the oath in question were themselves members of a society, and had themselves taken an oath not to disclose anything connected with that society at the time they administered the oath.

5 Sentence of transportation

i 'No discretion'

The trial was concluded in that one day, Monday 17 March 1834. But the judge did not sentence them on that day. He deferred it for two days until Wednesday 19 March. No doubt he talked it over with his brother judge. Then on the Wednesday the six were put to the bar to receive the sentence of the court. The judge said (as reported by *The Times*):

Having deliberated well and seriously upon the objections made for you – having deliberated well and seriously on what it is my duty to pronounce upon you – I feel I have no discretion in a case of this sort, but that I am bound to pronounce a sentence of the law, which the Act of Parliament has provided, and accordingly the sentence is that you and each of you be transported, etc., for seven years.

There was nothing to be done by way of appeal. At that time there was no appeal by a prisoner against conviction or sentence.

ii *Taken to Botany Bay*

Five of the men were taken to Portsmouth within a fortnight. George Loveless was ill and was taken later. They were locked on the outside of a coach with their hands and legs manacled, chained to each other. At Portsmouth they were rowed out to the 'hulks.' These were old wooden warships which, when their fighting days were over, were used as prisons. Afterwards they were taken in a lighter to a convict ship. In a few days it sailed for New South Wales. They were landed at Botany Bay, now Sydney.

George Loveless went through a similar ordeal a few weeks later but he was taken to Tasmania or Van Diemen's Land, as it was then called.

iii *Brutally treated*

All six were brutally treated. They had a terrible time. They worried about their wives and children at home. George Loveless had said to another brother, William, just before they sailed:

> William, do your best that the tyrants do not starve my dear wife and children. I care not for myself so that my wife and children be taken care of.

The trade union movement did so. They helped them, not only in money, but in careful regard.

6 Movement for release

i *A free pardon*

Meanwhile, throughout all England there was an ever-swelling movement for their release. Up and down the country and in the House of Commons protests were made against their sentence. It culminated in a mighty demonstration on 21 April 1834 when a huge procession of 50,000 people marched to Whitehall. After two years it had effect. On 14 March 1836 Lord John Russell (who had become Home Secretary) told the House that His Majesty had been pleased to grant a free pardon to the whole of the men. It was some time before they got back to England. George Loveless arrived on 13 June 1837. James Loveless, the two Standfields and James Brine reached Plymouth on 17 March 1838, exactly four years to the day since their trial. James Hammett came later.

ii *The churchyard at Tolpuddle*

At first the five settled in Essex on the edge of Epping Forest on farms provided by the trade union movement. But about 1846 all except James Hammett emigrated to Canada and settled in or near London, Ontario, where they lived and died.

James Hammett returned to Tolpuddle and lived there till nearly the end of his days when his sight became so bad that he went to the Poor Law Institution at Dorchester. He is buried in the churchyard at Tolpuddle.

3 The legal side

1 Were they Guilty?

i *The judge*

The judge, Mr Baron Williams, as I have told you, had only been appointed a fortnight. His practice at the Bar had been largely in paper work. He had little experience of court work. His main interest was in the classics. He had won all the prizes at Cambridge. He would recite Horace and Demosthenes by the hour – if he could find an audience. Nothing annoyed him so much as to hear counsel 'perpetrate a false quantity,' that is, pronounce a Latin syllable erroneously.

ii *The date of the offence*

In each count of the indictment, it was alleged that the oath was administered on 24 February 1834; but the evidence was that it was shortly before Christmas 1833. You might think that this was a fatal variance. But no one took the point, and for a good reason. Although a time and place had to be stated in the indictment, nevertheless

the prosecutor was not bound to the day laid but might prove the offence to have taken place on any other day or in any other month[1]

except when time was of the essence of the offence. Here time was not of the essence. If an oath was illegally

[1] *R v Brown* (1828) 1 Mood & M 163, 164; see also Blackstone *Commentaries* IV, 306.

115

administered, it did not matter whether it was in December, January or February.

iii *The preamble to the Mutiny Act 1797*

The preamble to the Mutiny Act 1797 showed that its purpose was to punish those who administered oaths to seamen and soldiers so as to prevent them disclosing acts of mutiny and sedition. Counsel for the prisoners submitted to the judge that the Act should be confined to cases of mutiny and sedition. But the judge ruled otherwise. I think that he was justified in so doing, because there was a decision of the full Court of King's Bench on the very point in 1802. It was *R v Marks*[1] where there was a trade dispute between the master clothiers and journeymen at Trowbridge concerning the rate of their wages. The accused were journeymen clothworkers who had administered an oath binding a clothworker to secrecy. It was held to be within the enacting part of the statute. Lawrence J said (at page 165):

It is true that the preamble and the first part of the enacting clause are confined in their objects to cases of mutiny and sedition: but it is nothing unusual in Acts of Parliament for the enacting part to go beyond the preamble.

iv *The Acts of 1824 and 1825*

Counsel for the defence referred to the Acts of 1824 and 1825.[2] He pointed out that under them workmen were now entitled to combine together to raise their wages. He said:

If, therefore, the prisoners had entered an association to raise the amount of wages, it would not be illegal, and if not illegal, then the administering of an oath to the members of a legal association would not be a violation of the 1797 Act.

The judge did not deal specifically with this point, but impliedly he rejected it. He must have thought that the later Acts of 1824 and 1825 could not affect the construction of the

[1] (1802) 3 East 157.
[2] 5 Geo IV c 95, 6 Geo IV, c 129.

earlier Act of 1797. In this he was wrong. Those Acts altered the whole position radically. Sir Stafford Cripps KC MP said in 1934:

It can never have been intended that a combination legal in itself should have been rendered illegal by the taking of an oath against which there was no prohibition in the Act legalising the combination.

A useful analogy can be found in two modern cases, *Tursi v Tursi*[1] and *Dyson Holdings Ltd v Fox*.[2]

On this ground I think that the judge should have withdrawn the case from the jury and directed them to find the six Not Guilty.

2 Was the sentence correct?

i *The conduct of the judge*

The judge's conduct was unforgivable. It was quite apparent that the Affpuddle men were reluctant to give evidence against the six Tolpuddle men. Even counsel for the prosecution could not get them to do so. Yet the judge himself took it up. He cross-examined them most severely and forced evidence out of them against the six. If there had been an appeal open to the prisoners – as there is today – the convictions would have been quashed on that ground alone, see *R v Cain*,[3] *R v Gilson and Cohen*[4] and *Jones v National Coal Board*.[5]

ii *The seven years*

The judge said:

I feel I have no discretion in a case of this sort . . . the sentence is that you and each of you be transported for seven years.

That was a grave error. The statute said 'for any term of

---

[1] [1958] P 54, 69 per Sachs J.
[2] [1976] QB 503, 509, 511.
[3] [1936] 25 Cr App R 204.
[4] [1944] 29 Cr App R 174.
[5] [1957] 2 QB 55, 64.

years not exceeding seven years.' That gave him a discretion to give one year, one month, or even one day. If ever there was a case for mitigation, this was it. Trade unions had been lawful ever since 1824. Up and down the country there had been oaths administered at these initiation ceremonies. No one had been prosecuted for them before. The Tolpuddle men administered the oath in December 1833. No caution was issued until 22 February 1834. The six might well believe their conduct was lawful. And they had done no harm to anyone – as George Loveless stressed in his statement to the judge. They had already been in prison for over three weeks. The proper sentence would have been four days from the commission day. That would have meant their immediate release.

iii *Conclusion*

The trial of the six Tolpuddle men is a blot on our legal history. The brutal treatment of them is a blot on our social history. But their steadfast courage is an example for all time.

4 150 years later

Introduction

You will find much of the subsequent history of trade unions in *The Closing Chapter* (pages 158–210). I covered there the years from 1834 to 1982. Then on 20 March 1984 came the 150th anniversary of the sentencing of the Tolpuddle Martyrs. I gave an address to the Bar Association for Commerce and Industry. I called it 'Trade Unions on Trial.' It was in Lincoln's Inn New Hall, filled to the full. Many had to stand. I brought the story up to date. I told more of the landmark cases on trade unions.

1 The *Taff Vale case*

i *Union liable in damages*

In 1900, the first year of the twentieth century, the judges were still deciding against trade unions: hitting them hard by awarding damages against them. There was the great *Taff Vale case*.[1] To understand it, you must know that the trade unions were virtually friendly societies. The members paid their subscriptions into a fund out of which benefits could be paid to members if they were ill or out of employment. Now in the *Taff Vale case* the railwaymen's union called a strike at the railway station at Cardiff. The men left work and set up

---

[1] *Taff Vale Rly Co v Amalgamated Society of Railway Servants* [1901] 1 QB 170, [1901] AC 426, HL.

peaceful pickets so as to persuade others not to go to work. The trains could not run, and the company lost money. The railway were advised to bring an action against the union itself, seeking an injunction and damages. The Court of Appeal threw out the action. But the House of Lords, in a startling judgment, overruled the Court of Appeal. They issued an interlocutory injunction against the trade union itself, restraining it from setting up the pickets, and said that the railway company could recover damages which could be enforced against trade union funds. Later, at the trial itself, the damages were assessed at £23,000 and that sum was paid out of the funds of the trade union. £23,000 in 1900. What would that be now?

ii *An outrageous decision*

In the eyes of trade unions, that was an outrageous decision. It meant that the railway company could take all the funds subscribed by the members so as to meet the damages. It meant that, in future, a trade union could never call a strike, else it would be in peril of losing all its funds. It meant virtually the end of trade unions. As G M Trevelyan says in his *History*: 'It struck at the very heart of trade union action.'

iii *Political consequences*

That case had immense political consequences. At the general election of 1906 there came into being a new political party. It was the Labour party. They ran a host of candidates themselves. They pledged complete immunity for trade unions. Many of the Liberal candidates gave the same pledge. The result of the general election was like an earthquake. Liberals had 397 seats. The new Labour party had 50 seats. The Conservatives only 157. It was a sweeping victory for the trade unions.

Parliament immediately passed the Trade Disputes Act 1906. It is probably the most important Act ever put into the Statute Book. It reversed all the judicial decisions against trade unions. The *Taff Vale case* was overruled. No trade union could thereafter be sued for damages for any wrongs done by its members. Its funds were unassailable.

2 The general strike of 1926

i *My truncheon*

On one occasion the trade unions over-reached themselves. It was in 1926 by calling a general strike. I remember it well. Together with other young members of the Bar, I joined as a special constable. We patrolled outside the great power station in Lots Road, whilst the soldiers were inside. We had our truncheons and arm-bands – I have mine still – whilst the soldiers had their rifles and bayonets at the ready. There were some threatening scenes but, as it turned out, no violence against us. The strike arose out of a trade dispute between the miners' union and the employers. The miners were backed by the Trades Union Congress. They called out all their affiliated unions in railway, transport and other trades. Pickets were set up so as to stop railway workers, merchant seamen and so forth going to work.

ii *The strike is held illegal*

But the seamen's union complained to the courts because their union rules had not been complied with. Mr Justice Astbury granted an injunction. He said:[1]

The so-called general strike called by the Trades Union Congress Council is illegal, and persons inciting or taking part in it are not protected by the Trade Disputes Act 1906 . . . No trade dispute does or can exist between the Trades Union Congress on the one hand and the Government and the nation on the other.

This interpretation of the law was reinforced by a speech by the Home Secretary, Sir John Simon, in the House of Commons. The trade unions accepted this interpretation of the law, and as they were not prepared to break the law, the strike collapsed.

[1] *National Sailors' & Firemen's Union v Reed* [1926] Ch 536, 539.

That was, however, an isolated case. Apart from it, for a great many years the trade unions successfully asserted their immunity. They enforced strict discipline over their members, compelling many to strike when they did not wish to do so.

3 The *Shah* case

i '*The Stockport Six*'

In the middle of 1983 Mr Shah published a paper called the *Stockport Messenger*. It was issued free to the public, being paid for by advertisements. He printed it at Warrington. Most of the men were non-union men, but six of them were, or became, members of the National Graphical Association (NGA). The NGA wanted it to become a 'closed shop.' Mr Shah refused. He sacked the six – called 'the Stockport Six.' Their dismissal may have been fair or unfair. We do not know. But if it was unfair, they could have complained to the Industrial Tribunal and sought reinstatement. But they do not appear to have done so. Instead, the NGA took up the cudgels on their behalf and demanded their reinstatement. Mr Shah refused. He did not give in to their demands.

ii *Mass pickets*

The NGA then took steps to organise mass pickets at Warrington outside the works of Mr Shah so as to prevent his delivery vans from leaving.

Now mass picketing is an offence under the criminal law. It is also a wrong under the civil law because it is intimidation – designed to make the employer do what he has a perfect right not to do. Before the 1982 Act the NGA would have had immunity from a civil action or an injunction because it would have been 'in contemplation or furtherance of a trade dispute.' But now it no longer has immunity.

iii *Fined £675,000*

Mr Shah obtained an injunction against the NGA to restrain the mass picketing. They disobeyed the injunction. They called thousands to Warrington and mounted a military operation to stop the delivery vans. There was a pitched battle between the police and the demonstrators. Mr Justice Eastham took a firm line. He fined the NGA for contempt of court. At first £50,000, then £100,000, then £525,000. The NGA did not pay. So the court ordered their funds to be sequestrated to meet the fines. Although the NGA are said to have assets of £10,000,000, they could not long stand fines of that magnitude. They did talk of more mass picketing but wiser counsels prevailed. They did not attempt any more.

iv *All newspapers stopped*

The NGA went, however, beyond mass pickets. They were so upset by the fines that they took action against the national newspapers who were not involved in the dispute in any way. They called a strike of all their members for one day. All the national newspapers were stopped, causing the loss of many millions of pounds. This was 'secondary action' which was claimed to be unlawful under the 1980 Act. Twelve national newspapers issued writs against the NGA, claiming damages up to the top limit of £250,000 each, making £3,000,000 altogether.

v *An important pronouncement*

The NGA threatened to call another one-day strike to stop the national newspapers. The newspapers got an injunction to stop it. The NGA sought to get the backing of the TUC. The TUC General Secretary, Mr Len Murray, made the important pronouncement that they could only support action that was lawful. They would not support it if it was unlawful. So the NGA did not go on with the strike. They decided to purge their contempt and to ask for their assets to be released from the sequestrator: but they said they would maintain their campaign in opposition to the 1980 and 1982 Employment Acts.

The whole country was grateful to Mr Murray and the moderate members of the TUC General Council for their pronouncement. It seemed to herald a new attitude of the trade unions towards the law.

vi *Mobocracy*

Under the 1980 Act Mr Shah was entitled to damages for the loss to his business. He got them. On 30 July 1984 Mr Justice Caulfield awarded him £125,000 against the Union. He said:

This was mobocracy at its worst and intimidation at its worst and I lay the blame on the Union.

4 GCHQ at Cheltenham

i *Secret surveillance network*

There was, however, more trouble brewing. It arose out of the Government Communications Headquarters (GCHQ) at Cheltenham. About 7,000 are employed there on highly secret intelligence work. They were members of the Civil Service trade unions. In 1981 these trade unions had called out their members on a one-day stoppage. They had issued a statement saying:

There will be a range of selective and disruptive action which will affect Britain's secret communications surveillance network. There will be both national and international repercussions.

ii *No trade unions*

The Government could not sit down under such a threat to our national security. They decided that the staff should not be permitted to belong to a trade union. So, early in 1984, they offered each person this option: £1,000 cash on resigning from the trade union; or being transferred to other work; or losing their jobs. The trade union movement was incensed. They called on their members to stop work for a half-day in protest – save for the staff at GCHQ. They were to continue to work normally. That was most illogical. If any persons had any grievance and were to strike, it would be the staff at Cheltenham. The calling out of the others for a half-day was quite unlawful. It was secondary action aimed solely at the Government. To make things worse, one of the printing unions – quite unlawfully – stopped publication of all the national newspapers for one day, causing them great loss.

iii *A telling defeat*

As it turned out, these unlawful actions were quite ineffective. The Prime Minister told the Commons on 1 March 1984 that well in excess of 90 per cent of the staff at Cheltenham had accepted the £1,000 and had given up their trade union membership. It was a telling defeat.

iv *A counter-attack*

The trade unions launched a counter-attack. They themselves resorted to the courts of law. They said that the Prime Minister had acted contrary to the rules of natural justice. At first instance they succeeded. But on appeal on 6 August 1984 the action of the Government was upheld.

5 The coal miners' strike

i *Pit closures*

In the first half of 1984, there was a new challenge. The National Union of Mineworkers flouted the law of the land. It arose out of the proposal by the National Coal Board to close some pits that were not economic. They were running at a loss. In order to mitigate the hardship to the men, the Board were ready to make substantial redundancy payments and alternatively offer work at other pits. The Union opposed the closures altogether. They said the pits should be kept open at all costs, whatever the loss might be.

The Union left each area to decide for itself whether to continue working normally or to come out on strike. Some areas like Nottinghamshire voted to stay at work. Others like Yorkshire voted to come out. This led to much bitterness between the various areas. One of the strengths of the trade union movement is the principle of 'solidarity.' It may be translated: 'Together we stand. Divided we fall.'

The Yorkshire miners and others were so incensed by the Nottinghamshire stand that they did all they could to stop it. They despatched pickets to the Nottinghamshire pits, relying on another principle of the trade union movement: 'Never cross a picket line.' It may be translated: 'No member of a trade union should cross a picket line (and go to work) no matter whether it is set up by his own or any other trade union.'

ii *Flying pickets*

A simple picket line of six men would not, however, deter the Nottinghamshire miners from going to work. So the Yorkshire men and others sent coach-loads of men to picket the Nottinghamshire mines. 'Flying pickets' they are called. They came in such numbers so as to intimidate the Nottinghamshire miners. At Ollerton, for instance, 500 pickets arrived at the pit. There were violent scenes. As a result, only a handful of miners were able to cross the picket line. Three policemen were injured. Violent scenes were repeated on the following evening. It was appalling and unacceptable. Such action by the flying pickets was a grave breach of the criminal law.

Every man in this country is entitled to go to work and earn his wages without being prevented or obstructed or intimidated by others. The police are under a duty to protect him in this right. For this simple reason: if the worker is obstructed, there is reason to apprehend a breach of the peace; and it is the bounden duty of the police to intervene and take reasonable steps to prevent a breach of the peace.

iii *Police reinforcements*

Acting on this principle, the police forces in Nottinghamshire were reinforced by other police forces in the country.
Thousands of police came to the aid of the men who wanted
to work. In March about 2,000 Yorkshire pickets arrived at
Babbington colliery in Nottinghamshire. There were only
20 police officers there at the time; 119 workers were due to
go to work and they were faced with 2,000 pickets. Police
reinforcements were called. Attempts were made by the
pickets to break through the police cordon. Stones were
thrown. Eighty-eight arrests were made, but 113 out of 119
men were able to go to work as they wished.

In the House of Commons some members attacked the
conduct of the police: but this attack was decisively repulsed.
The police acted calmly and well in pursuance of their duty
to preserve the peace.

Other steps were taken in support of the Union. Supplies
of coal and coke for steel works and electricity stations were
'blacked.' This too was quite unlawful. It was secondary
action contrary to the new Employment legislation.

iv *Why not go to the courts?*

All through the weeks, the question was being asked: Why
should it be left to the police to enforce the criminal law?
Why should not the National Coal Board go to the courts
and enforce the civil law? They did go – up to a point. They
did get an injunction to stop the mass picketing and
intimidation. But they did not follow it up. The Union
ignored the injunction. They sent out the flying pickets.
Why did not the National Coal Board proceed against the
Union for contempt of court? Why did they not get them
fined? and their assets sequestrated?

This must have been a matter of tactics by the National
Coal Board. If they had gone to the court and heavy fines
had been imposed on the Union – and their assets
sequestrated – it might have united all the miners. The
Nottinghamshire men might have joined the strike too. It

was better to let the miners fight between themselves rather than risk their being united.

v *Private hauliers do go to the court*

But two firms of hauliers in the Forest of Dean did go. The court granted an injunction against the South Wales section of the National Union of Mineworkers, ordering them not to interfere with the business of the hauliers. The Union disobeyed. They stopped the lorries. They stoned them. Mr Justice Park on 30 July 1984 fined the South Wales section £50,000. They did not pay. The judge ordered their assets to be sequestrated. We await the outcome.

On 31 July 1984 the judge was criticised by Mr Martin Flannery MP in the House of Commons. He said: 'There are tame Tory judges.' He refused to withdraw the charge. The Speaker named him. He was suspended by 260 to 80.

vi *There is a war on*

As I write this early in August 1984 there is a war on. Mr Arthur Scargill is urging the miners to defy the law. He is seeking the support of the TUC to close down the power and transport systems of the country. He says it is a 'fight to the finish.' The Prime Minister is calling on the rest of us to stand firm and to defeat 'the enemy within.' Who will win?

6 A trying time

i *What does the future hold?*

The trade unions are facing a crisis. They have to decide whether to obey the law of the land or not. For over 70 years they were immune. Now, if they disobey, they are liable to fines and damages and to having their assets sequestrated. This has made them concentrate their minds wonderfully. No trade union can survive for long with its assets seized, sequestrated and depleted.

What, then, does the future hold? What will the trade

unions do? Will they obey the law? Or will they resist it by force or by general strikes? Will they campaign for the repeal of the 1980 and 1982 Acts: and seek the restoration of the immunities which they had previously enjoyed since 1906? Would such a campaign have any chance of success? I should think not. The ordinary people of England will well remember the abuses to which immunities gave rise.

ii *Keep within the law*

Such is the impact of the new legislation. It does not mean the end of the trade unions. Far from it. They will still have much work to do for the well-being of their members. They will still have to consult with management and co-operate with it. In case of disagreement, they will still be able to call strikes – within the limits laid down by law. They will still be able to set up pickets – within the limits laid down by law. They will still be able to 'black' goods or transactions – within the limits laid down by law. But they must not go beyond those limits. They must keep within the law. That is fundamental in our constitution.

It is the lesson we have learnt over the centuries. The rule of law must be maintained. Just as in war 'England expects every man this day to do his duty' – so also in peace England expects every trade union every day to do its duty. And that is to obey the law.

iii *Put on probation*

But what, then, is to be your verdict? So far as the nineteenth century is concerned, it will be that the trade unions were persecuted and oppressed. But so far as the twentieth century is concerned, it will be that they exploited their immunities beyond measure. But what should be the sentence? Now that their immunities have to some extent been taken away, I would ask that they be put on probation. If they obey the law of the land, they should go free: for they have more useful things to do for their members. But if they should flout the law, they will find that their end will be at hand.

Part Five

Freedom of Assembly

Introduction

It was declared in the Universal Declaration of Human Rights of the United Nations Organisation:

Article 20 Everyone has the right to freedom of peaceful assembly and association. . . .

This freedom has only been won after much pain and anguish. It is bound up with the right to demonstrate. These demonstrations are made for various causes. Often it is to protest against the Government or against its doings. People march along the streets. They carry banners. They hear speeches. History shows how much Governments have disliked these demonstrations. So much so that they used to regard them as unlawful assemblies. They arrested the ringleaders and prosecuted them. Sometimes the demonstrations were for good causes, sometimes for bad causes. In principle, all these can and should be allowed by law so long as they are peaceful. But they are apt to result in violence on one side or the other. If they should threaten the peace of ordinary citizens in the neighbourhood, then the demonstrations become unlawful assemblies. The line is very difficult to draw. I will tell you of some of the most conspicuous in our history. I will start with William Penn and William Mead. I have sketched their trial before, but it is so dramatic and instructive that I tell it more fully now.

1 William Penn and William Mead

1 The Quakers

i *A peace-loving community*

The 'Quakers' is the name given to the Society of Friends which was formed in 1650. They were so called because they urged everyone to quake, that is, to 'tremble at the word of God.' They were a peace-loving society. They were averse to violence of any kind. They refused to bear arms or to take oaths. Their dress and their manners were plain and simple. They refused to bow or to curtsey as a mark of respect to their superiors. They refused to remove their hats as a sign of deference to a court of law. They held that Christian qualities mattered much more than Christian dogma. They had no priests, no sacraments, no churches. Only meeting places.

ii *'What shall I do?'*

It seems strange to us now that in the time of Charles II (1660–1685) these good people were persecuted simply because they would not subscribe to the doctrine of the Church of England and held religious meetings of their own. In England 4,000 were sent to prison, and 500 in London alone. Other dissenters were too. John Bunyan was imprisoned for 12 years in Bedford gaol for preaching the Gospel and not conforming to the established church. Yet he put it to good use. His *Pilgrim's Progress*, written in gaol, is one of the greatest works in the English language. It opens:

As I walked through the wilderness of this world, I lighted on a certain place where was a den,* and laid me down in that place to sleep: and, as I slept, I dreamed a dream. I dreamed; and, behold, 'I saw a man clothed with rags, standing in a certain place, with his face from his own house, a book in his hand, and a great burden upon his back.' I looked, and saw him open the book, and read therein; and, as he read, he wept and trembled; and, not being able longer to contain, he brake out with a lamentable cry, saying, 'What shall I do?'

2 William Penn – Preacher

i *No Cross, No Crown*

At the time of the trial, William Penn was only 26. He was a man of quality, the son of an admiral. He had been in prison already for his beliefs. Whilst there, he had written a famous book, *No Cross, No Crown*, in which he said:

True Godliness don't turn men out of the world, but enables them to live better in it and excites their endeavours to mend it.

He was tall and good-looking. His dress was well-cut and neat. He was a member of Lincoln's Inn and had studied law, which was to stand him in good stead.

William Mead was 42. He had been captain of a train-band: and was a wealthy linen-draper. He too had studied law.

ii *Sunday morning 14 August 1670 in Gracechurch Street*

Our story starts on Sunday 14 August 1670 at about 11 o'clock in the forenoon. It was in Gracechurch Street in the city of London. The Quakers' meeting-house there had been closed by the authorities. So the Quakers met in the street outside. About 300 or 400 people had gathered together. William Penn was standing up preaching to them. William Mead was nearby. After a little while the officers of the city came up and dispersed the crowd. They arrested William

* The gaol.

Penn and William Mead and took them before the Mayor of London. He committed them for trial.

iii *Charged with unlawful assembly*

An indictment was prepared charging them with unlawful assembly. It was in these terms:

That William Penn, Gent. and William Mead, late of London, linen draper, with divers other persons to the jurors unknown, to the number of 300, the 14th day of August in the 22d year of the king, about eleven of the clock in the forenoon, the same day, with force and arms, &c. in the parish of St. Bennet Grace-church in Bridge-ward, London, in the street called Grace-church street, unlawfully and tumultuously did assemble and congregate themselves together, to the disturbance of the peace of the said lord the king: and the aforesaid William Penn and William Mead, together with other persons to the jurors aforesaid unknown, then and there so assembled and congregated together; the aforesaid William Penn, by agreement between him and William Mead before made, and by abetment of the aforesaid William Mead, then and there, in the open street, did take upon himself to preach and speak, and then and there did preach and speak unto the aforesaid William Mead, and other persons there, in the street aforesaid, being assembled and congregated together, by reason whereof a great concourse and tumult of people in the street aforesaid, then and there, a long time did remain and continue, in contempt of the said lord the king, and of his law, to the great disturbance of his peace; to the great terror and disturbance of many of his liege people and subjects, to the ill example of all others in the like case offenders, and against the peace of the said lord the king, his crown and dignity.

If that indictment had been proved, it might well have been an unlawful assembly. The crucial element is contained in the words, 'tumultuously . . . to the great terror and disturbance of many of his liege people and subjects.' But, as you will see, there was no evidence of that element in the offence.

3 **Their trial**

i *1 September 1670 – They plead Not Guilty*

Just over a fortnight later, on Thursday 1 September 1670,

William Penn and William Mead were brought up for trial at the Old Bailey. On the bench there sat the Mayor, the Recorder, five aldermen and the two sheriffs, and below them the Clerk of the court. In the jury box there were twelve jurymen. The Clerk read out the indictment and said:

What say you, William Penn and William Mead, are you Guilty, as you stand indicted, in manner and form, as aforesaid, or Not Guilty?

William Penn asked for a copy of the indictment and that he might be given a fair hearing and the liberty of making his defence. So did William Mead. On these being promised, each of them pleaded:

Not Guilty in manner and form.

The trial did not start that day. The charge was for a misdemeanour. It had to wait until after the court had dealt with the felons and murderers. The Quakers waited five hours but their case was not reached that day. It was adjourned until Saturday 3 September 1670.

ii *3 September 1670   Hats off – Hats on – Hats off*

On Saturday 3 September 1670 the case came on. The Clerk called out:

Bring William Penn and William Mead to the bar.

Then there was much to-do about their hats. At first they were told to take them off and did so. Then they were told to put them on and did so. When they were brought to the bar, they had them on. Like other Quakers, they refused to remove them before the court. The Recorder exclaimed:

Do you not know there is respect due to the court?

Penn   Yes.

Recorder   Why do you not pull off your hat then?

Penn   Because I do not believe that to be any respect.

Recorder   Well, the court sets forty marks a piece upon your heads, as a fine for your contempt of the court.

137

The value of a mark was two-thirds of £1, so 40 marks were £26 – a very large fine in those days.

The report does not tell us whether the prisoners kept their hats on or not. But I imagine they took them off. It seems incredible to us now but in Cromwell's time there were many cases of Quakers being cast into prison by magistrates for not taking off their hats before the court: some even died in prison.[1]

iii *Penn was speaking to the crowd*

The jury were then sworn in the accustomed form in use down to my time:

> You shall well and truly try, and true deliverance make betwixt our sovereign lord the king, and the prisoners at the bar whom you shall have in charge, and a true verdict give, according to the evidence. So help you God.

Only three witnesses were called for the prosecution. They were officers of the city. They said that they saw a crowd of 300 or 400 people in Gracechurch Street. William Penn was speaking to them but there was such a noise that they could not hear what was said. They dispersed the crowd and arrested Penn and Mead. There was no suggestion of any violence or breach of the peace or that there was any tumult or terror or disturbance as charged in the indictment. Everyone knew that the Quakers were peaceable people and would not themselves resort to violence of any kind.

iv *Penn's vindication – to preach*

Then the prisoners were allowed to speak for themselves. Penn asserted that what they wished to do was

> to vindicate the assembling of ourselves to preach, pray, or worship the Eternal, Holy, Just God, that we declare to all the world, that we do believe it to be our indispensable duty, to meet incessantly upon so good an account.

The Clerk thought nothing of this vindication:

[1] See *Calendar of State Papers* (*Domestic*) (1652–1658).

You are not here for worshipping God, but for breaking the law; you do yourselves a great deal of wrong in going on in that discourse.

4 A dispute on the law

i *Penn's question: 'By what law?'*

Penn then asked to know the law which they were alleged to have broken:

I affirm I have broken no law, nor am I Guilty of the indictment that is laid to my charge . . . I desire you would let me know by what law it is you prosecute me, and upon what law you ground my indictment.

That was a most pertinent question. The Conventicles Act of 1663 (13 and 14 Car II c 1) had made it an offence to go to any separate meeting of more than five persons for religious worship other than according to the *Book of Common Prayer*. But that Act had expired in 1668. It was renewed in 1671 but this meeting in Gracechurch Street was in 1670 when there was no statute against it. The Recorder realised this. So in answer to Penn's question, 'By what law do you prosecute me?' the Recorder answered:

Upon the common law.

ii *Penn's follow-up: 'Where is that common law?'*

Penn took him up at once. He asked:

Where is that common law?

The Recorder was nonplussed. He did not know. So he prevaricated:

You must not think that I am able to run up so many years, and over so many adjudged cases, which we call common-law, to answer your curiosity.

Penn quite rightly considered that answer unsatisfactory. There were no cases to show what was an unlawful assembly at common law. So he retorted:

Am I to plead to an indictment that hath no foundation in law?

iii '*A saucy fellow*'

The Recorder could not answer the question. So he resorted to vulgar abuse. It recalls to my mind the story of the attorney who had to leave the case to his partner. His notes said: 'No case. Abuse other side's attorney.' Likewise here the Recorder said to Penn:

You are a saucy fellow, speak to the indictment.

Penn made a spirited reply:

Unless you shew me, and the people, the law you ground your indictment upon, I shall take it for granted your proceedings are merely arbitrary.

The Recorder resorted again to vulgar abuse:

You are an impertinent fellow, will you teach the court what law is? It is 'Lex non scripta,' that which many have studied 30 or 40 years to know, and would you have me to tell you in a moment?

Penn maintained his stand:

I have asked but one question, and you have not answered me . . . I design no affront to the court, but to be heard in my just plea.

iv '*Take him away*'

The Recorder could give no answer. His abuse having failed, he resorted to physical force. He called out to the warder: 'Take him away.'

Then, turning to the Mayor, he said:

My lord, if you take not some course with this pestilent fellow, to stop his mouth, we shall not be able to do any thing tonight.

The Mayor complied. He called out to the officers:

Take him away, take him away, turn him into the bale-dock.

The 'bale-dock' or 'bail-dock' is now simply the dock. It was at that time an enclosure set in the grounds some yards away. It was a place in which to keep prisoners pending trial. It was dirty and smelt so much that it was called a 'stinking hole.' Penn was 'rudely hauled into the stinking hole.'

140

5 Mead's case

i *He makes his defence*

William Mead was left in the court. It was now his turn to address the jury. He recalled that he, like other Quakers, was a peaceable man:

You men of the jury . . . I am a peaceable man. Therefore it is a very proper question what William Penn demanded in this case, an oyer of the law, on which our indictment is grounded.

The Recorder interrupted him:

I have made answer to that already.

That was untrue. The Recorder had not answered Penn.

ii *He quotes Coke*

Then Mead, turning his face to the jury, said:

You men of the jury, who are my judges, if the Recorder will not tell you what makes a riot, a rout, or an unlawful assembly, Coke, he that once they called the lord Coke, tells us . . .

Then he quoted the words from Coke's *Institutes* III 176 which show that an unlawful assembly is when three or more assemble themselves together to do an unlawful act and do it not, as to beat a man, or to enter forcibly into another man's land, to cut down his grass, his wood or break down his pales.

Both Penn and Mead quoted from Coke's *Institutes*. It was, I think the only authority then existing about an unlawful assembly. One hundred years later it was repeated by Blackstone in 1765 in his *Commentaries* IV 146:

An unlawful assembly is when three, or more, do assemble themselves together to do an unlawful act, as to pull down inclosures, to destroy a warren or the game therein; and part without doing it, or making any motion towards it.

The essence of it was the assembling together to do an 'unlawful act.' Here there was no evidence of any unlawful act.

iii *He also in the bale-dock*

When Mead quoted Coke, the Recorder interrupted him and said:

I thank you, sir, that you will tell me what the law is

scornfully pulling off his hat and adding:

I look upon you to be an enemy to the laws of England, which ought to be observed and kept, nor are you worthy of such privileges as others have.

To which Mead replied:

The Lord is judge between me and thee in this matter.

This appeal to divinity did not impress the Recorder. He ordered the officers to take Mead also into the bale-dock. They did so.

iv *The Recorder sums up*

The Recorder then summed up to the jury in the absence of Penn and Mead. It was very short:

You have heard what the indictment is. It is for preaching to the people, and drawing a tumultuous company after them, and Mr Penn was speaking; if they should not be disturbed, you see they will go on; there are three or four witnesses that have proved this, that he did preach there; that Mr Mead did allow of it: after this you have heard by substantial witnesses what is said against them: now we are upon the matter of fact, which you are to keep to, and observe, as what hath been fully sworn at your peril.

v *Penn appeals to the jury*

At this point Penn shouted out from the bale-dock in a loud voice:

I appeal to the jury who are my judges, and this great assembly, whether the proceedings of the court are not most arbitrary, and void of all law, in offering to give the jury their charge in the absence of the prisoners . . .

Mead added his voice to the protest but the Recorder gave

no heed to it. He commanded the jury to agree upon their verdict, 'the prisoners remaining in the stinking hole.'

6 Saturday afternoon 3 September 1670

i *The first verdict*

On Saturday afternoon 3 September 1670, the jury retired to an upstairs room. After one-and-a-half hours, eight came down again, but four remained in the room above. The court sent for these four. They came down, led by Edward Bushel. The Recorder said to Bushel:

Sir, you are the cause of this disturbance, and manifestly show yourself an abettor of faction; I shall set a mark upon you, sir. [That is, to fine him one mark.]

The twelve were then sent back to consider again. After some time they came back and said they were agreed. When asked whether Mr Penn was Guilty or Not Guilty, the foreman replied:

Guilty of speaking in Grace-church street.

ii *It is not accepted*

That verdict was quite understandable. The only evidence against Penn was of speaking in Gracechurch Street. There was no evidence of an unlawful assembly. The court were, however, angry. On hearing that verdict, the Recorder said:

Is that all?

Foreman That is all I have in commission.

The Recorder refused to accept it as a verdict. Technically, he was right. They had been asked to find 'Guilty' or 'Not Guilty.' Their verdict of 'Guilty of speaking in Grace-church street' was neither of these. It left the court with nothing to act upon. So the Recorder addressed them:

Gentlemen, you have not given in your verdict, and you had as good say nothing; therefore go and consider it once more, that we may make an end of this troublesome business.

iii *The second verdict*

The jury then asked for pen, ink and paper and were out for half-an-hour. When they came back, the foreman said:

Here is our verdict

holding forth a piece of paper on which was written:

We the jurors, hereafter named, do find William Penn to be Guilty of speaking or preaching to an assembly, met together in Grace-church street, the 14th of August last, 1670. And that William Mead is Not Guilty of the said indictment.

Each of them signed in his own hand: Foreman Thomas Veer, Edward Bushel, John Hammond, Henry Henley, Charles Milson, Gregory Walklet, John Baily, William Lever, Henry Michel, John Brightman, James Damask, Wil. Plumstead.

That verdict was perfectly understandable. The only evidence against Penn was of 'speaking or preaching to an assembly': that is all he was guilty of. Speaking or preaching was no offence at all. There was no evidence against Mead even of speaking or preaching. So he was Not Guilty. He ought to have been discharged at once.

But the court was furious with the jury. The Recorder addressed the jury in these words:

Gentlemen, you shall not be dismissed till we have a verdict that the court will accept; and you shall be locked up, without meat, drink, fire, and tobacco; you shall not think thus to abuse the court; we will have a verdict, by the help of God, or you shall starve for it.

iv *Penn's vigorous protest*

Penn made a vigorous protest:

My jury, who are my judges, ought not to be thus menaced; their verdict should be free, and not compelled . . .

The agreement of 12 men is a verdict in law, and such a one being given by the jury, I require the clerk of the peace to record it . . .

Then, looking upon the jury, he said:

You are Englishmen, mind your privilege, give not away your right.

The jury (led by Bushel) said:

Nor will we ever do it . . . We are agreed, we are agreed, we are agreed.

v *Locked up all night*

It was getting late. So the court decided to adjourn. They said they would sit at 7 o'clock the next morning, 4 September. Meanwhile, the jury were to be locked up all night. The court swore several persons, to keep the jury all night without meat, drink, fire, or any other accommodation; they had not so much as a chamber-pot, though desired.

7 Sunday 4 September 1670

i *The third verdict*

At 7 o'clock in the morning the court assembled again. The prisoners were brought to the bar. The jury were called in. Again they were asked:

Is William Penn Guilty or Not Guilty?

Again the jury gave the same reply:

William Penn is Guilty of speaking in Grace-church street.

The Mayor sought to add the crucial words 'To an unlawful assembly?' But Bushel answered:

No, my lord, we give no other verdict than what we gave last night; we have no other verdict to give.

ii *It is not accepted*

Then Penn reverted to the verdict which the jury had given in writing about Mead the night before, giving him 'Not Guilty.' Penn asked the Recorder:

Do you allow of the verdict given of William Mead?

The Recorder retorted:

It cannot be a verdict, because you were indicted for a conspiracy, and one being found Not Guilty, and not the other, it could not be a verdict.

Penn and Mead both protested vigorously. They had a good point as these interchanges show.

Penn   If Not Guilty be not a verdict, then you make of the jury and Magna Carta but a mere nose of wax.

Mead   How! is Not Guilty no verdict?

Recorder   No, it is no verdict.

Penn then took a good point.

Penn   I affirm, that the consent of a jury is a verdict in law; and if William Mead be Not Guilty, it consequently follows, that I am clear, since you have indicted us of a conspiracy, and I could not possibly conspire alone.

iii *The fourth verdict*

The Recorder would not accept their reasoning. He gave the jury yet another charge and told them to go to their chamber upstairs to consider again. Again they came back. Again they adhered to their previous verdicts on William Penn:

Guilty of speaking in Grace-church street.

Again the Recorder threatened Edward Bushel, one of the jurors:

You are factious fellow; I will set a mark upon you.

The Mayor added his threat:

I will cut his nose.

Again Penn protested:

It is intolerable that my jury should be thus menaced: Is this according to the fundamental laws? Are not they my proper judges by the Great Charter of England? What hope is there of ever having justice done, when juries are threatened, and their verdicts rejected?

The Recorder ordered the jury to go together and find another verdict. Again they steadfastly refused. They said they could give no other verdict than what they had already. The Recorder again threatened them:

Your verdict is nothing, you play upon the court; I say you shall go together, and bring in another verdict, or you shall starve; and I will have you carted about the city, as in Edward 3rd's time.

(I do not know the reference to Edward III's time: but I do know that in one case where a jury did not agree upon a verdict, they were to be carried round the circuit in a wagon until they were agreed.)

The foreman answered:

We have given in our verdict, and all agreed to it; and if we give in another, it will be a force upon us to save our lives.

By this time all Sunday had passed. Again the case was adjourned – till 7 o'clock on Monday morning. The prisoners were remanded to Newgate. The jury were again locked up. Again they were kept without meat, drink, fire or other accommodation. Next morning they and the prisoners were brought to court again.

8 Monday 5 September 1670

i *The fifth verdict*

By this time the jury had decided on their course of action. Instead of finding William Penn, 'Guilty of speaking in Grace-church street,' they decided to find him 'Not Guilty.' They drew up a paper, saying that 'We do find William Penn Not Guilty: and we do find William Mead Not Guilty.' They all signed it. Then when the Clerk asked them the crucial question, the foreman answered:

Here is our verdict in writing, and our hands subscribed.

On being asked formally, the foreman said they found Penn Not Guilty and Mead Not Guilty.

ii *Each separately – 'Not Guilty'*

The bench being unsatisfied with the verdict, commanded

that every person should distinctly answer to their names, and give in their verdict, which they unanimously did in saying 'Not Guilty.'

The reporter adds 'to the great satisfaction of the assembly.' No doubt all bystanders supported the jury.

iii *They are fined*

The Recorder was determined, however, to get his own back on the jury. He turned to them and punished them. He fined each of them 40 marks. He said to them:

I am sorry, gentlemen, you have followed your own judgments and opinions, rather than the good and wholesome advice which was given you; God keep my life out of your hands, but for this the court fines you 40 marks a man; and imprisonment till paid.

So the twelve jurors were taken off to Newgate and imprisoned there.

iv *Penn's request*

Penn then made a demand which was entirely justified:

I demand my liberty, being freed by the jury.

The Mayor was determined to keep him in prison. He remembered that Penn had been fined 40 marks for not taking off his hat. So he said:

No, you are in for your fines.

Penn Fines, for what?

Mayor For contempt of the court.

Penn made this final request:

I ask, if it be according to the fundamental laws of England, that any Englishman should be fined or amerced, but by the judgment of his peers or jury; since it expressly contradicts the 14th and 29th chapters of the Great Charter of England, which say, No freeman ought to be amerced but by the oath of good and lawful men of the vicinage.'

v *'Take him away'*

The Recorder had no answer to this, except to say:

Take him away, take him away, take him out of the court.

Penn I can never urge the fundamental laws of England, but you cry, 'Take him away, take him away.' . . . God Almighty, who is just, will judge you all for these things.

They hauled the prisoners into the bale-dock and from thence sent them to Newgate for the non-payment of their fines.

9 After events

i *Penn founds Pennsylvania*

We are told that William Penn's father, Admiral Sir William Penn, paid the fines of Penn and Mead and they were set free.

Some 10 years later, in 1682, at the age of 38 Penn went to the United States and founded Pennsylvania. Twenty years later, in 1702, he returned to England. He died in 1718 and was buried in ground belonging to the Quakers' meeting house at Jordans.

ii *The jurors are set free*

The jurors did not pay the fines on them. Instead, led by Bushel, they brought a habeas corpus before the Court of Common Pleas.[1] The sheriffs of London made their return, justifying the imprisonment on the ground that the jury had wrongly acquitted Penn and Mead: that the jury had done so contrary to full and manifest evidence of their guilt and contrary to the direction of the court on matter of law.

The case was argued with much learning. The court decided that the return was bad, and the prisoners were discharged. The reason given by the reporter was:

The reason given (*ut audivi*) was because the jury may know that of their

[1] *Bushel's case* (1670) Vaugh 135; Freem KB 1.

own knowledge which might guide them to give their verdict contrary to the sense of the court.[1]

In other words, the jury may have enough knowledge of their own to find the facts and apply the law better than the court itself. So they could not be said to have acted wrongly in any respect of fact or law.

That reasoning is, of course, not correct. The one thing that *Bushel's case* decided once and for all is that no judge can fine or imprison a jury for any verdict they may give, no matter how wrong the judge may think it to be, whether in fact or in law. There are ways and means by which a wrong verdict can be set aside, but no means by which a jury can be punished for giving it.

So, as I have said, Bushel and his fellow jurors were discharged. There is a plaque in the hall of the Central Criminal Court to commemorate it.

10 Legal points

i *Dress and manners in court*

It is shocking to read that Quakers were committed to prison for refusing to take off their hats. In 1657 Cromwell's Council disapproved of this punishment and recommended that – to avoid any further trouble – the court officers should take off their hats before bringing them before the magistrates.[2]

Even today there are parties and witnesses who come into court improperly dressed. Counsel may not be wearing a wig or gown, or he may come in a light suit or she in a colourful dress. The judge may say, 'I cannot see you' or 'I cannot hear you.' Counsel will be quick to conform, else he will get no more briefs. But it is not a contempt of court. I know of no case since that of Penn and Mead where anyone has been held guilty of contempt or been punished for not

---

[1] (1670) Freem 5.
[2] See *Calendar of State Papers (Domestic)* (1657–1658) 157.

conforming to accepted standards of dress or observing customary marks of respect.

ii *Contempt of court*

This case shows well how the courts in old days abused the power to convict for contempt of court – when there was no appeal to any higher court.

Penn's submissions, based on Magna Carta, were well justified. The modern power was fully considered in *Balogh v St Albans Crown Court*[1] which I have described in *The Due Process of Law*, pages 12–18. It is to be exercised by the judge of his own motion only when it is urgent and imperative to act immediately to prevent disorder: and then only as a temporary expedient. Steps should always be taken to enable the offender to be heard with legal representation as soon as possible. And there is always an appeal open to him.

iii *Keeping the jury together*

It is permissible for the judge to allow juries to separate at any time before they consider their verdict. This is the usual practice: they go out to lunch; they go home for the night; and so forth. The judge always warns them never to talk about the case to anyone outside their number. Once they are charged to consider their verdict, they must, as a rule, be kept together until they arrive at their verdict. In a long case, they may be provided with hotel accommodation.

Lately there has arisen the disquieting phenomenon of 'jury nobbling.' Friends of the accused may approach one or more of the jurors and seek to influence him by offering him money to stand out for 'Not Guilty' – or by threatening him with assault if he finds the accused Guilty. This evil was overcome to some extent by majority verdicts, as I described in *What Next in the Law*, pages 60–61. But the evil still remains. It was exploited by some who approached an honest juror with a bribe – expecting it not to be accepted – but expecting that he would report it to the

[1] [1975] 1 QB 73.

judge – and the judge would discharge the jury, thinking that the offer of a bribe would prejudice the jury against the accused. That, I hope, is being overcome: because most judges allow the case to go on, warning the jury not to be influenced by it.

But there still remains the risk that three or more jurors may be approached and be influenced to stand out.

iv *The presence of the prisoner*

It is not necessary for the accused to be in the dock. He can, with the permission of the judge, be seated in any convenient place. But usually the judge requires him to be in the dock.

In general, the accused has a right to be present at the trial in a place where he can hear and see all that goes on. But if he creates a disturbance – and will not desist – he can be removed and the trial can go on in his absence. So also for any other good cause.

During the trial of Stephen Ward, he was found unconscious, having taken an overdose of drugs. The judge concluded his summing-up in his absence, see the *Profumo Report*, page 229.

2 Henry Hunt and others

1 The movement for radical reform

i *Peterloo*

Everyone has heard of Waterloo. It was fought in 1815 near Brussels. But few nowadays have heard of Peterloo. It was fought in 1819 in Manchester. In a field called St Peter's Field. So people called it Peterloo. It led to a leading case on unlawful assembly, *R v Henry Hunt and others.*[1]

ii *Song to the men of England*

It was at a time when the working classes of England were in great distress. Their wages were very low. There was much unemployment and much misery – both in the agricultural south and in the industrial north. The poet, Percy Bysshe Shelley, was sorry for their plight. He wrote a *Song to the men of England:*

> Men of England, wherefore plough
> For the lords who lay ye low?
> Wherefore weave with toil and care
> The rich robes your tyrants wear?
>
> . . .
>
> With plough and spade, and hoe and loom,
> Trace your grave, and build your tomb,
> And weave your winding-sheet, till fair
> England be your sepulchre.

[1] (1820) 1 State Tr NS 171–495.

iii 'Orator Hunt'

The miseries of the working classes gave rise to a movement for radical reform. It was led by William Cobbett of *Rural Rides* and Henry Hunt, a Wiltshire farmer. He was a forcible speaker, known as 'Orator Hunt.' They preached the need to reform Parliament. They wanted the 'rotten boroughs' to be abolished: and replaced by proper constituencies with every man entitled to vote. They wanted the Corn Laws (which increased the price of bread) repealed. And so forth. They denounced violence and rioting. They wanted the reforms to be effected peacefully.

iv *Dangerous and subversive*

But the Government of the day was manned by the upper classes. They regarded the movement as dangerous and subversive to the constitution – in which they were supreme. They wanted to have the leaders arrested but had no evidence to do so. They decided to wait until evidence was available.

v *A demonstration is planned*

When the movement was in full swing, Henry Hunt and his friends planned a big demonstration in Manchester. They proposed to call a meeting on Monday 9 August 1819 but this was forbidden by the magistrates. So Henry Hunt gave notice for a meeting on 16 August 1819 and issued placards to this effect:

Manchester Public Meeting

> The undersigned give notice that a public meeting will be held on the area near St Peter's Church on Monday the 16th instant to consider the propriety of adopting the most legal and effectual means of obtaining RADICAL REFORM of the Commons House of Parliament. The chair to be taken by Henry Hunt, Esquire, at 12 o'clock.

Big preparations were made. The radical reformers called on all their supporters in the towns in and around Manchester to come to the meeting. Every town made a large banner carrying a slogan. Every town got its band practising patriotic tunes. Every town got its men together to march in procession and to drill in preparation.

vi *The Government are alarmed*

The Government were alarmed by these preparations. They feared that violence might result. Lord Sidmouth, the Secretary of State, called on the magistrates and on the military. (You will recall that there was no organised police force at this time. It was not forthcoming for another ten years.) The magistrates swore in about 300 special constables, all from the middle and upper classes. The military were stationed in barracks round about. There were troops of the Cheshire and Manchester Yeomanry. They were all volunteers of the upper classes. There were three squadrons of the 15th Hussars, a regular regiment. And two pieces of light artillery. Altogether 1,000 men, all armed.

2 The day arrives

i *The magistrates watch*

On Monday 16 August at about 10 o'clock, people began to assemble in St Peter's Field. It was only about as big as Trafalgar Square. Ten magistrates assembled in a house next to the field. They stationed themselves in an upper window from which they could see all that went on. The supporters of radical reform brought a cart on to the field and set it up as hustings from which Mr Hunt was to speak. This was about 100 yards from the magistrates' house. The constables were arranged in a line from the hustings to the magistrates' house. They were to keep the way clear so that, if Mr Hunt said anything seditious, he could be arrested and taken before the magistrates.

ii *The processions march in*

During the morning, the processions arrived from

Manchester and the neighbouring towns. It was a gloriously fine summer day. They came with banners flying, drums beating and bands playing. They were followed by thousands of men, women and children. The presiding magistrate, Mr William Hulton, himself described the scene as the contingents moved in:

All the bodies proceeded regularly, and in a remarkable manner, for they did not march straight to the hustings, but wheeled when they received the word of command. The persons in command went up to the hustings and deposited their colours. They were regularly received with loud huzzas. The men appeared to me to be beautifully exact in coming up to the hustings.

There were 16 contingents, each with its own flag or banner, having its own inscription, such as 'Annual Parliaments,' 'Universal Suffrage,' 'Vote by ballot,' 'Success to the Female Reformers of Stockport,' 'No Corn Laws,' 'No boroughmongering' and 'Unite and be Free.' Each contingent had its band. They played 'Rule Britannia' with the people saying, 'Britons never will be slaves.'

iii *'Orator Hunt' arrives*

At about midday, a carriage drove up with Mr Hunt and three of his principal supporters. A tremendous shout of welcome greeted them. They drove to the hustings and alighted. Mr Hunt took the chair. Then he stood up and started to speak. A bystander took down his words:

Gentlemen, I must entreat that you will be peaceable and quiet, and that every person who wishes to hear must keep order; and all I ask for is that during the proceedings you will be quiet.

3 The cavalry charge

i *The magistrates issue a warrant*

Meanwhile, the magistrates were trying to get information on which to issue a warrant. Eventually, one Richard Owen swore on oath:

Henry Hunt [and three others] at this time (now a quarter past one o'clock) have arrived in a car near St Peter's Church. An immense mob is collected. The town is in danger.

Thereupon a warrant was prepared and signed by all ten magistrates. It was addressed to the constables. It recited the information of Richard Owen and went on:

These are therefore, in his Majesty's name to require you forthwith to take and bring before us the bodies of Henry Hunt [and the three others].

ii *The constables cannot execute it*

Mr Hulton, the presiding magistrate, handed this warrant to the deputy constable, Joseph Nadin. Nadin said he could not do it with his constables:

It is out of our power to execute it without the aid of the military.

The reason was that the people had surged round the line of constables near the hustings. They had linked arms so as to prevent the constables getting to Hunt to arrest him.

iii *The military are called in*

The presiding magistrate then at once wrote a letter to Colonel L'Estrange, the commanding officer:

As chairman of the magistrates, I require the assistance of the military. The Civil Power is not sufficient.

The Colonel then ordered the troops forward. They were in the neighbouring streets awaiting orders. They were in full uniform with swords and pistols, and mounted on horses.

iv *16 killed and 600 wounded*

The first to arrive were the Yeomanry. They were in formation, with drawn swords. They trotted up towards the hustings. No doubt to arrest Hunt. As they came along, the men in the crowd closed in on them and tried to pull them off their horses. The women hissed and hooted. Then

157

Colonel L'Estrange looked up to the presiding magistrate
and asked:

What are your orders?

The magistrate replied:

For God's sake, see – they are attacking the Yeomanry. Save them.
Disperse the mob.

The Colonel gave orders at once to the Hussars. They
galloped in. They lashed out with their sabres. The people
fled in all directions. They could not get away fast enough.
The exits were blocked. Men, women and children were
struck down. Sixteen were killed and over 600 wounded, of
whom 113 were women, and 140 received sabre cuts.

4 Afterwards

i *The Government approve*

Orator Hunt and his colleagues were arrested and taken to
the New Bailey Courts at Manchester. They were detained
on a charge of high treason. But afterwards the Secretary of
State ordered it to be reduced to a treasonable conspiracy.

The Government emphatically approved of all that was
done. Lord Sidmouth sent a message to the magistrates
thanking them

for their prompt decision and effectual means for the preservation of the
public tranquillity.

ii *The City of London disapprove*

But all over the country meetings were held to express
sympathy with the demonstrators. The Common Council
of the City of London expressed the strongest disapproval of
the action of the Manchester authorities. They affirmed:

the undoubted right of Englishmen to assemble together for the purpose
of deliberating upon public grievances.

iii *'Rise like lions'*

Shelley wrote his *Masque of Anarchy*, but dared not publish it
at the time. It had this stirring refrain:

> Rise like lions after slumber
> In unvanquishable number.
> Shake your chains to earth, like dew,
> Which in sleep have fallen on you:
> Ye are many, they are few.

5 The trial of Hunt and others

i *Prejudice amongst jurors*

The trial was to have taken place at the assizes at Lancaster
but Hunt applied to the court in London for it to be held
elsewhere. He gave an interesting reason:

Among the military who attended there were the Manchester, Salford
and Cheshire Yeomanry, the privates of whom consisted chiefly, and the
officers entirely, of opulent manufacturers, and landed proprietors, in
Lancashire and Cheshire, and that a very great and general prejudice
existed throughout the county of Lancaster, and amongst the persons
who were likely to serve upon juries, as to the nature and object of the
meeting in question, and as to the share which the defendants had taken
in it; and, therefore, that they could not have a fair and impartial trial in
the county of Lancaster.

The court accepted this reasoning and ordered the case to
be tried, not at Lancaster, but at York.

ii *Seven long counts*

The trial was held at the Spring Assizes in York before Mr
Justice Bayley and a special jury in March 1820. The
indictments contained seven long counts which may be
shortened into:

1 Seditious conspiracy to the terror of His Majesty's
subjects.
2 Conspiracy to disturb the peace.
3 Conspiracy to excite discontent and disaffection.

4 Unlawful assembly to move His Majesty's liege subjects
to hatred and contempt of the Government and
constitution.
5 Unlawful assembly with menaces and offensive weapons.
6 Making a great riot.
7 Unlawfully, riotously and routously assembling.

iii *The jury's findings*

The judge in his summing-up shortened these seven counts
into two kinds of unlawful assembly. One was an assembly
to excite hatred and discontent of the Government. The
other was to assemble in a formidable and menacing manner
to the great alarm and terror of the peaceable subjects of the
King. The jury found Mr Hunt guilty of the first of those
two kinds of unlawful assembly, but not of the second. That
appears clear from the interchanges that took place when the
jury returned:

Mr Littledale (Junior for the prosecution)   This is very nearly in the
words of the fourth count, my Lord.

The judge You may take it on the fourth count.

Foreman We find Henry Hunt [and four others] guilty of assembling
with inflammatory banners an unlawful meeting for the purpose of
moving the liege subjects of our Lord the King to contempt of the
Government and Constitution of this realm as by law established.

iv *The effect of the verdict*

The judge asked them:

You do not mean to find that there was an intention to move the liege
subjects of the King to terror?

Foreman No, my Lord.

Mr Littledale Are the inflammatory banners part of the verdict then?

The judge No. That need not be included.

So we get the verdict:

Guilty of assembling an unlawful meeting for the purpose of moving the liege subjects of our Lord the King to contempt of the Government and Constitution of this realm as by law established.

When that verdict is analysed (Guilty on the fourth count but not guilty on all other counts), it is plain that the jury only found the accused had assembled together to criticise the Government and to urge the radical reform of the constitution. The jury negatived any conspiracy to disturb the peace, or to produce terror or fear or to excite discontent. They negatived any menaces or use of offensive weapons. They only found the truth, namely, that Hunt and his colleagues were radical reformers who had assembled this large gathering together as a demonstration to urge reform of our parliamentary system of government.

v *Guilty of unlawful assembly*

The judge treated that finding of the jury as a finding of 'Guilty of an unlawful assembly.' In so doing he was justified by the state of the law at that time. You must remember that in those days any publication which excited hatred or contempt of the Government was regarded as a seditious libel. It was a crime punishable with imprisonment. So also any demonstration which excited hatred and contempt of the Government. It was an unlawful assembly.

vi *Sentenced to two and a half years*

Mr Hunt applied to the full court to set the decision aside on the ground that some of the evidence had been wrongly admitted. But the full court refused his application.

The judge sentenced Hunt to be imprisoned for two and a half years in Ilchester gaol.

6 The trial of the military

i *Hit with a sword*

Afterwards, there was another case, *Redford v Birley and*

others.[1] It was against the military. A man, Thomas Redford, brought an action against an officer of the Manchester Yeomanry and a private called Alexander Oliver. He alleged that Oliver had cut him with his sword on the head. The action was tried at the Lancaster Assizes in April 1822. There was much doubt whether Redford was wounded at all, but in any case the judge directed the jury that it was the duty of the military, when requested by the magistrates, to execute warrants for the arrest of the leaders, to disperse the meeting, and to aid in preserving the peace.

ii *The warrant assumed to be good*

The trial of the military proceeded on the basis that the magistrates were justified in issuing the warrant. It was not suggested that the magistrates were wrong. On that basis, the military were justified in their action. The jury so found. They retired for about six minutes and found a verdict for the defendants.

iii *But was it wrong?*

But if the magistrates were wrong in issuing the warrant, it would be no defence to the military. As Lord Bowen said in his Report on the Featherstone Riots:[2]

If the military forces of the Crown are employed in suppressing a riot their status is that of ordinary citizens. The fact that they possess special arms and organisation is simply a reason for not lightly employing them . . . An order to take action from a magistrate who is present is required by military regulations; and wisdom and discretion are entirely in favour of such a practice. But the order of the magistrate at law has no legal effect. Its presence does not justify the firing if the magistrate is wrong, its absence does not excuse the officer in declining to fire when the necessity exists.

iv *Damages should have been recovered*

I must say that, looked at with modern eyes, I think the magistrates were wrong to issue the warrant for the arrest of

[1] (1822) 3 Starke 76.
[2] (1893) Parliamentary Papers, pp 9, 10.

Hunt. He had done nothing wrong. All he had done was to organise a great demonstration criticising the Government: and it had remained peaceful right up to that time. In any case it was wrong to attempt to execute the warrant by the use of that military force. If the constables could not execute the warrant themselves at that time, they should have waited for an opportunity to do so later in the day when they could do it peaceably.

If the case had been properly argued, I think the wounded man should have recovered damages against the military.

7 Legal points

i *What is an unlawful assembly?*

The judge's summing-up in *R v Hunt* has been treated as a correct statement of the law. He divided the offence of unlawful assembly into two branches: (1) an assembly to bring the Government into contempt; and (2) an assembly to cause terror and alarm to peaceable citizens.

That first branch has now gone. At the time the judge enunciated it, the law of seditious libel was still very active. It was invoked whenever a publisher attacked the Government of the day and brought it into contempt. It had been invoked against John Wilkes for his publication of the *North Briton No 45* and against the printers and publishers of the *Letters of Junius*; and, as I have said, in 1819 the poet Shelley wrote a series of poems called the *Masque of Anarchy* in which he ranged himself on the people's side against the Government, but he did not publish them then because it would have made him liable to a criminal prosecution for seditious libel.

That law is now obsolete. It was an undue restriction on the freedom of the press. Nowadays it is commonplace to read polemics against the Government and the constitution. They are the daily bread of journalists. No one troubles about them. With the end of seditious libel, there was an end of that branch of unlawful assembly. There is only one branch now left. It must be an assembly such as to produce 'terror and alarm in the neighbourhood,' that is, to innocent third parties, members of the public not participating in the assembly, see *Kamara v DPP*[1].

ii *The Law Commission's Report*

The Law Commission has recently criticised the common law on lawful assembly on the ground that it is too wide and too uncertain. They have issued a Report[2] recommending that the common law be replaced by two new statutory offences, namely, (1) violent disorder and (2) conduct intended or likely to cause fear or provoke violence. As a background to their proposals, I draw attention to some important cases where the offence of unlawful assembly has been considered – especially in regard to demonstrations.

[1] [1974] AC 104, 115–116 per Lord Hailsham of St Marylebone.
[2] See *Law Commission* No 123 (Cmnd no 85).

3 Later assemblies

1 The Chartists

The Reform Act of 1832 did something. It abolished the 'rotten boroughs.' But it did not do enough to satisfy the working classes. In 1839 came the Chartists. Their objectives were to effect more changes in the constitution of the country. (These were valid objectives which were achieved 30 years later.) They arranged meetings at which speakers appealed to the working classes to revolt and to use physical force for the purpose. Some of these meetings were at Newport in Monmouthshire where a Mr Vincent addressed crowds in words which invited the use of force and reasonable citizens were much alarmed. This led to the prosecution in *Vincent's case*.[1]

The judge told the jury:

I take it to be the law of the land that any meeting assembled under such circumstances as, according to the opinion of rational and firm men, are likely to produce danger to the tranquillity and peace of the neighbourhood is an unlawful assembly.

The defendants were found guilty of unlawful assembly.

2 The Salvation Army

i *The Skeleton Army*

In 1882 there was the case of *Beatty v Gillbanks*.[2] The

[1] (1839) 9 C & P 91, 109.
[2] [1882] 9 QBD 308.

Salvation Army formed processions and marched through the streets of Weston-super-Mare. They had a band, flags and banners, all in aid of their religious crusade. A body came out in opposition. They called themselves the 'Skeleton Army.' They deliberately collided with the Salvation Army. It led to a free fight, great uproar, blows, stone-throwing, and much disorder ensued. It caused great terror and alarm in the minds of the peaceful inhabitants of the town and was calculated to cause a breach of the peace. The court held that the Salvation Army were not guilty of an unlawful assembly. It follows that the Skeleton Army were guilty. Their ringleaders should have been prosecuted and not the Salvation Army.

ii *The band in Whitchurch Square*

In my own home town of Whitchurch there was a similar affair. In 1881 the Salvation Army held meetings and made processions quite peacefully. They were attacked by the 'Skeleton Army' of roughs. Cross-summonses were issued. But in view of *Beatty v Gillbanks* there were no convictions.

In 1889 the band of the Salvation Army met in the Square at Whitchurch and played hymns. They were opposed by the local brewers. They were prosecuted for 'obstructing the free passage of the highway, to wit, the Square.' The local magistrates found them guilty. Each was fined 10 shillings and costs or, in default of payment, 14 days' imprisonment on dry bread and cold water. They refused to pay the fines. They were handcuffed and taken to prison like felons. But a little later a big demonstration was held in their honour in Whitchurch. The leaders were charged. It was feared that they would not get a fair hearing before the local magistrates. So the case was transferred to the Central Criminal Court. They were triumphantly acquitted.

3 The Garden House Hotel

In 1970 the Garden House Hotel planned a 'Greek Week' in

Cambridge. They held a dinner and dance in the hotel. All expected a quiet evening. It was violently interrupted by students who were anti-Greek. They broke into the hotel. The police came. The students pushed them out of the way. They got into the dining room. They overturned tables. They smashed glasses. They tore down curtains. Chairs were brandished and thrown. A policeman and a proctor were seriously injured. The students were found guilty of unlawful assembly. One was sentenced to 18 months' imprisonment. The case was *R v Caird*.[1] Lord Justice Sachs said (page 504):

> The moment when persons in a crowd, however peaceful their original intention, commence to act for some shared common purpose supporting each other and in such a way that reasonable citizens fear a breach of the peace, the assembly becomes unlawful.

4 Red Lion Square

The National Front is on the extreme right wing of politics. They booked a large hall in Red Lion Square for a meeting on 15 June 1974. Liberation is an organisation very much left-wing in outlook. They booked a small hall in the same building for the same day. Each organisation planned a march to the hall on that afternoon. The police stationed a cordon at the corner of the Square. Some Liberation marchers made 'a deliberate, determined and sustained attack' on the police cordon. It was unexpected, unprovoked and viciously violent. It was the beginning of an afternoon's violence in which one young man was killed and a large number of demonstrators and 46 policemen were injured.

An inquiry was held by Lord Scarman. He pointed out that English law recognises as paramount the right of passage along a highway: a demonstration which obstructs passage along a highway is unlawful. Most certainly a 'mass picket' would be unlawful.

But he affirmed that the right to demonstrate exists,

[1] [1970] 54 Cr App Rep 499.

subject only to limits required by the need for good order and the passage of traffic.

5 The nuclear protesters

The Electricity Board proposed to build a nuclear power station. They wished to survey a possible site in Cornwall. They brought a rig on to the site. Demonstrators came and tried to stop the survey. They lay down in front of vehicles. They tied themselves to the rig. All this was a criminal offence. It was an unlawful assembly. It was also a breach of the peace. The police were entitled to use reasonable force to remove the demonstrators and move them off the site. The case was *R v Chief Constable of Devon and Cornwall, ex parte CEGB.*[1] I said (page 471):

I go further. I think that the conduct of these people, their criminal obstruction, is itself a breach of the peace. There is a breach of the peace whenever a person who is lawfully carrying out his work is unlawfully and physically prevented by another from doing it. He is entitled by law peacefully to go on with his work on his lawful occasions. If anyone unlawfully and physically obstructs the worker – by lying down or chaining himself to a rig or the like – he is guilty of a breach of the peace. Even if this were not enough, I think that their unlawful conduct gives rise to a reasonable apprehension of a breach of the peace. It is at once likely that the lawful worker will resort to self-help by removing the obstructor by force from the vicinity of the work so that he obstructs no longer. He will lift the recumbent obstructor from the ground . . .

If I were wrong on this point, if there was no breach of the peace nor apprehension of it, it would give a licence to every obstructor and every passive resister in the land. He would be able to cock a snook at the law as these groups have done. Public works of the greatest national importance could be held up indefinitely. This cannot be. The rule of law must prevail.

6 The violent miners

As I told you earlier, in the first six months of 1984 the miners have organised 'flying pickets.' They have carried

[1] [1982] 1 QB 458.

men long distances in coach or cars to mount mass pickets at collieries – to stop working miners from going to work. Sometimes to steel works to stop lorries carrying coke for the furnaces. In reply the police have organised protective cordons in hundreds so as to enable men to go to work. Violence has followed on a serious scale. These are unlawful assemblies at common law. But no charge of unlawful assembly has been brought against the perpetrators. The police have, quite understandably, charged the wrongdoers with obstructing the highway or obstructing the police in the execution of their duty. These are summary offences triable by the magistrates: whereas unlawful assembly is triable only on indictment.

7 The Law Commission's proposal

The Law Commission said[2] that this area of the law is closely connected with the exercise of fundamental liberties of the subject and it is necessary to move with caution. I agree. They have made recommendations which the Government are considering. A Bill is expected in the next session of Parliament.

[2] No 123, A2.2.

Part Six

Matrimonial Affairs

Introduction

To a practising lawyer it is always important to know: On whom is the burden of proof? What evidence is sufficient to discharge the burden? The problem arose nearly every day when I was first appointed a judge. That was in March 1944. It was so important that I made a special study of it. I wrote an article and submitted it to Arthur Goodhart, the editor of the *Law Quarterly Review*. He then gave me good advice:

When you state a proposition, always give some authority for it. Your readers will not check it up. That is what Coke did. He gave authorities for everything but, if you looked them up, they were authority for nothing. He got away with it time after time.

I called my article 'Presumptions and Burdens.' You will find it in the *Law Quarterly Review* for October 1945, page 379.

It was very unusual for a judge at that time to write an article for a Law Review or to give a lecture on law to a university: it was simply not done. When I gave the Hamlyn Lectures in 1949 Lord Jowitt LC wrote a letter rebuking me. But he was induced to do it because one of the government departments did not like what I had said.

The question of burden arose constantly in the divorce cases which I had to try. The only ground for divorce was proof of a matrimonial offence, such as cruelty or adultery. The leading authority on it was Sir William Scott, afterwards Lord Stowell. His judgments were so authoritative that I will tell you about him. Afterwards I will take some *causes célèbres* which turned on the burden of proof.

173

1 Sir William Scott

The elder brother

i 'Send Jack up to me'

I have told you of John Scott who became Lord Eldon. Now I tell you of his elder brother William who became Lord Stowell. He was six years older than John. He was a brilliant scholar. He gained a Fellowship at University College, Oxford, in 1766 at the age of 20. At that time their father made plans for John to be apprenticed, at the age of 15, to the trade of a coal-fitter. William wrote home: 'Send Jack up to me; I can do better for him here.'

Both brothers went in for law. But with a difference. William, the elder, became an advocate in Doctors' Commons. John, the younger, became a barrister practising in the Common Law Courts and in Chancery.

ii His judicial timetable

William was quite unlike John. He did not take much part in politics. He kept more to his professional career. His judicial timetable was rather like mine. In 1788, at the age of 43, he was appointed a judge of the Consistory Court; and in 1798 a judge of the High Court of Admiralty. He was on the bench for 39 years. He retired in 1827 at the age of 82.

iii One of our greatest judges

He was one of our greatest judges. During the Napoleonic

wars he laid down principles of Prize Law which have been
accepted throughout the world. He illuminated the law of
nations by his judgments on the slave trade. He expounded
the law of marriage and divorce with much care. His
judgments are expressed in clear, polished, exquisite
style – quite a contrast from the diffuse and obscure style of
his brother John. But they have one grave defect. They are
far too long. He examined the evidence in such detail as to
make them quite unreadable.

iv *Burden in cruelty*

When I was a divorce judge, I frequently quoted Lord
Stowell on the burden of proof in cruelty cases. He expressed
it eloquently in *Evans v Evans*.[1] A wife charged her husband
with cruelty. Sir William Scott took 100 pages to exculpate
the husband. But this passage is memorable. It gives his
reasons for maintaining the marriage bond (pages 36–38):

... Yet it must be carefully remembered that the general happiness of
the married life is secured by its indissolubility. When people understand
that they must live together, except for a very few reasons known to the
law, they learn to soften by mutual accommodation that yoke which
they know they cannot shake off; they become good husbands and good
wives from the necessity of remaining husbands and wives; for necessity
is a powerful master in teaching the duties which it imposes. If it were
once understood that upon mutual disgust married persons might be
legally separated, many couples who now pass through the world with
mutual comfort, with attention to their common offspring and to the
moral order of civil society, might have been at this moment living in a
state of mutual unkindness, in a state of estrangement from their
common offspring, and in a state of the most licentious and unreserved
immorality. In this case, as in many others, the happiness of some
individuals must be sacrificed to the greater and more general good.

That the duty of cohabitation is released by the cruelty of one of the
parties is admitted, but the question occurs, What is cruelty? ... This,
however, must be understood, that it is the duty of courts, and
consequently the inclination of courts, to keep the rule extremely strict.
The causes must be grave and weighty, and such as shew an absolute
impossibility that the duties of the married life can be discharged ...

... Mere austerity of temper, petulance of manners, rudeness of

[1] (1790) 1 Hag Con 35.

language, a want of civil attention and accommodation, even occasional
sallies of passion, if they do not threaten bodily harm, do not amount to
legal cruelty: they are high moral offences in the marriage-state
undoubtedly, not innocent surely in any state of life, but still they are not
that cruelty against which the law can relieve.

v *Burden in adultery*

In *Loveden v Loveden*[1] a wife was charged with adultery with
a Fellow of Merton College, Oxford. Sir William Scott in 53
pages found the charges proved. I quote (pages 2–3):

... It is a fundamental rule, that it is not necessary to prove the direct fact
of adultery; because, if it were otherwise, there is not one case in a
hundred in which that proof would be attainable: it is very rarely indeed
that the parties are surprised in the direct fact of adultery. In every case
almost the fact is inferred from circumstances that lead to it by fair
inference as a necessary conclusion; and unless this were the case and
unless this were so held, no protection whatever could be given to
marital rights ... The only general rule that can be laid down upon the
subject is that the circumstances must be such as would lead the guarded
discretion of a reasonable and just man to the conclusion.

vi *The change today*

When I was first a judge, we repeatedly quoted those words
of Sir William Scott. They set the standard of proof for the
judges. But they are never heard now. There is no longer any
binding knot for marriage. There is only a loose piece of
string which the parties can untie at will. Divorce is not a
stigma. It has become respectable. One-parent families
abound. But you may be interested to read of some famous
trials of the past.

[1] (1810) 2 Hag Con 1.

2 Queen Caroline's case

Introduction

Such were the principles applicable at the trial of Queen Caroline. It was in 1820. It was called a 'trial.' But it was really part of a debate in the House of Lords.

The King (George IV) was 58. The Queen was 46. He had just ascended the throne. He wanted a divorce. Lord Liverpool, at the instance of the King, brought a Bill to deprive the Queen of her title as Queen of England and to dissolve her marriage with the King.

1 George, Prince of Wales

i *Mrs Fitzherbert*

George (afterwards King George IV), when Prince of Wales, was a dissolute profligate spendthrift. In 1780, at the age of 18, he had an affair with an actress who blackmailed him. At 19, he carried on with the wife of a Hanoverian officer. Each year he had a different woman. He ran up enormous debts, until in 1784, when he was 22, he fell in love (or thought he did) with Mrs Maria Fitzherbert. She was 28 and was a very experienced woman. She was a Roman Catholic, too. She had already been married twice and widowed twice. She refused any sexual relations with the Prince unless he married her. So in 1785 he went through a marriage service with her according to the rites of the Church of England. It was performed by a clergyman who had been released from the Fleet prison. He was bribed to do it. The Prince promised him a bishopric when he came to the throne. The marriage was utterly invalid. The King had not given his consent to it.

ii *A desperate expedient*

In 1794, the Prince (then aged 32) was completely insolvent. He owed £500,000. He resorted to a desperate expedient. He decided to marry his cousin, Princess Caroline of Brunswick, then aged 20. The King (George III) was delighted. It would make an honest man of him. The couple were married on 8 April 1795. They spent the bridal night together, but never again afterwards. (Their daughter, Princess Charlotte, was born exactly nine months later on 7 January 1796.) The Prince did not live with his wife. He demanded a formal separation. He had an affair with one of the ladies of her bedchamber. He was a thoroughly bad lot and the whole country knew it.

2 Caroline, Princess of Wales

i *Her conduct is notorious*

So treated by her husband, the Princess Caroline herself drifted into bad society. She was guilty of levity and indecorum, if not adultery. In 1814, she left England for travels in Greece, Italy and the Holy Land. Her conduct there became notorious. A Chancery barrister was sent out to Milan to collect evidence against her.

ii *No prayers for her*

Then on 29 January 1820 the King, George III, died. George, Prince of Wales, became King. The Princess Caroline (still in Italy) became Queen of England. Then the King and his ministers acted very rashly. They directed that our *Book of Common Prayer* be altered. Up to that time, there had been a prayer for 'their Royal Highnesses the Prince of Wales, the

Princess of Wales' and all the Royal Family. They ordered that this should be struck out and that there should be a prayer for the new King George: but that there should be no prayer for 'our gracious Queen Caroline.' She learnt of this from the newspapers. She ordered post-horses and drove off for Calais at great speed. She hurried on board a packet boat, and landed at Dover where she was welcomed by an immense multitude. They had sympathy for her but not for her husband.

3 Her trial

i *Papers sent to Parliament*

The King was determined to get rid of her as Queen. He sent papers in a green bag to both Houses of Parliament respecting her conduct. The result was that a Bill was introduced to deprive the Queen of her title as Queen of England and to dissolve her marriage with the King. A special order was made by which counsel could be heard at the bar and witnesses examined. This took the form of a trial. It was always called afterwards 'the Queen's trial.' Nearly the whole talent of the Bar was engaged. Six on one side. Five on the other. All save one afterwards attained high judicial office.

ii *Brougham's opening speech*

But it was far from being a fair trial. If it had been an ordinary Bill for divorce before Parliament, there would have been a long-drawn-out procedure beforehand. It was summarised by Mr Brougham in his opening speech:[1]

It has been argued, I am informed, by the promoters of this bill, that my illustrious client is to be dealt with as if she were the lowest, not the highest, subject in the realm. God grant that she were in the situation of the lowest subject in the realm. God grant that she had never risen to a higher rank than the humblest individual who owed allegiance to his

[1] Campbell *Lives of the Lord Chancellors*, vol VIII, pp 308–309.

Majesty. She would then have been fenced round by the triple fence whereby the law of England guards the life and honour of the poorest female. Before such a bill could have been introduced against any other individual, there must have been a sentence of divorce in the Consistory Court, there must have been a verdict of a jury who might have sympathised with her feelings . . . She would have been tried by twelve honest, impartial, and disinterested Englishmen . . . She has, therefore, good cause to lament that she is not the lowest subject of his Majesty, and I can assure your Lordships that she would willingly sacrifice everything, except her honour, which is dearer to her than her life, to obtain the poorest cottage which has ever sheltered an Englishwoman from injustice.

iii *Wanting in natural justice*

The procedure at her trial was wanting in all the elements of natural justice. Mr Brougham on the Queen's behalf asked for particulars of the charges and places where she was supposed to have offended. His request was refused. He asked for a list of the witnesses. This too was refused. He asked to be allowed to give evidence of the King's own misconduct. He asked the Bishops who were present 'whether adultery is to be considered only a crime in woman.' He wanted to go into the King's marriage to Mrs Fitzherbert and his profligate life. This was always available in other divorce cases. It was called the 'right of recrimination.' But it was refused.

iv *The Italian witnesses*

All these reasonable requests being refused, the prosecution called their witnesses. They were mostly Italians. They had been brought over to this country at the expense of the Government. Several had fresh clothes, also at public expense. They were kept together in one large dormitory. They fed at a common table.

The first to be called was Teodoro Majocchi. He had been in the service of the Queen in Italy. In evidence in chief he said that in Naples the Queen and Bergami (with whom she was alleged to have committed adultery) had rooms next to one another with a communicating door between them: whereas the rest of her suite were distant and cut off.

v 'Non mi recordo'

But when Brougham cross-examined him, he repeatedly gave the answer *Non mi ricordo* (I do not remember). This phrase passed into common talk as denoting a liar.

The other witnesses all crumbled under cross-examination.

4 Brougham's final speech

i *The stolen bracelet*

Brougham spent the long vacation preparing his final speech. He himself considered it the most wonderful effort of genius recorded in the history of oratory. He gave instances from literature of women falsely accused of adultery. He took the villain in Shakespeare's play, *Cymbeline* – the Italian Iachimo who came to Britain, got into Imogen's bedroom by stealth and hid in a trunk. As she lay asleep he took off the bracelet from her arm and got back into the trunk. He went back to Rome and presented the bracelet as evidence of his and her adultery. Brougham quoted these lines:[1]

> . . . mine Italian brain
> 'Gan in your duller Britain operate
> Most vilely; for my 'vantage, excellent;
> And, to be brief, my practice so prevailed,
> That I returned with similar proof, enough
> To make the noble Leonatus mad,
> By wounding his belief in her renown.

Brougham also cited the case of Susanna who was falsely accused by the elders in the apocryphal book about Daniel and Susanna of which I will tell you later.

---

[1] Shakespeare *Cymbeline*, Act V, sc 5.

181

ii *17 times rewritten*

Brougham came to his peroration. He wrote it and rewrote it 17 times before he was satisfied with it. To modern ears, it is ridiculous hyperbole. It is so ornate that I smile as I read it. I have quoted it before in *What Next in the Law* (page 27). This is what he said:[1]

Such, my Lords, is the case now before you! Such is the evidence in support of this measure – evidence inadequate to prove a debt – impotent to deprive of a civil right – ridiculous to convict of the lowest offence – scandalous if brought forward to support a charge of the highest nature which the law knows – monstrous to ruin the honour, to blast the name of an English Queen! What shall I say, then, if this is the proof by which an act of judicial legislation, a parliamentary sentence, an *ex post facto* law, is sought to be passed against this defenceless woman? My Lords, I pray you to pause. I do earnestly beseech you to take heed! You are standing upon the brink of a precipice – then beware! It will go forth your judgment, if sentence shall go against the Queen. But it will be the only judgment you ever pronounced, which, instead of reaching its object, will return and bound back upon those who give it. Save the country, my Lords, from the horrors of this catastrophe – save yourselves from this peril – rescue that country, of which you are the ornaments, but in which you can flourish no longer, when severed from the people, than the blossom when cut off from the roots and stem of the tree. Save that country, that you may continue to adorn it – save the Crown, which is in jeopardy – the Aristocracy which is shaken – save the Altar, which must stagger with the blow that rends its kindred Throne! You have said, my Lords, you have willed – the Church and the King have willed – that the Queen should be deprived of its solemn service. She has instead of that solemnity, the heartfelt prayers of the people. She wants no prayers of mine.

iii *Raising his hands*

Then, raising his hands, with the palms open, at the same height above his head, he lowered his voice saying, solemnly and impressively:

But I do here pour forth my humble supplications at the Throne of Mercy, that that mercy may be poured down upon the people, in a larger

[1] Campbell *Lives of the Lord Chancellors*, vol VIII, pp 319–320.

measure than the merits of its rulers may deserve, and that your hearts may be turned to justice.

He called no evidence.

5 Case dismissed

i *The close vote*

The Lords were divided in opinion. Half of them were willing to degrade the Queen from her royal state and dignity; but they were not willing to find her guilty of adultery when the King himself had been guilty of adultery ten times more than she. They had no evidence before them of the King's adultery, but they felt in conscience bound to take it into account. They voted therefore against the Bill. The voting was so close that Lord Liverpool moved that 'further consideration of the bill should be adjourned for six months.' That was equivalent to its dismissal.

ii *The public applaud her*

During the whole progress of the trial, the excitement of the public was unbounded. They wholly discounted the evidence adduced against the Queen, declaring that the witnesses were suborned, and when the House was forced to abandon the Bill, the delight of the populace almost amounted to frenzy.

Brougham acquired great glory and popularity. The City of London gave him a fine gold ornamented snuff box which he presented to Lincoln's Inn. (It is still passed round after dinner.) Ordinary people contributed a penny apiece for a splendid candelabra. Inn signs carried Brougham's head.

iii *But no coronation for her*

The Queen, however, suffered a reverse. She wanted to be crowned Queen at the coronation of the King. But it was refused. She went early, between six and seven, to the Abbey. She tried to force her way in, but the crowd pushed her back with hisses. There was a great shout, 'Shame, shame, go to Bergami.' She got back into her carriage and wept. Soon afterwards she died.

iv *But she was Guilty*

No doubt on the evidence given at the trial, the verdict was properly Not Guilty. But other circumstances – not in evidence – such as the negotiation for a settlement – all point to her guilt. In any case, behind it all there was the gross misconduct of the King himself. It would have been most unfair to convict her whilst he went free. He was King for ten years: and he never did any good.

3 Lord Melbourne – Prime Minister

Introduction

Lord David Cecil has written two books of outstanding merit, *The Young Melbourne* and *Lord M*. Lord Melbourne was born in 1779. He was Home Secretary in 1834 when the Tolpuddle Martyrs were sentenced to transportation for life. He was Prime Minister in 1836 when he was sued by George Norton for criminal conversation; and in 1837 when Queen Victoria came to the throne. At 18 she adored him at 58.

1 His affairs

i *Criminal conversation*

Here I am concerned with the action for criminal conversation. If a wife committed adultery, her husband could sue her paramour for damages: on the footing that, although she was a guilty party, nevertheless he was responsible. This is the description of it, given by Blackstone in his *Commentaries*:[1]

Adultery, or criminal conversation with a man's wife, though it is, as a public crime, left by our laws to the coercion of the spiritual courts; yet, considered as a civil injury, (and surely there can be no greater) the law gives a satisfaction to the husband for it by action of trespass *vi et armis* against the adulterer, wherein the damages recovered are usually very large and exemplary. But these are properly increased and diminished by circumstances; as the rank and fortune of the plaintiff and defendant; the relation or connection between them; the seduction or otherwise of the wife, founded

[1] III, p 139.

on her previous behaviour and character; and the husband's obligation by settlement or otherwise to provide for those children, which he cannot but suspect to be spurious.

ii *He is most indiscreet*

Lord Melbourne's wife died in 1828 when he was 49. He then was most indiscreet in his affairs with women. He was sued by two husbands for criminal conversation with their wives – each separately, and at different times. Both husbands lost. Lord Melbourne was held not liable. But when he died in 1848 at the age of 69 he left annuities to both wives. So there may have been something criminal in the conversations with them after all.

The cases are not reported in the law books but Lord David Cecil has given vivid accounts of them.

iii *Lady Branden – Grapes and pineapples*

She was young and lovely. Her husband was a clergyman, The Revd Lord Branden. He got some compromising evidence about her relations with Lord Melbourne. He told her that he would overlook it if she would persuade Lord Melbourne to have him made a bishop. She rejected this suggestion. In 1829 Lord Branden brought an action for criminal conversation against Lord Melbourne. But all the evidence he could produce was first, that Lord Melbourne had sent her grapes and pineapples and, secondly, that a short gentleman had been seen leaving her house in the early hours of the morning – whereas Lord Melbourne was tall. The judge scornfully rejected it:

Pray call someone who will prove something to the purpose. You must get him a good deal nearer than this. You have not got him to the lady's house yet.

The action was dismissed.

2 Caroline Norton

i *Her husband out for money*

She was the grand-daughter of the playwright, R B

Sheridan. She inherited his literary gifts. She was 30 years younger than Lord Melbourne. She was very lively and exciting. They met constantly. Lord David Cecil tells the story admirably. Her husband, George Norton, was determined to make money out of this relationship if he could. So he sued Lord Melbourne for damages for criminal conversation. This is how Lord David Cecil puts it:

> He was intoxicated by the prospect of the fortune he was likely to get if he did contrive to win his case; alternatively, he thought Melbourne, for the sake of avoiding a public scandal, might pay up handsomely in order to persuade him to withdraw it. In either case he fancied he stood to win. He proceeded, therefore, to file a petition, accusing him of criminal conversation with his wife.

ii *'A handful of servants'*

Then Lord David Cecil goes on to tell us that

> The case came up for trial on 23 June. Public excitement was tremendous. Couriers waited all day ready to carry the news of the verdict to every important capital in Europe. From early morning, the law courts were besieged by huge crowds trying to get seats: so much so that the Attorney General, Sir John Campbell, who was appearing for Melbourne, had considerable difficulty in pushing his way through the throng . . . George Norton could not by law go into the witness box himself. Instead, he relied on the evidence of a handful of servants once in his employ, whom he had tracked down after months of search in the underworld of London and then persuaded by means of lavish bribes to come forward on his behalf. . . .

iii *Three little notes*

The chief documentary evidence brought forward were three notes from Melbourne. The first ran,

'I will call about quarter-past four. Yours, Melbourne.'

The second, 'How are you? I shall not be able to come today. I shall tomorrow.'

The third, 'No House today: I will call after the levee. If you wish it later I will let you know.'

Norton's counsel did what he could with these unpromising documents. He said they showed 'a great and unwarrantable degree of affection,' because they did not begin My Dear Mrs Norton, and added, 'there may be latent love like latent heat in the midst of icy coldness.'

(That trial was in 1836. Dickens wrote *Pickwick Papers* in 1837. So you can see the source of Serjeant Buzfuz's speech.)

iv 'Thunderous applause'

The proceedings, which lasted for nearly thirteen hours, were frequently interrupted by bursts of uproarious laughter. Campbell called no witness for the defence. Instead, rising at six o'clock and continuing till the candles guttered low in their sockets, he demolished the evidence offered on behalf of the plaintiff in a speech which all present agreed to be one of the most brilliant exhibitions of legal wit and eloquence ever heard in an English court of justice. The case ended just before midnight: the jury acquitted Melbourne without leaving the box. The verdict was received with thunderous applause.

4 Later cases

1 1857 – A turning point

i *Divorce only by Act of Parliament*

From a Prime Minister I turn to a hawker. You must remember that until 1857, adultery was not a ground for divorce. The husband could get a decree *a mensa et thoro* (from bed and board). The effect of it was that he was no longer bound to support his wife. But he could not sever the marriage bond so as to enable him to marry another woman. The only way of dissolving the marriage was by Act of Parliament. And that could only be obtained at great expense. The rich man could get it. But the poor man could not.

ii *The hawker's case*

This gave rise to a famous example of sustained irony by a judge. His words altered the whole course of law as to divorce. It was in 1844 at the Assizes at Warwick. Mr Justice Maule had before him a hawker who was charged with bigamy. When asked what he had to say, the hawker said that his wife had left the home and children to live with another man. He had never seen her since. And as she had deserted him, he had married the second wife.

iii *Sustained irony*

I will quote what Mr Justice Maule said, and when reading it

189

you will remember that £100 then would be infinitely greater now:

I will tell you what you ought to have done: and if you say you did not know, I must tell you that the law conclusively presumes that you did. You ought to have instructed your attorney to bring an action against the seducer of your wife for damages. That would have cost you about £100. When you had recovered damages against him, you should have employed a proctor and instituted a suit in the ecclesiastical courts for a divorce *a mensa et thoro* (from bed and board): that would have cost you £200 or £300 more. When you had obtained a divorce *a mensa et thoro*, you had only to obtain a private Act of Parliament for a divorce *a vinculo matrimonii*. The Bill might possibly have been opposed in all its stages in both Houses of Parliament and altogether these proceedings would cost you about £1,000. You will probably tell me that you have not a thousand farthings of your own in the world. But that makes no difference. Sitting here as an English judge, it is my duty to tell you that this is not a country where there is one law for the rich, and another for the poor. You will be imprisoned for one day.

Those words so struck the conscience of the country that it gave great impetus for a movement for divorce. In a few years there was passed the Matrimonial Causes Act 1857 which for the first time gave divorce by the courts so as to permit remarriage.

iv 'A Frankenstein monster'

The year 1857 marks a turning point in our social history. In that year jurisdiction in matrimonial causes was transferred from the ecclesiastical courts to civil courts then set up which were given power to pronounce a decree of divorce dissolving the marriage tie so as to permit the parties to remarry. The only ground on which divorce was permitted, however, was adultery. There was a difference between the sexes. Adultery by the wife was by itself sufficient ground to enable the husband to get a divorce. Adultery by the husband was, however, not sufficient to enable the wife to get a divorce unless it was coupled with cruelty or with desertion for two years. In the first year that that Act was in operation there were 300 divorces. That was considered so large that Lord Campbell noted in his diary what a

Frankenstein monster he had created. That monster has grown to the gargantuan proportions of 149,187 decrees granted in 1983.

2 1923 – Sex equality

i *Hotel bills*

It was not until 1923 that the sexes were put on an equal footing. In that year a wife was enabled to divorce her husband for adultery without having to prove cruelty or desertion, just as he was entitled to divorce her for adultery. No one could doubt the justice of this. A husband should keep as high a standard himself as that which he expects his wife to keep: but after 1923 there was an increase in the number of collusive divorces. When a marriage had hopelessly broken down, and the parties were both anxious for divorce, they would arrange that the husband should 'provide the grounds for divorce,' which meant that he would go to a hotel with a woman and send the hotel bill afterwards to his wife. The courts would, on such evidence, infer adultery. In fact, however, it might never have taken place. The woman he took might be his sister, or a woman who made a business of going to a hotel with a man for money but on the strict understanding that there was to be no adultery. Lord Merrivale was so uneasy about the position that he declined to act on hotel evidence, at any rate if the woman was unnamed; but the Court of Appeal overruled him. The Court of Appeal had in mind, no doubt, the considerable number of cases where the man declined to give the name of a woman with whom he had in fact committed adultery, so that it should not become public; but in so doing, it gave considerable scope to collusive divorces. When I sat as a divorce judge in 1944, we had hundreds of 'hotel bill' cases. They all went through 'on the nod.'

I would not go further into these cases about proof of adultery. This is not a treatise on our divorce laws.

5 Legal points

1 Burden of proof

In former times when adultery was considered a grave offence, the courts imposed a high burden of proof. In the present century, it is not regarded as an offence at all. It is simply one of the grounds on which a divorce can be obtained. So there is hardly any burden at all.

As in Queen Caroline's case, many a guilty person has been acquitted because the burden of proof has not been discharged. In criminal cases the jury are always told by the judge that the burden is on the prosecution to prove the case 'beyond reasonable doubt.' In a civil case it is to be 'on the balance of probability.' I ventured to explain the point in *Bater v Bater:*[1]

The difference of opinion which has been evoked about the standard of proof in recent cases may well turn out to be more a matter of words than anything else. It is of course true that by our law a higher standard of proof is required in criminal cases than in civil cases. But this is subject to the qualification that there is no absolute standard in either case. In criminal cases the charge must be proved beyond reasonable doubt, but there may be degrees of proof within that standard.

As Best CJ and many other great judges have said, 'in proportion as the crime is enormous, so ought the proof to be clear.' So also in civil cases, the case may be proved by a preponderance of probability, but there may be degrees of probability within that standard. The degree depends on the subject-matter. A civil court, when considering a charge of fraud, will naturally require for itself a higher degree of probability

[1] [1951] P 35, 36–37.

than that which it would require when asking if negligence is
established. It does not adopt so high a degree as a criminal court, even
when it is considering a charge of a criminal nature; but still it does
require a degree of probability which is commensurate with the
occasion. Likewise, a divorce court should require a degree of
probability which is proportionate to the subject-matter.

2 Bigamy

When I went the Western Circuit, the calendar at many an
Assize town contained three or four cases of bigamy. Now
there are hardly any cases of bigamy. This is due, no doubt,
to easy divorce, and the lessening respect for marriage. A
man and woman who want to live together do so without
troubling to get married. There is no stigma to it. Other
people just shrug their shoulders. They say it is just their
private affair.

6 Breach of promise

1 *Pickwick Papers*

i *He had not read it*

I was asked recently to broadcast for the World Service of the BBC. It was on *Good Books*. I chose *Pickwick Papers*. To my surprise, the interviewer had never read it. Yet when I was young everyone had read it. I have before me now the copy which I gave to my first wife in September 1922. Lord Goddard knew the trial of *Bardell v Pickwick* by heart. I suspect that many of you young people will know nothing of it. So I will tell you of it. It gives a picture of lawyers in the year 1830 – fictitious, but true to life. You will find it entertaining as well as instructive.

ii *Charles Dickens himself*

It was written by Charles Dickens. He was born in 1812, the son of a poor clerk who was imprisoned for debt. Charles, at the age of 12, started work labelling bottles for six shillings a week. His father soon withdrew him and sent him to school. At 15, he began work for a firm of attorneys in Gray's Inn. At 17, he was a freelance reporter in Doctors' Commons. Afterwards, he reported parliamentary debates. He was a keen observer of life. At 24, there appeared the first number of *Pickwick Papers*.

iii *Samuel Pickwick himself*

A distinctive feature of the book is the illustrations by Seymour and 'Phiz.' They depict Samuel Pickwick as a kindly, bespectacled, middle-aged gentleman, of the utmost respectability, wearing a black morning-coat, white waist-coat and white tights and gaiters. He founded the Pickwick Club with friends who accompanied him on travels into the countryside. They went by coach or carriage. There were no railways in those days. They had many exciting adventures which are told by Charles Dickens with inimitable skill. They did not form a collective story. They were published as a series of sketches.

iv *Its popularity*

The first numbers had little success, but then this is the description given by John Forster in *The Life of Charles Dickens*:[1]

. . . It sprang into a popularity that each part carried higher and higher, until people at this time talked of nothing else, tradesmen recommended their goods by using its name, and its sale, outstripping at a bound that of all the most famous books of the century, had reached to an almost fabulous number. Of part one, the binder prepared four hundred; and of part fifteen, his order was for more than forty thousand. Every class, the high equally with the low, were attracted to it. The charm of its gaiety and good humour, its inexhaustible fun, its riotous overflow of animal spirits, its brightness and keenness of observation, and, above all, the incomparable ease of its varieties of enjoyment, fascinated everybody. Judges on the bench and boys in the street, gravity and folly, the young and the old, those who were entering life and those who were quitting it alike found it to be irresistible.

A charming contemporary writer, Mary Russell Mitford, writing to a friend in Ireland, said:

It is fun – London life – but without any thing unpleasant; a lady might read it all *aloud*; and it is so graphic, so individual, and so true, that you could courtesy [sic] to all the people as you met them in the streets . . . Sir Benjamin Brodie takes it to read in his carriage between patient and patient; and Lord Denman studies 'Pickwick' on the bench whilst the

[1] (1872–4) (ed J W T Ley (1928)) pp 90–91.

jury are deliberating . . . It is rather fragmentary, except the trial, which is as complete and perfect as any bit of comic writing in the English language. You must read the 'Pickwick Papers.'

Now for *Bardell v Pickwick*. The story, as you read it, is most disjointed. Each incident of the Bardell story is separated by several chapters and pages from the next. I will try and tell them in sequence.

2 The preliminaries

i *Mr Pickwick broaches it delicately*

Mr Pickwick, when in London, had lodgings in Goswell Street. His landlady there was Mrs Bardell, a widow with one small boy. After Mr Pickwick had been there for about three years, he was minded to employ a man–servant named Samuel Weller. He had been 'boots' at the White Hart Inn in the Borough. He was a resourceful character, with a keen sense of humour. Mr Pickwick thought it would be useful to have Sam Weller in attendance on him at his lodgings in Goswell Street. So he approached Mrs Bardell to see if she could accommodate Sam in Goswell Street as well as himself. He had to broach it delicately because landladies can be troublesome.

He said to her:

'Do you think it a much greater expense to keep two people, than to keep one?'

'La, Mr Pickwick,' said Mrs Bardell, colouring up to the very border of her cap, as she fancied she observed a species of matrimonial twinkle in the eyes of her lodger; 'La, Mr Pickwick, what a question!'

ii *'You kind, good, playful dear'*

After a few more exchanges on the subject of the servant, Mrs Bardell seized her opportunity:

'Oh you kind, good playful dear,' said Mrs Bardell; and without more ado, she rose from her chair, and flung her arms round Mr Pickwick's neck, with a cataract of tears and a chorus of sobs.

'Bless my soul,' cried the astonished Mr Pickwick; 'Mrs Bardell my good woman – dear me, what a situation – pray consider – Mrs Bardell, don't – if anybody should come –'

'Oh, let them come,' exclaimed Mrs Bardell, frantically; 'I'll never leave you, – dear, kind, good, soul;' and, with these words, Mrs Bardell clung the tighter.

iii *Fainting in Mr Pickwick's arms*

'Mercy upon me,' said Mr Pickwick, struggling violently, 'I hear somebody coming up the stairs. Don't, don't, there's a good creature, don't.' But entreaty and remonstrance were alike unavailing: for Mrs Bardell had fainted in Mr Pickwick's arms; and before he could gain time to deposit her on a chair, Master Bardell entered the room, ushering in Mr Tupman, Mr Winkle, and Mr Snodgrass.

Mr Pickwick was struck motionless and speechless. He stood with his lovely burden in his arms, gazing vacantly on the countenances of his friends, without the slightest attempt at recognition or explanation. They, in their turn, stared at him; and Master Bardell, in his turn, stared at everybody.

iv *'An extremely awkward situation'*

One of Mr Pickwick's friends led Mrs Bardell down the stairs. Then:

'I cannot conceive – ' said Mr Pickwick, when his friend returned – 'I cannot conceive what has been the matter with that woman. I had merely announced to her my intention of keeping a man-servant, when she fell into the extraordinary paroxym in which you found her. Very extraordinary thing.'

'Very,' said his three friends.

'Placed me in such an extremely awkward situation,' continued Mr Pickwick.

'Very,' was the reply of his followers, as they coughed slightly, and looked dubiously at each other.

3 The lawyers

i *A solicitors' letter*

Then there is a break in the story for six chapters on other adventures. When they were back in London at The Angel, Sam Weller brought Mr Pickwick a letter:

'I don't know this hand,' said Mr Pickwick, opening the letter. 'Mercy on us! what's this? It must be a jest; it – it – can't be true.'

This was the letter:

Freeman's Court, Cornhill, August 28th, 1830.

Bardell against Pickwick

Sir,
Having been instructed by Mrs Martha Bardell to commence an action against you for a breach of promise of marriage, for which the plaintiff lays her damages at fifteen hundred pounds, we beg to inform you that a writ has been issued against you in this suit at the Court of Common Pleas; and request to know, by return of post, the name of your attorney in London, who will accept service thereof.

We are, Sir
Your obedient servants,
Dodson and Fogg.

Mr Samuel Pickwick.

Then there was the comment:

'It's a conspiracy,' said Mr Pickwick, at length recovering the power of speech; 'a base conspiracy between these two grasping attorneys, Dodson and Fogg. Mrs Bardell would never do it; – she hasn't the heart to do it; – she hasn't the case to do it. Ridiculous – ridiculous.'

'Of her heart,' said Wardle, with a smile, 'you should certainly be the best judge.'

ii *Served with a writ*

Mr Pickwick and Sam went to the offices of Dodson and Fogg and, after waiting awhile in an ante-room with their four clerks, Mr Pickwick was ushered in to see Messrs Dodson and Fogg. There were some exchanges. Then they served him with the writ:

'As you offer no terms, sir,' said Dodson, displaying a slip of parchment in his right hand, and affectionately pressing a paper copy of it, on Mr Pickwick with his left, 'I had better serve you with a copy of this writ, sir. Here is the original, sir.'

'Very well, gentlemen, very well,' said Mr Pickwick, rising in person and wrath at the same time; 'you shall hear from my solicitor, gentlemen.'

'We shall be very happy to do so,' said Fogg, rubbing his hands.

'Very,' said Dodson, opening the door.

'And before I go, gentlemen,' said the excited Mr Pickwick, turning round on the landing, 'permit me to say, that of all the disgraceful and rascally proceedings – '

'Stay, sir, stay,' interposed Dodson, with great politeness. 'Mr Jackson! Mr Wicks.'

iii 'You are swindlers'

'Sir,' said the two clerks, appearing at the bottom of the stairs.

'I merely want you to hear what this gentleman says,' replied Dodson. 'Pray, go on, sir – disgraceful and rascally proceedings, I think you said?'

'I did,' said Mr Pickwick, thoroughly roused. 'I said, sir, that of all the disgraceful and rascally proceedings that ever were attempted, this is the most so. I repeat it, sir.'

'You hear that, Mr Wicks?' said Dodson.

'You won't forget these expressions, Mr Jackson?' said Fogg.

'Perhaps you would like to call us swindlers, sir,' said Dodson. 'Pray do, sir, if you feel disposed; now pray do, sir.'

'I do,' said Mr Pickwick. 'You *are* swindlers.'

'Very good,' said Dodson. 'You can hear down there, I hope, Mr Wicks?'

'Oh, yes, sir,' said Wicks.

'You had better come up a step or two higher, if you can't,' added Mr Fogg. 'Go on, sir; do go on. You had better call us thieves, sir; or perhaps you would like to assault one of us. Pray do it, sir, if you would; we will not make the smallest resistance. Pray do it, sir.'

iv *Battledore and shuttlecock*

Sam Weller saw that Mr Pickwick was getting into trouble. He might be faced with a slander action by Dodson and Fogg.

'You just come away,' said Mr Weller. 'Battledore and shuttlecock's a wery good game, vhen you an't the shuttlecock and two lawyers the battledores, in which case it gets too excitin' to be pleasant. Come away, sir.'

Mr Pickwick went off and tried to see his own solicitor, Mr Perker, but as he had gone away for a week, he left the copy writ with Mr Perker's clerk and went off to Ipswich.

v '*Walentine's* day, *sir*'

Then there are other adventures for nearly 200 pages, including a Christmas visit to Dingley Dell. There is little mention of the action, save for the service of subpoenas on the three friends. Then we get to the conference of Mr Pickwick with his solicitor, Mr Perker, and afterwards with his counsel, Serjeant Snubbin, and his junior, Mr Phunky. The trial was fixed for 14 February 1830.

'This action, Sam,' said Mr Pickwick, 'is expected to come on, on the fourteenth of next month.'

'Remarkable coincidence that 'ere, sir,' replied Sam.

'Why remarkable, Sam?' inquired Mr Pickwick.

'Walentine's day, sir,' responded Sam; 'reg'lar good day for a breach o' promise trial.'

Mr. Weller's smile awakened no gleam of mirth in his master's countenance.

4 The trial itself

Then after another 40 pages we come to Chapter XXXIV which

IS WHOLLY DEVOTED TO A FULL AND FAITHFUL REPORT OF THE MEMORABLE TRIAL OF BARDELL AGAINST PICKWICK

As you read it, you must remember that at that date the parties themselves were not competent as witnesses. So neither Mrs Bardell nor Mr Pickwick could be called to give evidence. Serjeant Buzfuz appeared for Mrs Bardell. Serjeant Snubbin for Mr Pickwick. You should read the whole trial for yourself. I would pick out here the most amusing – and instructive – incidents.

i *Swearing the jury*

By way of introduction, I must tell you that at common law if there were not sufficient jurymen summoned or available to make up the twelve, the judge could award a *tales de circumstantibus*. It was a command to the sheriff to retain so many other qualified men as were present or could be found. (This is now replaced by the court summoning any persons in the vicinity [Juries Act 1974, s 6(1)].)

This being done, a gentleman in black, who sat below the judge, proceeded to call over the names of the jury; and after a great deal of bawling, it was discovered that only ten special jurymen were present. Upon this, Mr Serjeant Buzfuz prayed a *tales*; the gentleman in black then proceeded to press into the special jury, two of the common jurymen; and a green-grocer and a chemist were caught directly.

'Answer to your names, gentlemen, that you may be sworn,' said the gentleman in black. 'Richard Upwitch.'

'Here,' said the green-grocer.

'Thomas Groffin.'

'Here,' said the chemist.

'Take the book, gentlemen. You shall well and truly try – '

ii *The chemist has no assistant*

'I beg this court's pardon,' said the chemist, who was a tall, thin, yellow-visaged man, 'but I hope this court will excuse my attendance.'

'On what grounds, sir?' said Mr Justice Stareleigh.

'I have no assistant, my Lord,' said the chemist.

'I can't help that, sir,' replied Mr Justice Stareleigh. 'You should hire one.'

'I can't afford it, my Lord,' rejoined the chemist.

'Then you ought to be able to afford it, sir,' said the judge, reddening; for Mr Justice Stareleigh's temper bordered on the irritable, and brooked not contradiction.

'I know I *ought* to do, if I got on as well as I deserved, but I don't, my Lord,' answered the chemist.

'Swear the gentleman,' said the judge, peremptorily.

The officer had got no further than the 'You shall well and truly try,' when he was again interrupted by the chemist.

'I am to be sworn, my Lord, am I?' said the chemist.

'Certainly, sir,' replied the testy little judge.

iii *An errand-boy in the shop*

'Very well, my Lord,' replied the chemist, in a resigned manner. 'Then there'll be murder before this trial's over; that's all. Swear me, if you please, sir;' and sworn the chemist was, before the judge could find words to utter.

'I merely wanted to observe, my Lord,' said the chemist, taking his seat with great deliberation, 'that I've left nobody but an errand-boy in my shop. He is a very nice boy, my Lord, but he is not acquainted with drugs; and I know that the prevailing impression on his mind is, that Epsom salts means oxalic acid; and syrup of senna, laudanum. That's all, my Lord.' With this, the tall chemist composed himself into a comfortable attitude, and, assuming a pleasant expression of countenance, appeared to have prepared himself for the worst.

5 Serjeant Buzfuz opens the case

i *'The serpent was on the watch'*

Then Serjeant Buzfuz opened the case to the jury. He told how Mrs Bardell had put a notice in her parlour-window: 'Apartments furnished for a single gentleman. Inquire within.' Then he went on:

'... Did it remain there long? No. The serpent was on the watch, the train was laid, the mine was preparing, the sapper and miner was at work. Before the bill had been in the parlour-window three days – three days – gentlemen – a Being, erect upon two legs, and bearing all the outward semblance of a man, and not of a monster, knocked at the door of Mrs Bardell's house. He inquired within; he took the lodgings; and on the very next day he entered into possession of them. This man was Pickwick – Pickwick, the defendant.'

ii '*Systematic villany*'

Serjeant Buzfuz, who had proceeded with such volubility that his face was perfectly crimson, here paused for breath. The silence awoke Mr Justice Stareleigh, who immediately wrote down something with a pen without any ink in it, and looked unusually profound, to impress the jury with the belief that he always thought most deeply with his eyes shut. Serjeant Buzfuz proceeded.

'Of this man Pickwick I will say little; the subject presents but few attractions; and I, gentlemen, am not the man, nor are you, gentlemen, the men, to delight in the contemplation of revolting heartlessness, and of systematic villany.'

iii *The two letters*

There were only two letters in the case. These were little notes by Mr Pickwick, asking the landlady to get supper ready for him, and not to trouble about the warming-pan. (This was in the days before hot-water bottles.) Charles Dickens is said to have taken these letters from some which were in evidence in the case of Lord Melbourne (page 187).

Drawing forth two very small scraps of paper, Serjeant Buzfuz proceeded:

'And now, gentlemen, but one word more. Two letters have passed between these parties, letters which are admitted to be in the handwriting of the defendant, and which speak volumes indeed. These letters, too, bespeak the character of the man. They are not open, fervent, eloquent epistles, breathing nothing but the language of affectionate attachment. They are covert, sly, underhanded communications, but, fortunately, far more conclusive than if couched in the most glowing language and the most poetic imagery – letters that must be viewed with a cautious and suspicious eye – letters that were evidently intended at the time, by Pickwick, to mislead and delude any third parties into whose hands they might fall.

iv '*Chops and Tomato sauce*'

Let me read the first: – "Garraway's, twelve o'clock. Dear

Mrs B – Chops and Tomato sauce. Yours, PICKWICK." Gentlemen, what does this mean? Chops and Tomato sauce! Yours, Pickwick! Chops! Gracious heavens! and Tomato sauce! Gentlemen, is the happiness of a sensitive and confiding female to be trifled away, by such shallow artifices as these?

v *The warming-pan*

The next has no date whatever, which is in itself suspicious. "Dear Mrs B, I shall not be at home till to-morrow. Slow coach." And then follows this very remarkable expression. "Don't trouble yourself about the warming-pan." The warming-pan! Why, gentlemen, who *does* trouble himself about a warming-pan? When was the peace of mind of man or woman broken or disturbed by a warming-pan, which is in itself a harmless, a useful, and I will add, gentlemen, a comforting article of domestic furniture? Why is Mrs Bardell so earnestly entreated not to agitate herself about this warming-pan, unless (as is no doubt the case) it is a mere cover for hidden fire – a mere substitute for some endearing word or promise, agreeably to a preçoncerted system of correspondence, artfully contrived by Pickwick with a view to his contemplated desertion, and which I am not in a condition to explain? And what does this allusion to the slow coach mean? For aught I know, it may be a reference to Pickwick himself, who has most unquestionably been a criminally slow coach during the whole of this transaction, but whose speed will now be very unexpectedly accelerated, and whose wheels, gentlemen, as he will find to his cost, will very soon be greased by you!'

vi *The beautiful peroration*

Serjeant Buzfuz ended with this peroration:

'Damages, gentlemen – heavy damages – is the only punishment with which you can visit him; the only recompense you can award to my client. And for those damages she now appeals to an enlightened, a high-minded, a right-feeling, a conscientious, a dispassionate, a sym-pathising, a contemplative jury of her civilised countrymen.' With this beautiful peroration, Mr Serjeant Buzfuz sat down, and Mr Justice Stareleigh woke up.

6 The witnesses are called

i *Mr Nathaniel Winkle*

Then the witnesses were called – all subpoenad for Mrs

Bardell. They were her friend, Mrs Cluppins, and in addition, Mr Pickwick's three friends and Sam Weller. They had to attend and give evidence, however unwillingly. Mrs Cluppins said nothing of importance. Mr Nathaniel Winkle was called by Mr Skimpin, the junior for Mrs Bardell. He ought not to have cross-examined his own witness but he did so most effectively:

'Now, sir, tell the gentlemen of the jury what you saw on entering the defendant's room, on this particular morning. Come; out with it, sir; we must have it, sooner or later.'

'The defendant, Mr Pickwick, was holding the plaintiff in his arms, with his hands clasping her waist,' replied Mr Winkle with natural hesitation,
'and the plaintiff appeared to have fainted away.'

'Did you hear the defendant say anything?'

'I heard him call Mrs Bardell a good creature, and I heard him ask her to compose herself, for what a situation it was, if anybody should come, or words to that effect.'

ii *Ingenious dove-tailing*

'Now, Mr Winkle, I have only one more question to ask you, and I beg you to bear in mind his lordship's caution. Will you undertake to swear that Pickwick, the defendant, did not say on the occasion in question, "My dear Mrs Bardell, you're a good creature; compose yourself to this situation, for to this situation you must come," or words to *that* effect?'

'I – I didn't understand him so, certainly,' said Mr Winkle, astounded at this ingenious dove-tailing of the few words he had heard, 'I was on the staircase, and couldn't hear distinctly; the impression on my mind is – '

'The gentlemen of the jury want none of the impressions on your mind, Mr Winkle, which I fear would be of little service to honest, straightforward men,' interposed Mr Skimpin. 'You were on the staircase, and didn't distinctly hear; but you will not swear that Pickwick did not make use of the expressions I have quoted? Do I understand that?'

'No, I will not,' replied Mr Winkle; and down sat Mr Skimpin with a triumphant countenance.

iii *Samuel Weller*

Mr Pickwick's two other friends were also called. Then came Samuel Weller. In introducing him I must remind you that at common law hearsay evidence is not admissible. Counsel always shorten it, by referring to 'what the soldier said.' It comes from this passage:

Sam bowed his acknowledgments and turned, with unimpaired cheerfulness of countenance, towards Serjeant Buzfuz.

'Now, Mr Weller,' said Serjeant Buzfuz.

'Now, sir,' replied Sam.

'I believe you are in the service of Mr Pickwick, the defendant in this case. Speak up, if you please, Mr Weller.'

'I mean to speak up, sir,' replied Sam; 'I am in the service o' that 'ere gen'l'man, and a wery good service it is.'

iv *'What the soldier said'*

'Little to do, and plenty to get, I suppose?' said Serjeant Buzfuz, with jocularity.

'Oh, quite enough to get, sir, as the soldier said ven they ordered him three hundred and fifty lashes,' replied Sam.

'You must not tell us what the soldier, or any other man, said, sir,' interposed the judge; 'it's not evidence.'

'Wery good, my lord,' replied Sam.

v *'Have you a pair of eyes?'*

'Now, attend, Mr Weller,' said Serjeant Buzfuz, dipping a large pen into the inkstand before him, for the purpose of frightening Sam with a show of taking down his answer. 'You were in the passage, and yet saw nothing of what was going forward. Have you a pair of eyes, Mr Weller?'

'Yes, I have a pair of eyes,' replied Sam, 'and that's just it. If they wos a pair o' patent double million magnifyin' gas microscopes of hextra power, p'raps I might be able to see through a flight o' stairs and a deal door; but bein' only eyes, you see, my wision's limited.'

7 The summing-up

i *A glass of sherry*

Mr Justice Stareleigh summed up, in the old-established and most approved form. He read as much of his notes to the jury as he could decipher on so short a notice, and made running comments on the evidence as he went along . . . The jury then retired to their private room to talk the matter over, and the judge retired to *his* private room, to refresh himself with a mutton chop and a glass of sherry.

An anxious quarter of an hour elapsed; the jury came back; the judge was fetched in. Mr Pickwick put on his spectacles, and gazed at the foreman with an agitated countenance and a quickly beating heart.

ii *£750 damages*

'Gentlemen,' said the individual in black, 'are you all agreed upon your verdict?'

'We are,' replied the foreman.

'Do you find for the plaintiff, gentlemen, or for the defendant?'

'For the plaintiff.'

'With what damages, gentlemen?'

'Seven hundred and fifty pounds.'

Mr Pickwick took off his spectacles, carefully wiped the glasses, folded them into their case, and put them in his pocket; then having drawn on his gloves with great nicety, and stared at the foreman all the while, he mechanically followed Mr Perker and the blue bag out of court.

The story does not end there. Mr Pickwick refused to pay. He was sent to the Fleet prison. So was, in due course, Mrs Bardell because she had guaranteed the costs of Messrs Dodson and Fogg. They succeeded in getting their costs but Mrs Bardell did not get her damages. You will find it told in *What Next in the Law* (pages 83–87).

8 Legal points

i *Breach of promise*

It seems strange to us now that an action should lie at law for

207

breach of promise of marriage. Yet it was commonplace in the nineteenth century. Before the Reformation, it was a matter for the ecclesiastical courts. But afterwards it was introduced in the common law courts. In 1727 a girl of 15 was awarded £2,000 damages.[1] By 1830 there were many cases in the Court of Common Pleas. It had bad results. When an engagement was broken off, the girl sued the man for damages. The juries were sorry for her and awarded large sums. One young barrister was so frightened that, instead of breaking off the engagement, he married the girl and lived in misery ever after. He eventually committed suicide. He was James Shaw Willes (1814–1872), one of our most learned judges.

In 1869 Parliament intervened. By the Evidence (Further Amendment) Act 1869, the parties were made competent to give evidence themselves but it was provided that no plaintiff should recover a verdict 'unless his or her testimony shall be corroborated by some other material evidence in support of the promise.' If he gave her an engagement ring, that would be corroboration: but when he gave her his own signet ring, it was not, see *Wiedemann v Walpole*.[2]

When I was called to the Bar, there were still actions for breach of promise: but they became fewer. They were not ended until the Law Commission in 1969 recommended they should be abolished (Law Commission No. 26). They were abolished by the Law Reform (Miscellaneous Provisions) Act 1970 which said that an agreement to marry shall not have effect as a contract giving rise to legal rights.

ii *The rules of evidence*

One of the most interesting features of the case of *Bardell v Pickwick* is that it shows how important are the rules of evidence. The rights of the parties often depend on them.

It also seems incredible now but under the old common law for centuries every person having an interest, however

[1] *Holt v Ward* (1732) 2 Stra 937.
[2] [1891] 2 QB 534.

remote, in the result of the proceedings was barred from being a witness. There was a Latin maxim, *Nemo in propria causa testis esse debet*. That was why, in the year 1830, as I have told you, neither Mrs Bardell nor Mr Pickwick could go into the witness-box and give evidence. The reason was because it was assumed that each would be so biased in his own favour that his word, even on oath, could not be trusted. Nor could a husband give evidence in his wife's case: and vice versa. Nor could an accused man give evidence on his own behalf – until 1898.

Likewise in many cases a contract could not be enforced by action unless it was evidenced in writing. This goes back to the Statute of Frauds in 1677. Its object was to prevent frauds. But the effect of it was to promote them. It gave rise to thousands of cases in the courts and millions of pounds in the pockets of lawyers. It was not repealed until 1954 by the Law Reform (Enforcement of Contracts) Act 1954 but, even so, the repeal did not affect contracts of guarantee. Nor did it affect contracts for the sale of an interest in land. These still require to be evidenced by writing.

An engagement to marry did not, however, require to be evidenced in writing; nor did it require to be corroborated in any material particular. That is why Mrs Bardell succeeded, even though she had no writing and no engagement ring. The two letters produced by Serjeant Buzfuz were ridiculous.

iii *The conduct of counsel*

I have no doubt that in the time of Dickens, counsel did behave in the way that Serjeant Buzfuz did. Hectoring, bullying, distorting, accusing, behaving rudely and aggressively. That seems to have prevailed in those days. But not now. Counsel should be calm and restrained, never putting his case too high, courteous to the witnesses, never making any accusation of misconduct unless he has good grounds for it, always respectful to the court. In short, as they have it at the College at Winchester, *Manners makyth man*. They also make the good advocate.

Part Seven

Freedom of the Individual

Introduction

In 1949 I gave the first of the Hamlyn Lectures. I called it
Personal Freedom. I spoke of the writ of Habeas Corpus. This
is what I said:

The law says that no man is to be imprisoned except by judgment of the
King's courts or whilst awaiting trial by them. This freedom is
safeguarded by the most famous writ in England, the writ of habeas
corpus. Whenever any man in England is detained against his will, not by
sentence of the King's courts, but by anyone else, then he or anyone on
his behalf is entitled to apply to any of the judges of the High Court to
determine whether his detention is lawful or not. The court will then, by
this writ, command the gaoler or whoever is detaining him, to bring him
before the court; and, unless the detention is shown to be lawful, the
court will at once set him free.

This was not always so. In 1627, when the executive Government cast
Sir Thomas Darnel and four other knights into prison because they
would not subscribe money for the King, the Court of King's Bench, to
its disgrace, held that if a man were committed by command of the King
he was not to be delivered by habeas corpus.[1] Those were the evil days
when the judges took their orders from the executive. But the people of
England overthrew the Government which so assailed their liberties, and
passed statutes which gave the writ its present power. Never thereafter
have the judges taken their orders from anyone.

Now I wish to tell you of the greatest example of the value
of habeas corpus. It was in the abolition of slavery in
England.

---

[1] *Darnel's case* (1627) 3State Tr 1.

1 Slavery

1 The slave trade

i *15 million black slaves*

Over a period of 150 years, 15 million black slaves were transported by sea from the west coast of Africa to the West Indies and North America. They were put to work on the plantations there. They were bought and sold like animals. They were regarded as the absolute property of their masters.

England led the world in putting a stop to it. Now it is, or should be, non-existent. Article 4 of the Universal Declaration of Human Rights declared in 1948:

No one shall be held in slavery or servitude. Slavery and the slave trade shall be prohibited in all its forms.

ii *Slavery in the colonies*

In the seventeenth and eighteenth centuries, this was the law in our colonies:

A man who was a slave was obliged to serve his master for the whole of his life. He received in return food, clothing and shelter but no remuneration by way of wages. If he did not obey orders, the master could punish him by whipping or strokes or putting him on short rations. If the slave grew anything or made anything it belonged to his master. If a woman slave bore children – of any father – they belonged

214

to her master. The master could sell his slave for money and transfer all his rights over the slave to the purchaser. If the slave was ill-treated, he had no recourse to the courts of law for redress. He had no rights – no locus standi – to sue anyone. He was the property of his master – on the same footing as his horse or his cow, or his table or chair.

iii *Slavery in Roman law*

That law about slaves was derived from the Roman law. It divided men into two groups – those who are free and those who are slaves. Justinian in *Digest* I, 3 says:

Summa itaque divisio de iure personarum haec est, quod omnes homines aut liberi sunt aut servi (The great division in the law of persons is that all men are either free or slaves).

Moyle summarises it in these words:[1]

Slavery is a condition of absolute 'rightlessness.' A slave could have no rights against either his master or any one else; . . . a slave was not a 'person' at all . . . The Roman lawyers looked upon him as a 'res,' and applied to him, as an object of property, the same rules which they laid down as to domestic animals. . . .

except that he could be freed by manumission, that is, by going through the prescribed procedure.

iv *Baptism in England*

But in England itself there was no such law about slavery. We had the institution of villeinage, but this was very different. In *Smith v Brown and Cooper* Sir John Holt, the Chief Justice, tried his own hand at emancipation. He went so far as to say:[2]

As soon as a negro comes into England, he becomes free: one may be a villein in England, but not a slave.

Others did not go so far. They said that, if a negro came into England *and was baptised here* – thus becoming a

[1] Moyle *Imperatoris Justiniani Institutiones* (1923, 5th edn) 109.
[2] (1705) 2 Salk 666, Holt 495.

Christian – he became free. But if he was not baptised – and remained an infidel – he was still a slave. That was based on two cases in 1678 and 1696, *Butts v Penny*[1] and *Gelly v Cleve.*[2] In consequence, there were many cases where slaves (who had been brought to England by their masters) absconded, were baptised by sympathetic clergymen, and were employed by their 'godfathers.' Sometimes their former masters discovered their whereabouts, recaptured them, and took them back to the plantations. But sometimes they escaped altogether.

v *It does not make him free*

This law so upset the planters and merchants that in 1729 they asked the Attorney-General and Solicitor-General for their opinion on it. These were two of the greatest lawyers of their time or of any time: Sir Philip York, afterwards Lord Hardwicke, Lord Chancellor; and Sir Charles Talbot, afterwards Lord Talbot, also afterwards Lord Chancellor. I give their opinion in full from the book of Mr Granville Sharp:[3]

In order to certify a mistake, that slaves become free by their being in England, or being baptized, it hath been thought proper to consult the King's Attorney and Solicitor General in England thereupon; who have given the following opinion, subscribed with their own hands:

OPINION

We are of opinion, that a Slave by coming from the West Indies to Great Britain, or Ireland, either with or without his master, doth not become free; and that his master's property or right in him, is not thereby determined or varied; and that baptism doth not bestow freedom on him, nor make any alteration in his temporal condition in these kingdoms: we are also of opinion, that the master may legally compel him to return again to the plantations.

P. YORK

Jan 14, 1729 C. TALBOT

[1] (1678) 2 Lev 201.
[2] Referred to in *Chamberlin v Harvey* (1696) 1 Ld Raym 147.
[3] He was a leading abolitionist. The book was published in 1769, called *A Representation of the Injustice and Dangerous Tendency of Tolerating Slavery.*

2 The case of Jonathan Strong

i *The great liberator*

That opinion was treated as good law for the next 40 years. It was invoked by the planters in the case of an African slave, Jonathan Strong. But it was challenged by the great liberator, Granville Sharp.[1] In 1765, his master brought this slave, Jonathan Strong, over from Barbados as his servant. He took lodgings in Wapping but there treated the slave 'in a barbarous manner . . . by beating him over the head with a pistol.' His head swelled, his eyes were afflicted, and he was very ill. In this condition he was useless to his master who let him go whither he pleased. Mr Granville Sharp had pity on him. He got him baptised, with two godfathers. He took him to an apothecary who restored him to health. His old master then happened to see him robust and well. He determined to get him back. He got men to seize him (without any warrant) and to take him to the Poultry-counter (at the end of Cheapside where poultry and slaves were bought and sold). He was there sold for £30 to Mr John Kerr. The purchaser arranged for him to be taken on the ship *Thames* and carried to Jamaica.

ii *He is rescued*

His godfathers went to Mr Granville Sharp. He applied to the Lord Mayor for Strong to be released. The lawyers for the purchaser cited the opinion of York and Talbot. The Lord Mayor did not decide the legal issue. He discharged Strong simply because he had been taken up without a warrant. Thereupon the ship's captain seized Strong and said aloud: 'Then I now seize him as my slave.' But Mr Sharp was equal to this. He put his hand on the shoulder of the ship's captain and said:

I charge you, in the name of the King, with an assault upon the person of Jonathan Strong, and all these are my witnesses.

---

[1] The story is told by Clarkson in his book, *The History of Slavery*, pp 66–67.

The ship's captain was so taken aback that he let Strong go: and Mr Granville Sharp took him away.

So this slave was rescued by Mr Granville Sharp: but many others were less fortunate. They were recaptured, sold in London, and carried back to the West Indies.

3 The case of James Somerset

i *Seized by force*

Such cases disclosed a great issue between the planters and merchants on the one side and the abolitionists on the other side. They decided to bring a test case to settle the law. It was the case of James Somerset.[1]

James Somerset was a negro slave in Africa. He was carried in a slave ship from Africa to Virginia to be there sold. He was put up for sale. Charles Stewart bought him. He owned a plantation in Virginia. On 1 October 1769 Stewart, his master, embarked on a voyage to England, taking Somerset with him. He was to attend him during the voyage and during his stay in England, and to return with him afterwards to Virginia. They arrived in London on 1 November 1769. Somerset served Stewart in London for nearly two years until 1 October 1771. Then he absconded. Stewart employed men to recapture him. They seized him by force and carried him down to the river Thames. They put him on a vessel called the *Ann and Mary*. It was about to sail for Jamaica. Stewart told Captain Knowles, the master of the vessel, that he was to be securely kept on board and carried to Jamaica and there sold. Knowles accepted the instructions. He took charge of Somerset. He kept him in irons on the vessel to prevent him escaping.

ii *A writ of habeas corpus*

At that point Mr Granville Sharp made an application for a writ of habeas corpus. Lord Mansfield ordered a writ to issue

---

[1] *Somerset v Stewart* (1772) Lofft 1 (sometimes spelt *Sommersett* as in 20 State Tr 1).

directed to Captain Knowles, requiring him to bring the body of Somerset before his Lordship with the reason for detaining him. On 9 December 1771 Captain Knowles produced the body of Somerset before Lord Mansfield and gave the above history as the reason.

The case was argued with great learning by the counsel on both sides. Lord Mansfield in his judgment was troubled by the impact on commerce – if the slave was set free. He said that there were 14,000 or 15,000 slaves in England, selling at £50 each. If they were all set free, it would mean a loss of £750,000 to the owners. He pointed out that

contract for sale of a slave is good here: the sale is a matter which the law properly recognises and will maintain the price according to the agreement.

iii *The air of England*

Yet he came to the final conclusion:

The state of slavery is so odious that nothing can be suffered to support it, but positive law. Whatever inconvenience, therefore, may follow from the decision, I cannot say that the case is allowed or affirmed by the law of England: and therefore the black must be discharged.

That is the formal report, but Lord Campbell tells how Lord Mansfield put it more eloquently:

Every person coming into England is entitled to the protection of our laws, whatever oppression he may heretofore have suffered and whatever the colour of his skin. The air of England is too pure for any slave to breathe. Let the black go free.

The phrase, 'the air of England is too pure for any slave to breathe,' was not original. It was taken from the argument of Francis Hargrave.

As a result of Somerset's case, 14,000 or 15,000 slaves in England were freed. Some stayed with their masters as ordinary servants, receiving pay for their services. Some took work with other masters. Others were in the workhouses.

4 Slavery still lawful abroad

i *A call for freedom*

But that was only in England. Everywhere else slavery was lawful: and the slave trade was lawful. William Cowper in 1788 was shocked by it. He wrote:[1]

> ... dear as freedom is and in my heart's
> Just estimation prized above all price,
> I had much rather be myself the slave,
> And wear the bonds, than fasten them on him.
> We have no slaves at home. Then why abroad?
> Slaves cannot breathe in England; if their lungs
> Receive our air, that moment they are free;
> They touch our country, and their shackles fall.
> That's noble, and bespeaks a nation proud
> And jealous of the blessing. Spread it then,
> And let it circulate through every vein
> Of all your empire; that where Britain's power
> Is felt mankind may feel her mercy too.

It was a long haul before slavery elsewhere was abolished. Several leading cases came before our courts about it.

ii *150 slaves thrown overboard*

In 1782, ten years after *Somerset's case*, a slave vessel was carrying 300 negroes from Guinea in the West Indies to Jamaica. The voyage was delayed and they were in want of water. Sixty of the slaves died of thirst. Forty out of frenzy threw themselves overboard and were drowned. The master and crew threw 150 into the sea – to drown or be eaten by sharks – so as to save themselves and the other 50. The owner of the negroes claimed on his insurance policy for the value of the 150 thrown overboard, alleging that they were lost by 'perils of the sea.' The owner recovered against the underwriters at first instance, but the verdict was set aside on appeal and a new trial ordered, see *Gregson v Gilbert*.[2]

---

[1] *The Task*, Bk ii, *The Timepiece*.
[2] (1783) 3 Doug KB 232.

iii *William Wilberforce*

Then William Wilberforce appeared on the scene. He was
one of the most gifted men of his time. Eloquent, sincere and
handsome, he was instrumental in getting a series of Acts
from 1806 to 1811 prohibiting the slave trade in Britain or
on British ships. But our legislation could not affect foreign
ships.

Many here regarded the slave trade as contrary to the law
of nations: and the slave traders as pirates to be captured.

5 Britannia undone

i *English sailors board a slaver*

This came before our courts in *Le Louis:*[1] In 1816, a French
slave vessel, *Le Louis*, sailed from Martinique in the West
Indies on a voyage to the coast of Africa. She had arranged to
pick up slaves at Mesurada. Before she got there, she was
sighted by an English cutter, *The Queen Charlotte*. She
sought to escape but the English vessel overtook her and
boarded her. In the engagement, 12 lives were lost on the
British side and three on the French side. Several on both
sides were wounded. The English vessel took the French
vessel into Sierra Leone, a British colony. The Court of
Admiralty there held that she was engaged in the slave trade
contrary to the general law of nations and condemned her.
The French vessel appealed to the Court of Admiralty here.

ii *A judge rules against them*

A great judge, Sir William Scott (afterwards Lord Stowell),
of whom I have already told you, held that the English cutter
was in the wrong. The French vessel was on the high seas in
time of peace. She was doing what was lawful by the law of
France. The English vessel had no right to stop her or search
her, even in pursuit of a good end. Sir William Scott said:

[1] (1817) 2 Dods 210.

... It was not piracy either by the law of nations, or the law of Great Britain. It was not by the law of nations, because to make it so, it must either have been so considered and treated in practice by all the civilised states in Europe, or made so by virtue of a general convention; whereas, on the contrary, it had been carried on by all nations, even by Great Britain herself, until within a few years, and was at this moment carried on by Spain and Portugal, and not even at the present hour prohibited altogether by France ... All nations had a right to seize pirates, because they were general robbers, *hostes humani generis*; their violence was not confined to one nation, but was universal; and the general law of self-preservation gave a right to all to seize persons so conducting themselves. But in the slave trade it was quite different.

He then went on to say that a good end does not justify a bad means:

... To procure an eminent good by means that are unlawful is as little consonant to private morality as to public justice ... A nation is not justified in assuming rights that do not belong to her merely because she means to apply them to a laudable purpose; nor in setting out upon a moral crusade of converting other nations by acts of unlawful force. ...

iii *Was the judge right?*

I think that Sir William Scott missed a great opportunity to develop the law of nations. Slavery was so repugnant to human rights that he could and should have declared that it was contrary to international law. He should have held the English sailors to be justified.

6 The Emancipation Act 1834

In 1834 the efforts of William Wilberforce, Granville Sharp and others secured the emancipation of the slaves in all the British Colonies. In this year 1984 – 150 years later – we attended a Service of Commemoration and Thanksgiving at St Margaret's, Westminster, where the resounding words of the statute were recited:

... from and after the said First Day of August One thousand eight hundred and thirty-four Slavery shall be and is hereby utterly and for ever abolished and declared unlawful throughout the British Colonies, Plantations, and Possessions Abroad.

7 Rule Britannia

i *The Navy to the rescue*

Other countries lagged far behind us. Even after 1834 France, Spain, Portugal and the United States all maintained the slave trade. Our Navy did a great deal to suppress it. This was shown in 1840 by the great case of *Buron v Denman*.[1] Commander Denman RN was a son of the Lord Chief Justice, Lord Denman. He had the command of three of Her Majesty's ships off the coast of West Africa. His instructions were to suppress the slave trade. Now at that time Sierra Leone was a British colony where the slaves had all been emancipated. But two of them – a negro woman named Fry Norman and her boy, British subjects belonging to Sierra Leone – had been abducted and taken to a place along the coast called the Gallinas, under the sovereignty of native chiefs. But some Spaniards had gone there and erected factories in which they housed slaves ready to transport to North America. They had gunpowder, spirits and goods of all descriptions for use in their slave traffic.

ii *They free the slaves*

On 11 November 1840 Commander Denman entered the Gallinas river with the British vessels, *Wanderer*, *Rolla* and *Saracen*, and an armed force of about 120 men. They had a justifiable reason for their invasion. They were going to release the British subjects, the woman Fry Norman and her son. The Spanish slave dealers saw them coming. In great haste they got into canoes and carried off with them as many slaves as they could. They deserted the factories. They let loose the slaves and drove them up into the country. The British landed. They made arrangements with the native chiefs under which they set fire to the slave factories in the villages. They threw the gunpowder into the river: and the casks of spirits as well, because they had been poisoned. They were there a fortnight. The British liberated all the slaves.

[1] (1848) 2 Exch 167.

Then they re-embarked and went to Sierra Leone, taking with them 841 slaves who were there emancipated.

iii *Lord Palmerston approves*

All this was reported to London where Lord Palmerston approved it in this letter on 6 April 1841:

> ... Lord Palmerston is of opinion that the conduct of Commander Denman, in his proceedings against the slave factories at the Gallinas, ought to be approved. And I am to add, that Lord Palmerston would recommend that similar operations should be executed against all the piratical slave trade establishments which may be met with on parts of the coast not belonging to any civilised power. ...

8 The Spaniard makes a claim

i *He has a* prima facie *case*

Then one of the slave dealers, named Senor Buron, sued Commander Denman in the courts of England. He alleged that he had lost 4,000 slaves of the value of £100,000 (£25 each) and goods and chattels, and claimed damages for trespass.

The court followed the decision of Sir William Scott in *Le Louis*. It held that in the Gallinas it was lawful for Senor Buron to possess slaves and that he had a *prima facie* case. The only defence available to Commander Denman was that it was an 'act of state' which was not actionable in the English courts. But there was this difficulty: Commander Denman had not been given any authority to invade the Gallinas. His instruction 'to suppress the slave traffic' only extended to his 'stopping ships at sea' – that was under a treaty with the Spanish Crown. But that did not extend to his invading the Gallinas.

ii *But he is defeated by 'act of state'*

So Commander Denman had to rely on the letter of Lord Palmerston – written long after the invasion. By it, the

British Crown had ratified the conduct of Commander
Denman so that it was just as good as if he had been given
previous instructions. The court accepted this argument.
Parke B said (page 190):

> If this act, by adoption, becomes the act of the Crown, the seizure of the
> slaves and goods by the defendant is a seizure by the Crown, and an act of
> state for which the defendant is irresponsible, and, therefore, entitled to a
> verdict on the plea of Not Guilty.

Outside England there remained much to be done. In the
United States the movement towards emancipation was
given great impetus in 1852 by the famous novel by Mrs
Harriet Beecher Stowe, *Uncle Tom's Cabin*, based on real life.
It hastened the Civil War between the North and South in
the United States. In 1865, slavery was abolished there.
France abolished it in 1868 and Portugal in 1875.

9 Legal points

i *The law of nations*

There was at one time a school of thought which held that
the rules of international law – sometimes called the law of
nations – did not change. But this was held recently to be
erroneous. In *Trendtex Trading Corporation v Central Bank of
Nigeria*, I said:[1]

> International law does change: and the courts have applied the changes
> without the aid of any Act of Parliament. Thus, when the rules of
> international law were changed (by the force of public opinion) so as to
> condemn slavery, the English courts were justified in applying the
> modern rules of international law: see the 'Statement of Opinion' by Sir
> R Phillimore, Mr M Bernard and Sir H S Maine appended to the *Report
> of the Royal Commission on Fugitive Slaves* (1876), p. XXV, paras. 4 and 5.
> Again, the extent of territorial waters varies from time to time according
> to the rule of international law current at the time, and the courts will
> apply it accordingly: see *R v Kent Justices, ex parte Lye* [1967] 2 QB 153,
> 173, 189. The bounds of sovereign immunity have changed greatly in the
> last 30 years. The changes have been recognised in many countries, and
> the courts – of our country and of theirs – have given effect to them

[1] [1977] QB 529, 554.

without any legislation for the purpose, notably in the decision of the Privy Council in *The Philippine Admiral* [1977] AC 373.

. . . International law knows no rule of stare decisis. If this court today is satisfied that the rule of international law on a subject has changed from what it was 50 or 60 years ago, it can give effect to that change – and apply the change in our English law – without waiting for the House of Lords to do it.

I think we may now say that, whereas in the time of Sir William Scott, international law did permit of slavery and the slave trade, now it does not permit it. It is contrary to international law which is expressed in the Universal Declaration of Human Rights. If we should find it being practised anywhere, we should be entitled to seize any ship or to invade any country so as to put it down.

ii *Act of state*

Senor Buron was a Spaniard. Suppose he had been Mr Smith, a British subject. Could he have sued Commander Denman? It has often been said that the doctrine of act of state does not apply to a British subject. I cannot think this is right. I cannot think that, if Mr Smith had been a slave dealer in the Gallinas, he would have succeeded against Commander Denman. Lord Pearson gave these illustrations in *Nissan v Attorney-General*:[1]

. . . What is the position if, in a foreign country, a British army or truce force seizes in one operation a row of 10 houses of which one belongs to a British subject and the other nine to foreigners? What is the position if, in a foreign country, a British army or truce force seizes a building and goods both belonging to a partnership, of which some partners are British subjects and others are foreigners?

I should have thought that, if the foreigners could not sue, the British subjects could not sue. But in *Nissan v Attorney-General* Lord Reid said (page 213):

. . . I am of opinion that a British subject – at least if he is also a citizen of the United Kingdom and Colonies – can never be deprived of his legal right to redress by any assertion by the Crown or decision of the court that the acts of which he complains were acts of state.

[1] [1970] AC 179, 240.

226

If this be correct, then Mr Smith could have successfully sued. But I venture to think Lord Reid was wrong.

The truth is that no judge – and no professor of law – has ever been able to define what is, or is not, an act of state. I venture to think that, whenever the Crown or its officers or government department does some act in a foreign country, which is wrongful or unlawful by the law of that country, in each case that arises the court will decide, as matter of public policy, whether the plaintiff should recover damages or not. In *Buron v Denman* it was clearly contrary to public policy that Senor Buron should recover damages. It would be the same with Mr Smith. That is because the slave trade is so obnoxious. But in the case put by Lord Pearson, the innocent householders ought to recover compensation, no matter whether British subjects or not.

To make things clear I ought to add that if the Crown or a government department does an unlawful act *in this country* – either against a British subject or an alien – it is no defence to say that it is an act of state, see *Nissan v Attorney-General* (page 207 by Lord Reid).

2 Security of the state

1 The problem

i *If our freedom is attacked*

I trust that I have been as vigilant as anyone to preserve the freedom of the individual. But I have to confess that it has on occasion had to take second place. If our society is attacked by one or more who would destroy us and our freedoms, then we must have the means to defend ourselves. We must stop them at every point of their attack – before they launch their offensive if we can – and after it is launched. If the danger is grave and imminent, we may have to detain them without trial; we may have to act on secret intelligence; and we may have to modify the rules of natural justice. All this may be necessary to protect ourselves lest we ourselves be destroyed.

ii *The state must defend us*

The problem was squarely faced by Lord Gardiner and his colleagues in their Report in 1975 on terrorism in Northern Ireland (Cmnd 5847):

... Some of those who have given evidence to us have argued that such features of the present emergency provisions as the use of the Army in aid of the civil power, detention without trial, arrest on suspicion and trial without jury are so inherently objectionable that they must be abolished on the grounds that they constitute a basic violation of human rights. We are unable to accept this argument. While the liberty of the subject is a human right to be preserved under all possible conditions, it is not, and cannot be, an absolute right, because one man may use his liberty to take away the liberty of another and must be restrained from doing so. Where freedoms conflict, the state has a duty to protect those in need of protection.

In these pages I will illustrate the principles.

2 Regulation 18B

i *Young King's Counsel*

The first cases which illustrate this conflict are those in the Second World War under Regulation 18B. It provided that

If the Secretary of State has reasonable cause to believe any person to be of hostile origin or associations . . . and that by reason thereof it is necessary to exercise control over him, he may make an order against that person directing that he be detained.

Under that Regulation, during the war, nearly 2,000 persons were interned in the Isle of Man and elsewhere. They were not *proved* to be enemies or to have done anything actively hostile. They were detained simply on suspicion that they might do something harmful to our war effort. They were not charged with any offence. They were not tried by any court. But they were interviewed by legal advisers. These were young King's Counsel who were assigned as legal advisers to each region. Norman Birkett in London, Hartley Shawcross in the South-East, I myself in the North-East, and so on. We had information from intelligence sources. This was often highly confidential. It could not be disclosed to the suspect, lest he or his associates use it to identify those sources and destroy them. We did, however, give the individual as much information as we could – so that he could dispel any suspicion that rested on him. In short, we acted as fairly as we possibly could. Then we made our recommendation to the Secretary of State or his deputy, the Regional Commissioner.

ii 'The Nazi parson'

I remember one case well, and I mentioned it in *The Family*

Story. A clergyman had a living in a remote vicarage in Yorkshire. I had received statements from the police and intelligence sources about him, but he did not see these or have any opportunity of cross-examining. These statements showed that he had gone on holidays to Germany and had frequent conclaves with the Nazi party. He had been there just before the outbreak of the war. He was known locally as 'the Nazi parson.' On interviewing him, I formed the view that he was of hostile associations and would help the enemy if he could. I thought that, if he remained at large in his lonely vicarage, there was a danger that he might afford help to any German parachutists who dropped down there. He might direct them to vital bridges and installations which they could sabotage. On my recommendation he was detained under Regulation 18B. The Bishop of Ripon sent a telegram of protest to the Regional Commissioner, Lord Harlech, but the order was maintained.

iii *We were in peril*

Those of you who have not known war may be surprised at the decision. But you must realise the great peril in which we were. The enemy had overrun Holland, Belgium and France. Many of our soldiers had escaped from Dunkirk – by a miracle – without their arms. The enemy were the other side of the Channel, ready to pounce. We were fighting alone for our very lives. We could take no risk of traitors in our midst.

3 *Liversidge v Anderson*

i *The request for particulars*

Many of those detained were followers of Sir Oswald Mosley and his British Union of Fascists. Some challenged the validity of their detention in the courts. They failed in such cases as Trevor Lees ([1941] 1 KB 72); Benjamin Greene ([1942] 1 KB 87); and Henry Budd ([1942] 58 TLR 212).

This brings me to the great case of *Liversidge v Anderson*.[1]
It was not really a great case at all. It was decided on a point
of pleading. Liversidge had been detained in Brixton prison
under Regulation 18B. We do not know the information
which led to his detention. It must have been sufficient to
satisfy the legal adviser that he should be detained. He then
brought an action in the courts for false imprisonment. This
put on the Home Secretary the burden of justifying the
detention. In his defence, the Home Secretary pleaded that
Liversidge was detained under Regulation 18B. He (the
Home Secretary) pleaded that he had 'reasonable cause to
believe' that Liversidge was of hostile associations and that it
was necessary to control him. Thereupon, Liversidge asked
for 'particulars' of the grounds on which the Home
Secretary had 'reasonable cause to believe.' All the judges in
all the courts (save Lord Atkin) held that Liversidge was *not*
entitled to the particulars. I thought then, and still think, that
all the judges (save Lord Atkin) were right. If the Home
Secretary had been ordered to give those particulars, he
would have had to disclose all the most confidential reports
from his intelligence sources, or state the gist of them. Such
disclosure would be most detrimental to those sources and
might put them in peril of their lives. So it was absolutely
right for the judges to refuse those particulars.

ii *Lord Atkin's dissent*

Lord Atkin, however, dissented. He did it, not on any
ground of principle, but on a most technical interpretation
of the statute. He read the regulation as if it was to be
construed *objectively*: 'If *there is* reasonable cause to believe;'
whereas all the other judges read it *subjectively*: 'If he (the
Home Secretary) has reasonable cause to believe.' Read
subjectively there was no ground for giving particulars. No
particulars were ever ordered of a state of mind.

iii *His wild rhetoric*

If Lord Atkin had stopped there – at his wrong inter-

[1] [1942] AC 206.

pretation of the statute – no one would have worried. His dissent would have passed unnoticed. But he went on to indulge in what Professor Heuston calls 'the passionate, almost wild, rhetoric of the three concluding paragraphs.'[1] It is so good an example of our English prose that, although I have quoted part of it before, I must remind you of it:[2]

> I view with apprehension the attitude of judges who on a mere question of construction when face to face with claims involving the liberty of the subject show themselves more executive minded than the executive . . . In this country, amid the clash of arms, the laws are not silent. They may be changed, but they speak the same language in war as in peace. It has always been one of the pillars of freedom, one of the principles of liberty for which on recent authority we are now fighting, that the judges are no respecters of persons and stand between the subject and any attempted encroachments on his liberty by the executive, alert to see that any coercive action is justified in law. In this case I have listened to arguments which might have been addressed acceptably to the Court of King's Bench in the time of Charles I.
>
> I protest, even if I do it alone, against a strained construction put on words with the effect of giving an uncontrolled power of imprisonment to the minister. . . .

iv *It gives much offence*

That outburst gave much offence to the judges sitting with him. Lord Maugham, who presided, wrote an indignant letter to *The Times*. Lord Atkin was reproved privately by Lord Simon, the Lord Chancellor, and by Lord Caldecote, the Lord Chief Justice. The letters are given in full in Professor Heuston's article.

Yet those offending passages have been applauded by lawyers and laymen ever since. This is because of the emphasis they put on the independence of the judges. The sentiments find an echo in the hearts of every Englishman. But this should not blind us to the fact that Lord Atkin's dissent was wrong. He was construing the words of Regulation 18B in their objective sense: whereas they should have been construed – and were construed by all the

---

[1] 'Liversidge v Anderson in Retrospect' (1970) 86 LQR 33, 36.
[2] *Liversidge v Anderson* [1942] AC 206, 244.

others – against the background of the danger we were in and the necessity of combating the enemies in our midst.

v *Look at* Hansard

I would also ride my favourite hobby-horse. If reference had been made to *Hansard*, it becomes clear that Parliament intended the Regulation to operate in just the way that all the judges (save Lord Atkin) held that it did operate. Professor Heuston has done much valuable research on it. In his article he says:[1]

... The clause was attempting to make it plain beyond argument that Parliament was validly delegating to the King in Council power to issue Regulations authorising internment without trial. The point was taken by T E Harvey, Independent Member for the Combined English Universities, who moved to leave out the words 'Secretary of State,' and to insert instead the words 'satisfaction of a judge of the High Court.' Thereupon the Home Secretary, Sir Samuel Hoare, stated that he could not accept the amendment, because the act in question was an executive and not a judicial one. But on the Home Secretary giving an undertaking to establish an Advisory Committee and other safeguards for the liberty of the subject, Harvey withdrew his amendment, and the clause received the Royal Assent in the form set out above ... the conclusion must be that in 1939 Parliament intended to give a power of internment to the Home Secretary the exercise of which could not be questioned in the courts.

Let us leave it there.

4 Dangers in peacetime

i *Hosenball deported*

That was in time of war. Now I turn to time of peace. In 1977 there was the case of Mark Hosenball.[2] He was a young journalist of 25 who had come, at the age of 18, from the United States of America, and had been here for seven years. Then suddenly the Home Secretary ordered him to be deported and excluded from England because his presence

[1] (1970) 86 LQR 33, 62–63.
[2] *R v Home Secretary, ex parte Hosenball* [1977] 1 WLR 766.

was not conducive to the public good. He was given a hearing before an advisory committee, but he was not told the nature of the information against him. So it was not in accordance with natural justice. Yet the necessity of national security prevailed and he was deported. I have told all about it in *The Due Process of Law* (pages 85–88).

ii *Terrorism in Northern Ireland*

The conflict – between freedom and security – has been acute in Northern Ireland for the last nine years. A body of men, calling themselves the Irish Republican Army, have declared war against the United Kingdom. They lie in wait for the security forces and seek to destroy them. They come over to England and plant bombs, killing and injuring hundreds of innocent people. At one time there was legislation giving power of detention – internment – of suspects without trial. Now that has been discarded. But there is the power of exclusion. Under the Prevention of Terrorism (Temporary Provisions) Act 1976 (re-enacted in 1984), residents in Northern Ireland can be excluded from entry into England. And residents in England can be excluded from going to Northern Ireland. This is a serious deprivation of the liberty of the subject – restricting his freedom of movement within the United Kingdom. These exclusion orders are made by the Secretary of State without any trial, but with an inquiry by advisers. There has been much discussion as to whether they should be continued or not. Inquiries have been held by men of high standing in the state – Lord Shackleton and Earl Jellicoe.

iii *Freedom takes second place*

It has been held, right up to the present day, that the freedom of the individual must take second place to the security of the state. This is what Lord Jellicoe said in para 191:[1]

Exclusion is a matter of public policy. It is based not merely on the conduct of the excluded person, but also – once his terrorist in-

[1] Cmnd 8803.

volvement is established – on matters such as the security situation at the time exclusion is considered and the danger the person poses to the public at large. Neither the courts nor any form of tribunal could properly be expected to carry out an examination of all these issues and to reach a binding decision. It is noteworthy that Lord Gardiner's committee which in the mid-1970s examined, amongst other things, the procedures governing internment in Northern Ireland recommended that the final decision should rest not with any body or tribunal, but solely with the Secretary of State.[1] The Secretary of State is and should remain accountable to Parliament for the way he discharges this onerous responsibility. It is the duty of Parliament to ensure that this accountability has real meaning. I should add that, although in practice the Advisers' recommendations have almost invariably been accepted, the Advisers themselves have indicated to me that they would not favour a system where their decisions were binding.

iv *Some would have been killed*

And in the subsequent debate in the House of Lords, Lord Harris of Greenwich (who was a Minister of State at the Home Office for five years) said there was no doubt that

as a result of the exclusion power being on the statute book a number of people are alive today who otherwise would have been dead. As a Home Office Minister for five years, I have absolutely no doubt that that is correct.[2]

He added:

If the people concerned were IRA terrorists we should of course have preferred to bring them to trial and get them convicted in an English court. But the evidence which we had in many of these cases left me in no doubt that although the person concerned was an IRA terrorist, it would not have enabled us to secure his conviction in an English court. That is why the Bill was introduced in the first place. The fact is that if it had been known to some of the people who have been subject to such orders what the character of the evidence was and the identity of some of the people who had brought these matters to the attention of the security authorities, then there is no doubt that those people would have been murdered.

v *The correct principle*

That shows conclusively that the principle is correct: when a

[1] Cmnd 5847, para 159.
[2] *Hansard* 23 February 1984, col 899.

person is suspected of being a terrorist, the Secretary of State can make an exclusion order against him without a trial. It can be made on the evidence of intelligence officers of whom the suspect knows nothing and whom he has no opportunity of cross-examining. It can be made without even telling him the nature of the information against him. All this is very contrary to the fundamental principle of natural justice. But natural justice must take second place in extreme cases to the national security. By which I mean, it must take second place to the duty of the state to protect the lives of ordinary people.

vi *Trade unions are banned*

There has just been a striking instance of this. I told you earlier (page 124) of the security headquarters (GCHQ) at Cheltenham. The staff had for many years been members of the Civil Service Unions. But those unions on several occasions took disruptive action which upset the most sensitive areas of our intelligence network. It was so serious that the ministers of the Crown decided that the unions should be banned from Cheltenham. The ban was put into effect by the Prime Minister who is responsible for national security. She did it under a Royal Prerogative to control the Civil Service. She banned any of the staff from joining trade unions. Her action was contrary to the European Convention which says that 'Everyone has the right to form and join trade unions.' It was also contrary to natural justice because she did not consult the trade unions or hear their case. But on 6 August 1984 her action was held by the Court of Appeal to be lawful. It was because national security had to come first. Lord Lane, the Lord Chief Justice, said:

The actions taken by the Government with regard to trade union membership at GCHQ were clearly actions taken on the ground of national security . . . The ministers were sole judges of what the national security required . . . Their actions could truly be said to have been taken in the interests of national security to protect this country from its enemies or potential enemies.

vii *Religious cults*

At the outset of this chapter, I quoted Lord Gardiner:

Where freedoms conflict, the state has a duty to protect those in need of protection.

This is well illustrated by the freedom of religion on the one hand and the respect for family life on the other hand. There are many 'religious cults' which use the freedom of religion so as to destroy the family life of young people and their respect for their homes. They use a technology of brainwashing with strange words and ideas so as to get young people to attach themselves to the cult and detach themselves from their families. I have received many tragic letters from parents greatly distressed by their children being torn away.

On 11 July 1984 in the House of Lords I asked this question of the Minister of State:

My Lords, is the noble Lord the Minister aware that the pernicious activities of these cults have been exposed in the courts of law from time to time and have been proved to the satisfaction of juries, especially in the Moonies case? Is he also aware that the promoters of these cults have amassed huge fortunes? They are often outside this country and cannot be got at, and such funds as are here have been registered as charities and therefore not followed. So these cults are making enormous profits and causing enormous damage. Is it not time that there was a comprehensive inquiry into all their activities?

The Minister did not accede to my request.

On 23 July Mr Justice Latey criticised the Church of Scientology in these words:

It is dangerous because it is out to capture people, especially children and impressionable young people, and indoctrinate and brainwash them so that they become the unquestioning captives and tools of the cult, withdrawn from ordinary thought, living, and relationships with others.

When a judge speaks thus – Is it not time for the Minister to do something to protect those in need of protection?

3 Misprision

1 Informers

i *Identity kept secret*

One of the most useful means of combating terrorism is to get information from informers. It has long been held that his identity can be kept secret. In 1820 the reason was expressly stated to be

> the ground of danger to the public good, which would result from disclosing the sources of such informations – for no person would become an informer, if his name might be disclosed in a court of justice, and if he might be subjected to the resentment of the party against whom he had informed.[1]

But then I come to a point of much importance. Suppose that a man gets to know that terrorists are going to plant a bomb in a public house in Birmingham or outside Harrods in London. Is he under any duty to inform the police? so that they may intervene to stop the explosion and thus save lives. A like question arises where robbers are planning a raid on a bank. If a man gets to know of it, ought he not to tell the police? No doubt there is a moral duty. But is there a legal duty?

You may say that the man has a right to keep silent. But I do not think so. It is another case where the security of the state takes priority over the freedom of the individual.

ii *An old French word*

It came up for consideration in the case of *Sykes v DPP*.[2]

---

[1] *Home v Bentinck* (1820) 2 Brod & Bing 130, 162.
[2] [1962] AC 528.

Sykes was convicted of an old offence called 'misprision of felony.' The word 'misprision' is derived from an old French word 'mésprendre' which means to act wrongly, and in early times it meant simply a wrong action or omission. If a man knew that a felony had been committed, or was about to be committed, it was his duty to report it to the proper authority. If he did not do so, he was guilty of misprision of felony.

2 A weapon armoury

i *Guns for sale*

In 1960 thieves got into the weapon armoury at a United States Air Force station in Norfolk. They stole 100 pistols, 4 submachine-guns and about 1,960 rounds of ammunition. They hired a taxi and took the stolen goods to Manchester. They took them into the house of a man named Kenny. Kenny wanted to sell them. So he got hold of a man he knew called Sykes and asked him if he could find a purchaser for them. Sykes thought that there might be a ready buyer in Ireland. So Sykes went up to an Irishman who was a waiter in a Manchester club. He asked him: 'Have you any contacts with the IRA?' The waiter said: 'Maybe I have. What do you want?' Sykes said: 'I know of some guns for sale,' and told him where they were.

ii *Sentenced to five years*

Now that Irish waiter was a good citizen. He told the police and they recovered the weapons from Kenny's house. Kenny was charged with receiving them knowing them to have been stolen. He was convicted and sentenced to seven years. Sykes was charged originally with being an accessory *after* the fact, but the prosecution dropped that charge because there was no evidence that he had taken any active steps to conceal the theft. He was only charged with misprision of felony. The jury convicted him and he was sentenced to five years.

There was an appeal to the House of Lords. I presided. Lord Goddard sat beside me. He had retired from being Lord Chief Justice. Mr Edward Clarke QC submitted that the offence of misprision was obsolete. We held that it was still in force. I did much research into the old books. You may be interested in some parts of it:[1]

3 Old law

i *Hue and cry*

My Lords, it has been an offence for the last 700 years or more, not always under the name 'misprision of felony,' but still an offence. Ever since the days of hue and cry, it has been the duty of a man, who knows that a felony has been committed, to report it to the proper authority so that steps can be taken to apprehend the felon and bring him to justice. In the thirteenth century it was his duty 'to raise hue and cry,' that is to say, he had to report it to the sheriff of the county or his officer or to the constable of the town; whereupon it was the duty of that officer to levy hue and cry, that is, to shout aloud calling on all able-bodied men over the age of 15 to pursue the offender and arrest him: and it was their duty to join in the pursuit. The duty on the officer to levy hue and cry and on the citizens to join in pursuit was reinforced by various statutes and particularly by the Statute of Westminster (1275) 3 Edw 1, st 1, c 9.

ii *Address to the Grand Jury*

In 1852 Parke B when he went on the Home Circuit addressed the Grand Jury at Lewes in these words as recorded in *The Times* of March 18, 1852: 'In the western division particularly a great many felonies were committed of which the parties who were the sufferers by them gave no information to the authorities or the police. He therefore felt himself called upon to say publicly, that it should be known that this proceeding, which was known to the law by the name of "Misprision of Felony" was a very serious offence, and subjected the persons who were convicted of it to imprisonment for a year. The law with regard to this matter had certainly fallen into desuetude, but it was very necessary that it should be known it still existed, and during the last 20 years he had himself been called upon to make use of it in the county of Durham, and he had sentenced two persons to a year's imprisonment for having wilfully withheld information relating to an act of felony that had been committed.'

[1] Ibid at 555, 560, 564.

iii *Not out of date*

My Lords, it was said that this offence is out of date. I do not think so. The arm of the law would be too short if it was powerless to reach those who are 'contact' men for thieves or assist them to gather in the fruits of their crime; or those who indulge in gang warfare and refuse to help in its suppression. There is no other offence of which such persons are guilty save that of misprision of felony.

I am not dismayed by the suggestion that the offence of misprision is impossibly wide: for I think it is subject to just limitations.

iv *Planned felonies*

My Lords, there was some discussion before us whether a man was bound to disclose a contemplated felony which comes to his knowledge, such as a planned raid on a bank. There is a striking passage in Lambard's Eirenarcha (1614), p 289, which says that failure to do so is misprision of felony. So does Dalton's Country Justice (1619), p 211, and Hawkins' Pleas of the Crown, 8th edn, vol 2, chap 29, s 23, p 444. These are weighty authorities and the commissioners who reported on the Criminal Law in 1843 were clearly in favour of it. They said: 'The necessity for making such disclosures extends, perhaps, with greater force, to the knowledge of a meditated crime, the perpetration of which may, by means of such a disclosure, be prevented, than it does to the knowledge of one already committed.' This is good sense and may well be good law.

4 Modern law

i *An indictable offence*

Lord Goddard (whose knowledge of the criminal law was unequalled) put it in these words:[1]

In my opinion, therefore, misprision of felony is today an indictable misdemeanour at common law, and a person is guilty of the crime if knowing that a felony has been committed he fails to disclose his knowledge to those responsible for the preservation of the peace, be they constables or justices, within a reasonable time and having a reasonable opportunity for so doing. What is a reasonable time and opportunity is a question of fact for a jury, and also whether the knowledge that he has is so definite that it ought to be disclosed. A man is neither bound nor would he be wise to disclose rumours or mere gossip, but if facts are

[1] Ibid at 569.

within his knowledge that would materially assist in the detection and arrest of a felon he must disclose them as it is a duty he owes to the State.

ii *Now abolished*

In 1965 the Criminal Law Revision Committee recommended (Cmnd 2659) that the distinction between felonies and misdemeanours should be abolished: and that, with its abolition, the law about misprision of felony should be reconsidered. I do not know whether it was much reconsidered. The offence of misprision of felony was never expressly abolished. But it was done impliedly in the Criminal Law Act 1967. By section 5(1) it was made an offence to accept a bribe for not disclosing information to the police: thus inferring that, if he did not accept a bribe, it was no longer an offence to conceal the information.

iii *Revived for terrorism*

The offence of misprision has, however, been revived for terrorism connected with Northern Ireland affairs. By section 11 of the Prevention of Terrorism Act 1984, if a person has information which he knows would be of material assistance in preventing an act of terrorism or apprehending an offender of it, then it is his duty to disclose it to a competent authority. If he fails without reasonable excuse to disclose it, he is guilty of an offence punishable with imprisonment up to two years.

In the debates in the Lords some disquiet was expressed about this offence. I urged that it should remain. After all, if he has a reasonable excuse for not telling the police, he is not guilty. At the report stage, there was a division upon it. The clause was retained by a majority of 129 to 92.

I should like the matter to be reconsidered for other offences too, such as robbery or bank raids. Nowadays these are often complex military operations, which require much planning beforehand. If any citizen gets to know of a planned raid, he ought to tell the police – so as to prevent it happening.

242

Part Eight

International Terrorism

Introduction

One of the most alarming features of modern times is the spread of international terrorism. Terrorists from one country go to another and commit violent crimes there. They kidnap individuals. They hijack aircraft. They threaten to kill hostages unless their demands are met. They ask for prisoners to be released or ransom paid. It is blackmail of the worst description.

At other times it is simply one political group attacking another – not in their own country but in another – seeking to exterminate them. It is violent murder of the worst description.

This has led to intense security precautions at the airports of the world and in the capital cities. Passengers are 'frisked.' Packages are scanned. Armed guards stand by.

This evil was vividly exposed when a policewoman was shot dead in London. Yet the murderers went scot-free. They claimed diplomatic immunity. It is such a landmark that I tell you of it.

1 The Libyan Embassy

The outrage

i *Colonel Gaddafi's exploits*

Colonel Gaddafi is head of the Government of Libya. He has many opponents both in his own country and outside it. From 1980 onwards he declared that he proposed to liquidate his opponents living abroad. In England his adherents were responsible for outrages. A well-known Libyan journalist was assassinated outside the mosque in Regent's Park. A Libyan lawyer was murdered in his London home. A student opponent of Colonel Gaddafi was stabbed to death in Manchester. In March 1984, 29 people were injured in bomb attacks. The perpetrators were never caught.

ii *So-called 'students'*

Many Libyan supporters of Colonel Gaddafi came to England on student visas. Some of them were pretty middle-aged students – gentlemen in their late 30s – yet they were admitted. They had been enrolled in some of our private educational establishments.

There were other Libyan students admitted also. These were opponents of Colonel Gaddafi. So there were representatives of each faction here in London.

iii *The Libyan People's Bureau*

Libya did not have a proper embassy here. But they had a building here in St James's Square which was called the Libyan People's Bureau. At first it was not recognised as a diplomatic mission, but afterwards many countries, including Great Britain, accorded it diplomatic status. And several of the staff were accredited as diplomats entitled to diplomatic privilege.

iv *A policewoman is killed*

At 10 am on 17 April 1984 there was a peaceable demonstration in St James's Square outside the Libyan People's Bureau. Some Libyan residents in this country were demonstrating so as to show their disapproval of the Gaddafi régime in Libya. The police had been forewarned. They were firmly in control. There was no problem of public order.

Suddenly, without any warning, a machine-gun opened fire. A hail of bullets came from a first-floor window of the Bureau. They struck down people in the Square. Twelve were wounded. A woman police-constable, Yvonne Fletcher, was shot through the stomach and died shortly afterwards.

v *The miscreants go free*

You might have thought that our police would have entered the building at once – in defence of our people – and have arrested the miscreants. But no. None of our police or security forces entered the building. No one was arrested or searched. The premises were kept under strict surveillance but that was all. After a week or two, on 26 April 1984, the people in the building were allowed to leave. All their belongings went also, weapons and all, in 'diplomatic bags' *alias* crates. They walked free under police protection from the building, into cars, on to Sunningdale where they were questioned by police, on to Heathrow and on to an aircraft for Libya. Not one of them will ever be brought to justice.

vi *All wondered why*

All the ordinary people in England were astonished. Why, why were these murderers allowed to go free? The reason given by the Government was that they were covered by diplomatic immunity. On the television screen extracts were shown from the Vienna Convention of 1961, saying that the premises were 'inviolable': and that the persons of the diplomats were 'inviolable:' and that diplomatic bags could not be 'opened or detained.'

2 The Vienna Convention

1 My speech in the Lords

i *It is welcomed*

The matter was debated in the House of Lords on 16 May 1984. I looked up the law and made a speech. It was welcomed by all the newspapers. The *Daily Telegraph* next day had a headline:

DENNING'S LAW ON EMBASSIES STUNS LORDS

Lord Denning shook the Government rigid last night with the news that it was 'entirely wrong' in law not to enter the Libyan Embassy.

The *Sunday Mirror* on 20 May had a big heading:

IS LORD DENNING RIGHT?

ii *My opening*

My speech is reported in *Hansard* but, as few people read it, I reproduce it here. I opened in these words:

My Lords, a few weeks ago a most wicked crime was committed in one of our public places – in St James's Square. It was in England that it was committed. A woman police constable was murdered but the criminal went free. He was not arrested. The premises from which the shot was fired were not searched. It is said that the miscreants had diplomatic privilege under the Vienna Convention. I do not believe it. Those who interpret the Vienna Convention in that way are entirely wrong.

2 My argument

i *What does 'inviolable' mean?*

The Vienna Convention was made, by the Diplomatic Privileges Act 1964, part of our English law. It is to be interpreted and can be interpreted again by our English lawyers just the same. It starts off with a word known in international law but very little known in our English law. It states that the premises of the embassy, or whatever it may be, are to be 'inviolable.' It adds that the person of the diplomatic agent is to be 'inviolable.' Does that mean without exception? Under the preamble to the convention it is said that it is only the expressed terms that apply, but still the old customary rules of international law go with it. Article 41 of this convention states:

'The premises of the mission must not be used in any manner incompatible with the functions of the mission as laid down in the present Convention or by other rules of general international law.'

The mission was being used in contravention of every elementary principle of international law.

ii *The exception of self-defence*

Let me take the first instance – the personal privilege of the ambassador or the diplomatic agent. Article 29 states:

'The person of a diplomatic agent shall be inviolable. He shall not be liable to any form of arrest or detention. The receiving State shall treat him with due respect and shall take all appropriate steps to prevent any attack on his person, freedom or dignity.'

Is there not a correlative to that? If we are to protect him from any attack, surely he is not allowed to attack us; to attack our personal freedom or dignity by firing weapons and guns from the embassy. Let me take illustrations from our international law and quote Hugo Grotius – almost a founder of it. He gave the illustration that if an ambassador attacked a man, that man in self-defence could kill that ambassador. Grotius himself said that. It is the principle of self-defence. So did Oppenheim in his later edition of *International Law*, or the more modern ones. There is the exception of self-defence in the case I have given.

iii *The exception of emergency*

There is the exception of emergency. The drunken diplomat with a loaded gun in a public square: is he not to be arrested? Is he not to be detained? Cannot our police deal with such a position? Clearly they could.

There is the principle of self-defence; the principle of emergency and, indeed, there is the principle which Dr F A Mann pointed out in a letter to *The Times*. Supposing an ambassador goes out with a machine gun and starts shooting down people in a public street? Is he entitled to privilege from arrest or detention? It cannot be. There are exceptions written by international law for this convention which were not put in but ought to have been put in.

iv *The embassy on fire*

I have dealt with the personal position of the ambassador or the diplomatic agent himself. But what about the premises, the mission where he resides? Are those premises inviolable? Article 22 states:

'The premises of the mission shall be inviolable.'

It goes on to say:

'The premises of the mission ... shall be immune from search, requisition, attachment or execution.'

That is what the convention expressly says; but impliedly international law writes in the exceptions. If an embassy is on fire and likely to spread to adjoining premises are not our firemen and police entitled to go into that residence or that mission to put out the fire and save the houses next door? If there is a gunman inside shooting and firing at our ordinary peaceful people outside, are we not allowed to go in? If you plead the principle of self-defence, or whatever exception one calls it, we are entitled to search the premises and arrest the miscreants and prevent these crimes from being committed.

v *Hoards of arms*

As my noble friend, Lord Kennet, said, when in 1973 Pakistan discovered that the Government of Iraq had hoards of arms in its embassy the Pakistan authorities were quite right and entitled to go in – despite what Iraq said. They did go in and found hoards of arms there. This so-called principle of inviolability is subject to many exceptions in international law which are written impliedly into the convention when the position is abused by those of the sending authority. I have dealt with that.

vi *Scan the diplomatic bag*

Neither does the diplomatic bag have all that much exemption. That is also covered by Article 27. It is true that it says:

'The diplomatic bag shall not be opened or detained.'

It goes on to say:

'The packages constituting the diplomatic bag must bear visible external marks of their character and may contain only diplomatic documents or articles intended for official use.

Supposing that provision is breached, and the diplomatic bag contains narcotics, bombs or whatever else it may be. It seems to me that that provision does not prevent proper steps being taken to discover it, whether by scanning or whatever else. Such action is perfectly lawful for our authorities. They need not actually open the bag these days. By scanning and other scientific means they can well see things. We have these things at the airports. They can well see whether there is any metallic substance or the like there.

3 The difficulty

i *Tit for tat*

I have gone through the terms of the convention, because, as I said, they are part of our English law, but what is to be done? I know the difficulty of the position. If we had taken steps here, what would have been done by those others in Libya to our own residents there? Would they play just tit for tat? I do not know whether they would or not. But on the other hand, I can see the difficulty, which is why the decision was not taken, as I suggest it could have been, to enter the premises, seize, search and arrest.

ii *An advisory opinion*

But if I am wrong about that, what is to be done? As my noble friend Lord Broxbourne says, it is not much good trying to review this convention and get all the states of the world to agree to a modification. Let us do all that we can. One thing that has occurred to me is that we could take the advisory opinion from the International Court of Justice. It could say whether the exceptions which I have indicated are existent in international law. It could say whether those exceptions which I have indicated are correct or not. If the International Court of Justice affirmed that, you would have guidance for all the countries for the future so as to know what could be done.

iii *Co-operate with others*

Otherwise, there are other means. As my noble friend Lord Kennet said, we can do everything we can by co-operation with others to stop this evil of our day – this international terrorism. All I would say is that, as I view this Vienna Convention, and as I view the Diplomatic Privileges Act, they did not give privilege to those criminals who were shooting from the embassy in St James's Square.

3 Another point of view

Further consideration

i *Consideration by the Government*

In the debate Baroness Young for the Government said:

> ... The noble and learned Lord, Lord Denning, raised a number of very interesting and important points. I would like to confirm that we are reluctant without the most careful and balanced consideration of the implications to advocate exceptions to the basic rules of inviolability or to enter into the dangerous game of claiming rights of retaliation in response to a breach of the convention. But this certainly does not mean that the fundamental right of self-defence, either in international law or in domestic law, is irrelevant in this context....

ii *An expert opinion*

After the debate Lord Greenhill of Harrow, who has had a most distinguished career in the Diplomatic Service, wrote me a letter setting out a most cogent argument. It is so pertinent that, with his permission, I venture to reproduce it.

> When I was serving in an iron curtain country some years ago I was astonished one morning to read in the newspapers of my involvement in a spy 'trial.' During 'the trial' the defendants said that I had instructed them to undertake certain spying missions. The whole thing was totally fictional. In due course I was expelled and the defendants were imprisoned without justification.
>
> Let us suppose that during this 'trial' the witnesses had stated (under instructions of course) that I was responsible for the murder of a citizen of that iron curtain country. Let us suppose that the court 'accepted' this

allegation and, with feigned indignation, had asked for me to be handed over for trial on a criminal charge.

Compare this imaginary scenario with the events in St James's Square. Her Majesty's Government (rightly) claimed that Libyans had shot the policewoman. The Libyan Government (falsely) denied it and claimed full immunity. In the imagined situation in my last paragraph the Government of that iron curtain country would have claimed (falsely) that I had murdered one of their citizens. HMG would have (rightly) denied it. But the case on the other side would have been presented as entirely reasonable and their objective that justice should be done. In that situation I do not imagine that you would have advocated that the British Minister out there should have waived the diplomatic immunity of his Mission, given access to the Legation and handed me over for trial.

Such a situation was not entirely fanciful then and is even less so now.

iii *What do you think?*

International law differs from municipal law in that it has no sanctions for breach of it. It has no police, no sheriffs, no magistrates, no punishments. The only reason why diplomatic immunity is well established is because it is in the interest of each country to adhere to it. If we were to arrest an ambassador of another country here, we would find that our ambassador might be arrested there. If we were to enter the mission premises here, there might be retaliation by entry into our embassy there. Each country is persuaded to adhere to the Vienna Convention by the fear of tit for tat. The only sanction that is available is expulsion. If a diplomat abuses his diplomatic privilege, he can be expelled. In return, the other country expels one of ours.

But even so, it is important that the rules about diplomatic privilege should be as clear as possible. If it be permissible by international law to open a diplomatic bag (or crate) to see if there are any bombs, narcotics or weapons there, why should we not do so? Need we fear any tit for tat? Even if the other country should open our diplomatic bags they would, I trust, not find any bombs, narcotics or weapons in them. They would only find confidential documents, containing secret information. Ah, there is the rub. The disclosure of this secret information may be just as dangerous as bombs, narcotics or weapons.

So there it is. What do you think? Would you hold diplomatic privilege to be 'inviolable' in all circumstances without exception? or would you admit exceptions? and if so, in what circumstances? It is so difficult that I would like to see it answered by the International Court of Justice.

iv *The rich Nigerian Mr Dikko*

The question has become more urgent by one of the strangest stories ever. On Thursday 5 July 1984, about midday, a rich Nigerian Mr Umaru Dikko was receiving guests at his expensive London house. He was surrounded and overpowered. Drugs were pumped into him. He was made unconscious and bundled off in a van. He was taken to a place where two large wooden crates were awaiting his arrival. His unconscious body was packed into one of these, together with a man who was fully conscious and had drugs and syringes. Two other men – fully conscious – were packed into the other crate. At about 4 pm these two large crates arrived at Stansted airport. They were to be loaded on a Nigerian Airways cargo aircraft. Our police had been told of Mr Dikko's disappearance and were on the look out. Some members of the Nigerian High Commission were already at Stansted. Our police opened the crates and found the contents. They took the unconscious Mr Dikko to hospital. They arrested the others.

The truth then came out. The Nigerian authorities regard Mr Dikko as a conspirator who had robbed Nigeria of vast sums of money and hoarded them in this country and elsewhere. They felt that extradition proceedings would mean long delay and much uncertainty. So they took this extraordinary means of getting him back to Nigeria.

As a result of inquiries, four men, three Israeli nationals and one Nigerian national, have been charged with kidnapping and with administering drugs with intent to kidnap. They have not yet been brought to trial. The Nigerian Government are applying for the extradition of Mr Dikko. They deny that the High Commissioner or any of their responsible Ministers were involved in the kidnapping.

It was said that these crates were marked 'diplomatic property,' but they did not have the visible markings that a diplomatic bag normally has, and there was no courier such as normally accompanies a diplomatic bag. So our police were quite entitled to open them. But if the diplomatic markings had been in order, would these crates have been free from search? Would the Vienna Convention serve to cover them? I hope not.

Part Nine

General Warrants

Introduction

In the eighteenth century personal freedom was grossly infringed by the executive government. The Secretary of State claimed the right to issue general warrants. These warrants authorised the officers of the Crown to search premises for libellous papers, to arrest the authors and publishers thereof and to bring them before the Minister. All this was done without any previous notification or charge at all. This practice had started in 1688 with the trial of the Seven Bishops.[1] The Bishops had been arrested and committed to the Tower by virtue of such a warrant issued at the instance of the Privy Council. Sir Robert Wright the Chief Justice, and two other judges, held this to be lawful. They held that a charge of libel was a charge of breach of the peace. One judge, Mr Justice Powell, dissented. This ruling held sway until it was challenged in the great cases of which I will now tell you.

[1] (1688) 12 State Tr 183.

1 John Wilkes

1 *The North Briton*

i *John Wilkes himself*

In 1762 John Wilkes was aged 35. He founded in that year *The North Briton*, a weekly political paper in which he attacked the Government of the day. It led to some important constitutional cases which have reverberated in our own time.

But I would tell you first a little of John Wilkes himself. He was extremely ugly, with a hideous squint, but with a wit and charm that carried all before him. He led a life of dissipation and debt and a duel. He was a member of the Hell-fire Club at Medmenham Abbey near Marlow. He lived up to its motto, taken from Rabelais, 'Fay ce que voudras' (Do what you like). He was withal fluent and courageous. If you please, he was a profligate demagogue. He became the idol of the citizens of London. He was for a time a Member of Parliament. In 1774, at the age of 47, he was Lord Mayor of London itself.

ii *Sir Charles Pratt (Lord Camden)*

Next, I will tell you something of his complete opposite, Sir Charles Pratt, afterwards Lord Camden. He tried all the important cases arising out of *The North Briton* No 45. He was Lord Chief Justice of the Common Pleas from 1762 to 1766, and afterwards Lord Chancellor. He was a universal favourite, of spotless character, with an attractive gentleness and a graceful eloquence. There is a fine portrait of him in Guildhall. It was painted by Sir Joshua Reynolds, with a Latin inscription written by Dr Johnson. It says with simple truth that he was the 'zealous supporter of English liberty by law.'

iii The North Briton *No 45*

The first number, No 1, of *The North Briton* came out in June 1762. John Wilkes wrote much of it and edited it himself but he did not disclose the fact. It came out every Saturday at a price of 2½d a copy. It sold about 2,000 copies a week. No 44 appeared on 2 April 1763. Then there was a gap of three weeks whilst John Wilkes was in Paris. In between, on 19 April 1763 there was a new session of Parliament. The King made his speech from the throne.

iv *Powers of invective*

No 45 appeared on Saturday 23 April 1763. In it, John Wilkes used all his powers of invective to condemn the King's speech. It had, of course, been prepared for the King by the ministers. This is an extract from what John Wilkes wrote in No 45:[1]

The ministers' speech of last Tuesday is not to be paralleled in the annals of this country. I am in doubt, whether the imposition is greater on the sovereign, or on the nation . . . They have sent the spirit of discord through the land, and I will prophesy, that it will never be extinguished, but by the extinction of their power . . . I lament to see it [meaning the honour of his said majesty's crown] sunk even to prostitution.

v *The King is angry*

Nowadays vilification of that kind is commonplace among political enemies. It is shrugged off as beneath contempt. But at that time it was regarded by ministers as treasonable. It was a seditious libel which threatened the security of the state. It was a crime punishable by heavy fine and long imprisonment.

[1] 19 State Tr 1385, 1386, 1387.

The young King – he was only 25 – was angry. So was the Government. Over the weekend they asked the Law Officers for advice. They said that it was a seditious libel and that a general warrant should be issued by the Secretary of State to arrest those responsible and search their premises. There were many precedents for such a warrant.

2 General warrant issued

i *Set out verbatim*

No time was lost. On Tuesday 26 April 1763 the Secretary of State issued a 'general warrant.' I set it out verbatim. Read it carefully. You will see that it did not name John Wilkes or anyone in particular. It referred in quite general terms to the 'authors, printers, and publishers.' That was why it was called a 'general warrant.' It was addressed to the King's messengers for them to execute:[1]

George Montagu Dunk Earl of Halifax, Viscount Sunbury and Baron Halifax, one of the lords of his majesty's most honourable privy council, lieutenant-general of his majesty's forces, and principal secretary of state: These are in his majesty's name to authorize and require you (taking a constable to your assistance) to make strict and diligent search for the authors, printers, and publishers of a seditious and treasonable paper, intitled, THE NORTH BRITON, NUMBER XLV. SATURDAY, APRIL 23, 1763, *printed for G Kearsley in Ludgate-street, London, and them, or any of them, having found, to apprehend and seize, together with their papers, and to bring in safe custody before me to be examined concerning the premises, and further dealt with according to law; and, in the due execution thereof, all mayors, sheriffs, justices of the peace, constables, and all other his majesty's officers civil and military, and loving subjects whom it may concern, are to be aiding and assisting to you as there shall be occasion; and for so doing this shall be your warrant. Given at St. James's the twenty-sixth day of April in the third year of his majesty's reign.*

Dunk Halifax.

To Nathan Carrington, John Money, James Watson, and Robert Blackmore four of His Majesty's messengers in ordinary.

[1] *R v Wilkes* (1763) 2 Wils 151.

ii *The King's messengers*

On the next day, Wednesday 27 April 1763, the King's messengers made their first arrests under the warrant. But not John Wilkes on that day. They went to the premises of Dryden Leach, a printer. They took a constable with them. They spent six hours there searching through Mr Leach's premises. They found one of the early copies of *The North Briton* and some papers being prepared for the next, No 46. They thought – as it turned out quite wrongly – that he must have printed No 45 as well.

iii *'Beef-steaks and beer'*

So they arrested Mr Leach himself and one of his journeymen printers, Huckle. They took them off to the office of the Secretary of State and treated them well. They only kept Huckle for six hours but they 'used him very civilly by treating him with beef-steaks and beer.'[1] They were then satisfied that he had nothing to do with No 45. So they released him. But they kept Mr Leach for four days because the Secretary of State was too busy to see him. Then Lord Halifax did see him. He was satisfied 'that the said Dryden Leach did not print the said seditious libel intitled *The North Briton*, No 45, Saturday, April the 23rd, 1763.'[2] So Mr Leach too was released.

iv *Wilkes arrested*

Having got nothing from the printers, the King's messengers turned their attention to the man whom they believed to be the author and publisher of No 45. No other than John Wilkes himself.[3] In the morning of Saturday 30 April they

---

[1] *Huckle v Money* (1763) 2 Wils 205.
[2] *Money v Leach* (1765) 3 Burr 1742, 1744.
[3] I have described it also in *What Next in the Law*, pp 196–197.

went to his house in Great George Street, Westminster. They searched his premises. They got a smith who broke open the locks of the drawers. They swept up all his papers, put them into a sack and carried them off. His private pocket-book filled the mouth of the sack. They arrested him and took him off.

Thenceforward the timetable shows the court acting with great expedition.

3 Habeas corpus

i *Issue forthwith*

Just before 12 noon, Serjeant Glynn came into the Court of the Lord Chief Justice, Sir Charles Pratt and said:

Serjeant Glynn My Lord, two of the King's messengers have this morning entered into the house of my client, John Wilkes. They claim to be acting under the authority of a general warrant issued by the Secretary of State. They have arrested him and seized his papers. I would ask your Lordship to allow a writ of habeas corpus to issue instantly, returnable forthwith.

Lord Chief Justice This is a most extraordinary warrant. Let an habeas corpus be issued immediately, returnable forthwith.

ii *They 'jumped the gun'*

The officers for the Crown soon heard of this. They knew that a habeas corpus would be issued. But they also knew that it would take four or five hours to get the writ of habeas corpus prepared and issued and served on the King's messengers. So they 'jumped the gun.' They decided to get John Wilkes out of the custody of the King's messengers before the writ was served: and into the Tower.

iii *Committed to the Tower*

At about 1 pm they went to the Secretary of State and got him to sign a warrant to commit John Wilkes to the Tower of London. 't was directed to the Constable of the Tower and was in these words:[1]

Charles Earl of Egremont, and George Dunk Earl of Halifax, lords of his majesty's most honourable privy council, and principal secretaries of state: These are in his majesty's name to authorize and require you to receive into your custody the body of John Wilkes esq herewith sent you, for being THE AUTHOR AND PUBLISHER OF A MOST INFAMOUS AND SEDITIOUS LIBEL, INTITLED, THE NORTH BRITON, NUMBER XLV. TENDING TO INFLAME THE MINDS AND ALIENATE THE AFFECTIONS OF THE PEOPLE FROM HIS MAJESTY, AND TO EXCITE THEM TO TRAITOROUS INSURRECTION AGAINST THE GOVERNMENT, AND TO KEEP HIM SAFE AND CLOSE, *until he shall be delivered by due course of law; and for so doing this shall be your warrant. Given at St. James's the 30th day of April 1763, in the third year of his majesty's reign.*

Egremont, Dunk Halifax.

To the Right Honourable John Lord Berkley of Stratton, constable of his majesty's Tower of London, or to the lieutenant of the said Tower, or his deputy.

iv Incommunicado

At about 2 pm, the King's messengers, armed with the warrant, took John Wilkes to the Tower. His solicitor asked time and again to be allowed to see him but it was refused time and again. The lieutenant on duty at the Tower said:

I have received orders from the Secretary of State not to admit any person whatsoever to speak with or see Mr Wilkes. I will not and cannot disobey orders.

So John Wilkes remained in the Tower *incommunicado* over the weekend.

v *Another habeas corpus*

On Monday 2 May the King's messengers came to the Lord Chief Justice to make their return of the writ of habeas corpus. They said they could not produce John Wilkes because they were not served with the writ until 5 pm on the

[1] *R v Wilkes* (1763) 2 Wils 151, 152–153.

General Warrants

Saturday: and by that time, he had been removed to the Tower. Serjeant Glynn for John Wilkes was ready to overcome this device:

I ask for another habeas corpus to issue, this time directed to the Constable of the Tower of London.

Lord Chief Justice We grant it and make it returnable without delay.

4 The return of the warrant

i *Wilkes brought to the Bar*

This is the scene as described by the reporter in *R v Wilkes*:[1]

At the sitting of the Court (which was crowded to such a degree as I never saw it before) in the morning Mr Wilkes was brought to the Bar, and sat among the serjeants, (next to the reporter, on his left hand,) when the Lieutenant of the Tower returned upon this second writ of habeas corpus the warrant of commitment of Mr Wilkes to the Tower by the two Secretaries of State, (before set forth), which being read, Serjeant Glynn moved the Court that Mr Wilkes might be discharged out of custody without bail. . . .

Serjeant Glynn put forward three grounds for his motion. The first two went to the sufficiency of the warrant of commitment to the Tower. The third was that John Wilkes was a Member of Parliament: and as such he was entitled to privilege to be free from arrest in all cases except for three offences – treason, felony and actual breach of the peace – for which he could be arrested: and these did not apply here.

ii *Parliamentary privilege*

The Lord Chief Justice held that John Wilkes was entitled to freedom from arrest: because a libel (with which John Wilkes was charged) was not treason or felony or a breach of the peace. The court refused to follow the case of *The Seven Bishops* in this entertaining passage (pages 159–160):

[1] (1763) 2 Wils 151, 154–155.

266

We are all of opinion that a libel is not a breach of the peace: it tends to the breach of the peace, and that is the utmost. But that which only tends to the breach of the peace cannot be a breach of it. Suppose a libel be a breach of the peace, yet I think it cannot exclude privilege, because I cannot find that a libeller is bound to find surety of the peace, in any book whatever, nor ever was, in any case, except one, viz. the case of *The Seven Bishops*, where three Judges said, that surety of the peace was required in the case of a libel: Judge Powell, the only honest man of the four Judges, dissented, and I am bold to be of his opinion, and to say that case is not law; but it shews the miserable condition of the State at that time. Upon the whole, it is absurd to require surety of the peace or bail in the case of a libeller, and therefore Mr Wilkes must be discharged from his imprisonment: whereupon there was a loud huzza in Westminster-Hall. He was discharged accordingly.

It is said that a great part of the population of London was in Westminster Hall, Palace Yard and the adjoining streets and the 'huzzas' were heard with dismay at St James's Palace (the King's place of business).

5 General warrants held illegal

i *A spate of actions*

Although the legal reason was parliamentary privilege, nevertheless thenceforward the profession took the view that general warrants were illegal. There was a spate of actions – by Mr Leach the printer, Mr Huckle the journeyman printer, and many others – against the King's messengers for damages. All had been arrested under the general warrant..The Lord Chief Justice ruled that they were illegal. Their actions came for trial in 1763 and 1764. The jury in each case were asked to assess the damages. They gave Mr Leach £400, Mr Huckle £300 and 15 others £200 each. Those were very large sums in those days.

ii *Wilkes awarded £1,000*

John Wilkes himself brought an action against a Mr Wood who had come to his house with the King's messengers and told them what to do. This case was tried by the Lord Chief

Justice on 6 December 1763. The jury found a verdict of £1,000 damages.

These large sums were awarded by way of exemplary damages. I have told you of them when discussing exemplary damages in *What Next in the Law*, pages 196–198.

iii Leach's case – *Usage does not justify*

In *Leach's case*,[1] an appeal was taken by a writ of error to the Court of King's Bench. It raised two points: First, was the general warrant lawful or not? Second, even if it was, did it cover Mr Leach who was not the printer of No 45?

The case was first argued in Trinity term 1765. The main argument for the King's messengers was that general warrants in this form had been issued ever since the Revolution of 1688 and had never been questioned. Lord Mansfield rejected this argument in these words (page 562):

It is said that usage will justify it, and it appears, that the same form subsisted at the Revolution and has been continued ever since. Usage has great weight, but will not hold against clear and solid principles of law . . . The form of the warrant probably took its rise from a law for licensing the press (13 & 14 Charles II, chap 33), which is law no more: it arose from a law, which is now expired . . .

Wilmot J – I have not the least doubt, nor ever had, that these warrants are illegal and void.

Yates J – So totally bad, that an usage, even from the foundation of Rome itself, would not make them good.

Aston J – I am of the same opinion, that this is a void and illegal warrant.

The case was set down for argument on Friday 8 November 1765: but the Attorney-General declined to argue it because he could not get over the objection that Mr Leach was not the author, printer or publisher of the libel. Lord Mansfield approved this course, saying (page 563):

This is a warrant to take up the authors, printers, and publishers; and the messengers have taken up persons who fall under none of those descriptions.

[1] *Money v Leach* (1765) 1 Wm Bl 555.

6 *Entick v Carrington*

i *Warrants are issued*

Although those cases about *The North Briton* No 45 hit the headlines, there were other cases which made the law. They arose out of a weekly paper called *The Monitor*, or *British Freeholder*, published six months earlier. I do not know whether John Wilkes was behind it, but it also published matter that was offensive to the Government of the day. So offensive that on 6 November 1762 the Secretary of State issued warrants for arrest and search. These were similar to the general warrant in *The North Briton*, but differed in that these warrants gave the names of the persons affected. One of them was John Entick. He was a clerk who was concerned in the publishing of *The Monitor*. He lived in Stepney. The only change from the general form was to insert these words:[1]

> . . . *make strict and diligent search for John Entick, the author, or one concerned in the writing of several weekly very seditious papers, intitled* THE MONITOR OR BRITISH FREEHOLDER, *No 357, 358, 360, 373, 376, 378, 379, and 380; London, printed for J Wilson and J Fell in Paternoster-Row; which contain gross and scandalous reflections and invectives upon His Majesty's Government, and upon both Houses of Parliament.* . . .

ii *Search of Entick's house*

Armed with that warrant, on 11 November 1762 at 11 o'clock in the day-time the King's messengers (without any constable) went into John Entick's house in Stepney. They went through the rooms in his house. They rummaged through his bureau and writing-desk and several drawers. They were there four hours in all. Then they took away several of his papers. But they did not arrest him or take him with them. They let him go free.

[1] (1765) 2 Wils 275.

iii *Arrest of Beardmore*

A similar warrant was issued on the same day, 6 November 1762, in respect of Arthur Beardmore.[1] He was an attorney living in Wallbrooke. A similar entry, search and seizure was made on the same day, 11 November 1762. But his treatment was worse than that of Entick. They arrested Beardmore and took him off. They kept him for six and a half days. In reasonable comfort, be it said. He was then released on bail.

iv *He is awarded £1,000*

Each brought an action against the four King's messengers. Beardmore's action was tried first. It came before the Lord Chief Justice. He tried it with a jury, but only on the question of damages. The King's messengers had no defence on liability: because Arthur Beardmore was simply an attorney for the publisher and had no concern in the writing of *The Monitor* at all. He did not come within the warrant. The jury awarded him £1,000 damages. The messengers asked for the verdict to be set aside for excessive damages. The Lord Chief Justice refused (page 250):

> The Court must consider these damages as given against Lord Halifax: and can we say that £1,000 are monstrous damages as against him, who has granted an illegal warrant to a messenger who enters into a man's house, and prys into all his secret and private affairs, and carries him from his house and business, and imprisons him for six days. It is an unlawful power assumed by a great minister of state. Can any body say that a guinea per diem is sufficient damages in this extraordinary case, which concerns the liberty of every one of the King's subjects?

7 A test case

i *Three years elapse*

Entick's case was tried next in Westminster Hall before the Lord Chief Justice. It was treated as a test case so as to decide

---

[1] *Beardmore v Carrington* (1764) 2 Wils 244.

whether the warrants were lawful or not. So the judge asked the jury to find a 'special verdict,' that is, to set out the facts and ask the full court to decide the law. They did so. They assessed the damages at £300 if the defendants were liable in law.

It took three years before the law was argued. It was in Michaelmas term 1765 before the full court. The King's messengers relied on the long usage for nearly a century. Nevertheless, the court held the warrants unlawful.

ii *Lord Camden's judgment*

The Lord Chief Justice (then raised to the peerage as Lord Camden), giving the judgment of the court, said:[1]

. . . The warrant in our case was an execution in the first instance, without any previous summons, examination, hearing the plaintiff, or proof that he was the author of the supposed libels; a power claimed by no other magistrate whatever (Scroggs CJ always excepted); it was left to the discretion of these defendants to execute the warrant in the absence or presence of the plaintiff, when he might have no witness present to see what they did; for they were to seize all papers, bank bills, or any other valuable papers they might take away if they were so disposed; there might be nobody to detect them . . . In the case of *Wilkes*, a member of the Commons House, all his books and papers were seized and taken away; we were told by one of these messengers that he was obliged by his oath to sweep away all papers whatsoever; if this is law it would be found in our books, but no such law ever existed in this country; our law holds the property of every man so sacred, that no man can set his foot upon his neighbour's close without his leave; if he does he is a trespasser, though he does no damage at all; if he will tread upon his neighbour's ground, he must justify it by law . . . Upon the whole, we are all of opinion that this warrant is wholly illegal and void. . . .

[1] *Entick v Carrington* (1765) 2 Wils 275, 291, 292. (I have taken the extract from that report which is authentic, whereas the report in *State Trials*, vol XIX, 1029, 1066 is different and is not authentic.)

2 Outlawry

1 Wilkes flees the country

i *He goes to Paris*

Although John Wilkes had successfully claimed parliamentary privilege, this privilege might well be taken from him. The House of Commons were determined to expel him for the seditious libel in No 45. He saw this coming. It meant that, if he was no longer a Member of Parliament, he would no longer be privileged from arrest for misdemeanour or for debt: and he had many creditors waiting for him. So he went off to Paris, seeking to escape the impending avalanche.

Whilst he was gone, his worst fears came to pass. On 20 January 1764 the House of Commons did expel him.

ii *Informations for libel*

The Solicitor-General laid an information against him for publishing a seditious and scandalous libel in *The North Briton* No 45: and another for an obscene and impious libel in his *An Essay on Woman* (a parody of Pope's *An Essay on Man*). The trial was fixed for 21 February 1764. Our law at that time did not allow his flight to France to be any excuse for not appearing at the trial. Flight was treated as a confession of guilt. So the case proceeded on 21 February 1764 in his absence. The jury found him Guilty on both informations.

iii *He is outlawed*

As he had fled from England to avoid arrest, he was liable to be outlawed. That was a very complicated procedure, but the prosecution went through it all. Demands were made for him to appear at five county courts in succession. On 5 August 1764 the Sheriff of Middlesex read a proclamation at the great door of St Margaret's, Westminster, ordering him to appear. He did not appear. On 1 November 1764 he was, by the law and custom of the realm, OUTLAWED. That was a fearful sentence on him. It meant the forfeiture of his goods and chattels and all the profits of his real estate; and perpetual imprisonment with many incapacities.

2 **Wilkes returns**

i *Elected to Parliament*

After nearly four years' absence in France, John Wilkes returned to England. He had a good plan in his mind. It was to get himself elected a Member of Parliament so that he could once again claim the privilege of parliament. He stood for the county of Middlesex. During the campaign, a heckler called out:

Vote for you, Sir! I'd as soon vote for the Devil.

Wilkes retorted at once:

But in case your friend should not stand?

He was elected by a huge majority on 28 March 1768.

ii *A writ of error*

Pending the election, the authorities could have had him arrested as an outlaw, but they held their hand – on his promise to surrender himself to the court on the first day of Easter term 1768. On that day John Wilkes voluntarily made a personal appearance before the court. He surrendered himself to the outlawry but asked that it be reversed. He brought a writ of error for the purpose. Meanwhile he was kept in custody.

iii *A technical flaw*

Serjeant Glynn appeared for him and made many technical objections to the outlawry. Lord Mansfield disallowed them all but he found a most technical objection of his own. The Sheriff of Middlesex in his return had said:

At my County Court held at the Three Tuns in Brook-Street near Holborn in the county of Middlesex

whereas he ought to have inserted the two words 'of Middlesex' in two places so that it should have read

At my County Court *of Middlesex* held for the county *of Middlesex* at the Three Tuns in Brook-Street near Holborn in the county of Middlesex.

iv *Outlawry reversed*

Lord Mansfield justified this technicality in these words:[1]

From the precedents we have seen, it appears, that a series of judgments have required a technical form of words, in the description of the County Court at which an outlaw is exacted: that after the words 'at my County Court,' should be added the name of the county, and after the word 'held,' should be added – 'for the county of ———,' (naming it). Whereas here, the sheriff says 'at my County Court,' without adding – 'of Middlesex:' and he says – 'held at the house, &c.' without adding the words 'for the county of Middlesex,' after the word 'held.'

It was solely by reason of the technical objection discovered by himself that Lord Mansfield reversed the outlawry. John Wilkes was accordingly set free.

v *Resounding rhetoric*

I can understand it perfectly. Outlawry was such a fearful punishment that any technical objection would serve to set it aside. I would have done it myself. But I would not have prefaced it with the resounding rhetoric that he used. I know

---

[1] *R v John Wilkes* (1770) 4 Burr 2527, 2563.

274

it by heart, I have repeated it on many occasions. I have set it out in full in *The Family Story* (page 173):

The Constitution does not allow reasons of State to influence our judgments: God forbid it should! We must not regard political consequences; how formidable soever they might be: if rebellion was the certain consequence, we are bound to say 'Fiat justitia, ruat caelum' [Let justice be done though the heavens fall].

I am afraid that Lord Mansfield had his tongue in his cheek. He did have regard to political consequences. He did not want to make John Wilkes a martyr. So he found a technicality by which he set him free.

vi *Sentenced*

Although the outlawry was reversed, the conviction of John Wilkes was still valid. He had to be sentenced for it. On 18 June 1768 in respect of *The North Briton* No 45 he suffered a fine of £500 and imprisonment for ten calendar months: and in respect of *An Essay on Woman* a fine of £500 and imprisonment for twelve calendar months to follow the first ten months. He paid the fines and served his sentences. He was released on Easter Tuesday 1770.

3 Legal points

1 Obsolescent laws

i *Outlawry proceedings*

These were most uncommon even in Lord Mansfield's time. They were often reversed on the most technical grounds. After the reversal in *Wilkes's case*, they fell into disuse. They were formally abolished by section 12 of the Administration of Justice Act 1938.

ii *Parliamentary privilege disappears*

In granting John Wilkes parliamentary privilege from arrest, the Court of Common Pleas were only dealing with the warrant of commitment to the Tower of London. They released John Wilkes on the ground that, as a Member of Parliament, he was privileged, that is, free from arrest for writing and publishing a seditious libel. In this respect the court were mistaken. As soon as Parliament reassembled in November 1763, it was resolved by both Houses:

That privilege of Parliament does not extend to the case of writing and publishing seditious libels, nor ought to be allowed to obstruct the ordinary course of the laws in the speedy and effectual prosecution of so heinous and dangerous an offence.

And in 1831 the Committee of Privileges said:

Since that time it has been considered as established generally, that privilege is not claimable for any indictable offence.

Nor indeed for any criminal offence.

So far as civil cases are concerned, in the old days when there was imprisonment for debt, a Member of Parliament could claim privilege from arrest: but now that imprisonment for debt has disappeared, the privilege has disappeared also.

Nevertheless, although the Court of Common Pleas mistakenly granted him the privilege, there was a better reason for releasing John Wilkes. It was because a general warrant was unlawful and illegal: and therefore an arrest in pursuance of it was also unlawful and illegal. That is how the decision was understood. No general warrant was issued by any Secretary of State after the release of John Wilkes.

2 Modern applications

i *Habeas corpus*

The case of John Wilkes is a good illustration of the efficacy of the writ of habeas corpus. John Wilkes had been arrested and detained by the authority of the Secretary of State. Yet the court required him to be produced at once to inquire whether his detention was lawful or not. This principle was applied by the House of Lords recently in regard to an immigrant. It was in *R v Home Secretary, ex parte Khawaja*.[1] The House approved what I said in *R v Governor of Pentonville Prison, ex parte Azam*:[2]

. . . If a man can make a prima facie case that he is not an illegal entrant, he is entitled to a writ of habeas corpus as of right: see *Greene v Home Secretary* [1942] AC 284, 302 by Lord Wright. The court has no discretion to refuse it. Unlike certiorari or mandamus, a writ of habeas corpus is of right to every man who is unlawfully detained. If a prima facie case is shown that a man is unlawfully detained, it is for the one who detains him to make a return justifying it.

ii *Searching for papers*

Very recently in the *Rossminster case*[3] a search warrant was

---

[1] [1983] 1 All ER 765.
[2] [1974] AC 18, 32.
[3] *R v IRC, ex parte Rossminster* [1980] AC 952.

issued in very general terms. It authorised the officers of the Inland Revenue to search for papers when they suspected that a tax fraud had been committed. The warrant did not specify any particular tax offence. It was very general, in these words, 'an offence involving fraud in connection with or in relation to tax.' The Court of Appeal held that the warrant was bad. I gave reasons very like those given in *Entick v Carrington*. I said (page 974):

So here. When the officers of the Inland Revenue come armed with a warrant to search a man's home or his office, it seems to me that he is entitled to say: 'Of what offence do you suspect me? You are claiming to enter my house and to seize my papers.' And when they look at the papers and seize them, he should be able to say: 'Why are you seizing these papers? Of what offence do you suspect me? What have these to do with your case?' Unless he knows the particular offence charged, he cannot take steps to secure himself or his property. So it seems to me, as a matter of construction of the statute and therefore of the warrant – in pursuance of our traditional role to protect the liberty of the individual – it is our duty to say that the warrant must particularise the specific offence which is charged as being fraud on the revenue.

If this be right, it follows necessarily that this warrant is bad. It should have specified the particular offence of which the man is suspected. On this ground I would hold that certiorari should go to quash the warrant.

But the House of Lords reversed us. They held that the warrant was good. As I have told you before,[1] they were criticised by *The Times*. In a leading article *The Times* said:

If our liberties had to be protected by them, they would prove a leaky umbrella.

iii *The new Bill*

Under the Police and Criminal Evidence Bill now going through Parliament, the law about search warrants will become very complicated. The existing powers of magistrates are retained. They can already issue warrants to search for stolen goods, drugs, firearms, explosives and other *prohibited* goods. But the Bill will give the magistrates power to issue warrants to search for *evidence* of serious crime, such

---

[1] *The Closing Chapter*, p 222.

as murder weapons, blackmail notes, and papers evidencing fraud and conspiracy. Some papers are *excluded*, such as items subject to legal privilege, journalistic material and confidential papers. Other papers are subject to a special procedure requiring application to a circuit judge. In the debates I expressed my concern at these complications.

iv *A point not argued*

In reversing the outlawry of John Wilkes, Lord Mansfield went on an extreme technicality of his own – invented by himself without hearing argument upon it. I see nothing improper in his conduct. Normally a judge would not decide a case on a new point of his own without inviting counsel to make their submission on it. But on occasion it may be done. I did it in *Goldsmith v Sperrings Ltd* where I said:[1]

An erroneous proposition should not be accepted as good law simply because counsel have passed it by in silence and have not sought to challenge it. By that means it gains currency and is never remedied. Better to correct it now while the opportunity offers rather than let it continue to disturb the course of justice. If this be error, and upon me proved, it at least opens the way for the House of Lords to put things right for the future.

[1] [1977] 1 WLR 478, 486.

Part Ten

Freedom of the Press

Introduction

There is one great lesson to be learnt from the nineteenth century. It is the freedom of the press: and in particular its freedom to criticise the Government of the day. In those times any criticism in the press of the King or his Ministers was considered to be a seditious libel. The reason was that it was feared that it would shake the constitution. I have already told you of the cases about *The North Briton* and *The Monitor*. Although the courts held that the general warrants were illegal, no one at that time questioned the law of seditious libel. John Wilkes was held guilty of it. He was fined and sent to prison.

The judges were themselves much at fault in all this. They were 'lions under the throne' – lions that were fierce to spring upon any jackal that ventured to yell against the Government. They said that the question of 'libel or no libel' was for them, the judges, and not for the jury. And they invariably held that criticism of the King or his Ministers was a libel. There was a great constitutional crisis. It took 30 years before the freedom of the press was secured.

In this Part I will tell of two great judges who were at variance about it. They were Lord Camden and Lord Mansfield. Of these two, Lord Camden was much the greater. Lord Mansfield was the less. If the story becomes a little technical at times, please forgive me. It is of such constitutional significance that all should know it.

I will also tell you of blasphemous libel which has recently been revived.

1 Seditious libel

1 *The Letters of Junius*

i *Who was he?*

From 1769 to 1771, many letters were published containing trenchant criticisms of the Government of the day. They were signed *Junius*. That was a pseudonym. The writer used it to conceal his identity. If he had been discovered, he would certainly have been prosecuted for seditious libel. Many have tried to find out who he was. The evidence points strongly, but not certainly, to his being Sir Philip Francis (1740–1818), an educated stylist who was high up in the War Office and had access to inside information. The letters stopped when Francis went to India.

ii *His attack on the King*

The letters were published by Henry Woodfall in the weekly *Public Advertiser*. They were reprinted in the *London Evening Post*, the *London Museum* and other periodicals. They were immensely popular. The merchants of London were delighted to read the condemnations which *Junius* poured on the unpopular and misguided Government of the day. But the ministers were furious.

On 19 December 1769 *Junius* went further than ever before. He brought the King, George III, into it. The King was then only 31. The letter was couched in the form of giving advice to the King but reproaching him for allowing himself to be misled by his ministers. These are typical passages:

> Sir, it is the misfortune of your life, and originally the cause of every reproach and distress which has attended your government, that you should never have been acquainted with the language of truth, till you found it in the complaints of your subjects. . . .

After describing the affection of the people for the King when he began his reign, *Junius* went on:

> Such, Sir, was once the disposition of a people, who now surround your throne with reproaches and complaints. Do justice to yourself, banish from your mind those unworthy opinions, with which some interested persons have laboured to possess you. Distrust the men who tell you the English are naturally light and inconstant, that they complain without a cause. Withdraw your confidence equally from all parties, from ministers, favourites, and relations, and let there be one moment in your life in which you have consulted your own understanding.

iii *The ruling of the judges*

Nowadays nobody would take much notice of stuff of that sort. But in those days the ministers regarded it as a seditious libel. It was a threat to the Government. It was a crime to be punished by imprisonment. The judges took the same view. What is more, they were determined to keep it in their own hands. They were not going to let it go to the jury. So they ruled that, as matter of law, it was for the judges themselves to rule on the intention of the article – whether it was seditious or not – whether it was innocent or criminal – and not for the jury. The only thing for the jury to decide was whether the accused published it. If the accused had published it, the jury were to find him guilty. The judge would sentence the man to a fine or imprisonment or both.

I ought to add that if there was any innuendo alleged, such as filling in a blank – 'K' means 'King' – the jury were to decide whether the words bore that sense or meaning. This was usually obvious.

2 A previous case in 1752

i *Mr Pratt's defence*

That ruling by the judges had gone back a long time. It had been invoked nearly 20 years earlier in 1752. A young counsel, Mr Charles Pratt (afterwards Lord Camden) was appearing for a printer, Mr Owen. He was charged with a seditious libel on the Speaker of the House of Commons. Mr Pratt took a line different from that taken by the judges. He told the jury that they were bound to look to the nature and tendency of the supposed libel and to acquit the defendant unless they believed that by it he *intended* to sow sedition and to subvert the constitution. He said:

Are you impannelled merely to determine whether the defendant had sold a piece of paper value two-pence?

ii 'Not guilty, my Lord'

The presiding judge, Lord Chief Justice Lee, directed the jury that the *one* question for them was whether the printer did publish the paper by selling it. It was not for them to consider his intention. The jury retired, and after being out two hours they returned a general verdict of Not Guilty. The judge called them back and put it to them again. The foreman was at first 'a good deal flustered;' but the question being again repeated to him, 'Did the printer sell the paper?' the foreman said in a firm voice, all his fellow jurors nodding assent:

'Not guilty, my Lord; not guilty! That is our verdict, my Lord, and we abide by it!'

Upon which there was a loud shout of exultation.

That case was in 1752. Mr Pratt remembered it afterwards in the great controversy about the letter of *Junius*. I will tell you about it.

3 Juries refuse to convict

i *The papers are sold out*

The letter to the King (of which I have given extracts) was published in the *Public Advertiser* on 19 December 1769 and in other papers soon after. There was a rush to buy them. All were sold out in a few hours. They were reprinted time and again. The Attorney-General regarded it as grossly seditious libel. He laid informations against Henry Woodfall, the publisher of the *Public Advertiser*, John Miller, the publisher of the *London Evening Post*, and John Almon, a bookseller.

The trial of John Almon came on first, but I will not take up your time with telling you about it. It turned on the sufficiency of evidence.

ii *Woodfall is prosecuted*

The trial of Henry Woodfall, the printer and publisher, came on next on 13 June 1770. Lord Mansfield directed the jury in the accustomed way. He told them that the words in the information alleging 'intention, malice, sedition, or any other still harder words' were 'mere formal words, mere inference of law, with which the jury were not to concern themselves.'

iii *Out for ten hours*

The report goes on:

About twelve the jury withdrew. At half an hour after three lord Mansfield began to whisper with serj Davy, who had been out of court and returned, with the Attorney General, with Mr Wallace, and the other crown lawyers. In the space of a quarter of an hour he sent three times to the jury to know if they were not agreed in their verdict. He said he would not sit longer than four, if the other business of the Court should be over. The jury not returning, lord Mansfield proposed to Mr Lee that he should sign an agreement with Mr Attorney General, that the jury might give their verdict to lord Mansfield privately at lord Mansfield's house. After some time and persuasion from lord Mansfield, Mr Lee consented, and signed such agreement; after which lord Mansfield pulled off his hat, and said, Mr Lee, you have done right to consent. Lord Mansfield then adjourned the Court, and retired. The jury continued undetermined till near ten at night, when they agreed upon their verdict, and went in hackney coaches from Guildhall to lord Mansfield's house in Bloomsbury-square, and gave their verdict in these words: 'Guilty of printing and publishing only.'

iv 'Guilty of publishing only'

Lord Mansfield stood at his parlour door, and made the jury give their verdict in his hall where the footmen were, and when they had given it, he withdrew, without saying a word.

That verdict, 'Guilty of publishing only,' gave rise to a serious question. Was it equivalent to a verdict of 'Guilty'? or was it ambiguous? This was a matter for argument before the full court. The case was adjourned for the purpose.

v Miller is prosecuted

Meanwhile, during the adjournment, there took place the trial of John Miller, the publisher of the *London Evening Post*. It had also published the letter to the King. The trial took place on 18 July 1770 at Guildhall. Lord Mansfield directed the jury in much the same way as he did in Woodfall's case, ending with the words:

. . . I will repeat it to you again, you must be satisfied as to the meanings laid down in the information, and concerning the persons, and you must be satisfied with regard to the publication; if you are satisfied you will find him guilty; if not you will find him not guilty.

vi 'Not guilty' – The loudest huzzas

The report goes on:

The trial began about nine o'clock in the morning, and was finished about twelve. The jury retired into a private room, and continued locked up, till half an hour past seven in the evening, at which time they were agreed in their verdict; and the Court being broke up, they carried it to lord Mansfield, at his house in Bloomsbury-square. His lordship met them at his parlour door, in the passage, and the foreman having pronounced their verdict Not Guilty, his lordship went away without saying a word. But there being a vast concourse of people in the square, who had followed the jury from Guildhall, they, as soon as the verdict was known, testified their joy, by the loudest huzzas.

That was the end of that case. Even Lord Mansfield could not go against the verdict of Not Guilty. It meant in practice that none of these prosecutions would succeed. But there was a point of law left. In the case of Woodfall, the court had reserved judgment on the verdict of 'Guilty of printing and publishing only.'

vii *Woodfall would be acquitted*

On 20 November 1770 Lord Mansfield gave an elaborate judgment, trying to find out what the jury meant by adding the word 'only.'[1] In the end the court decided that the word 'only' could not be rejected as meaningless. They said:

. . . If a doubt arises from an ambiguous and unusual word in the verdict, the court ought to lean in favour of a *venire de novo*, that is, in favour of a new trial. . . .

There was no new trial. The prosecution did not go on with the case against Woodfall. They knew that Miller had been found Not Guilty: and that, if Woodfall was tried again, he would be acquitted also.

4 *Junius* attacks Lord Mansfield

i *Salvoes against Lord Mansfield*

Meanwhile, after the acquittal of Miller, *Junius* had opened up his guns again. This time they were not aimed at the King. They were aimed at Lord Mansfield himself. *Junius* wrote to Woodfall the publisher, asking him to publish a letter against Lord Mansfield:

I don't think you run the least risque. We have got the rascal (Lord Mansfield) down, let us strangle him if it is possible.

Junius's first salvo was fired on 14 November 1770. It was addressed to Lord Mansfield:

[1] *R v Woodfall* (1770) 5 Burr 2661.

Our language has no term of reproach, the mind has no idea of detestation, which has not already been happily applied to you, and exhausted . . .

I see, through your whole life, one uniform plan to enlarge the power of the Crown at the expense of the liberty of the subject.

. . . When you invade the province of the jury in matter of libel, you in effect attack the liberty of the press; and, with a single stroke, wound two of your greatest enemies. . . .

ii '*Prosecute us if you dare*'

Junius ended with a warning to Lord Mansfield not to prosecute the printer of the letter:

. . . Beware how you indulge the first emotions of your resentment; this paper is delivered to the world, and cannot be recalled; the persecution of an innocent printer cannot alter facts, nor refute arguments. . . .

iii *Lord Mansfield does not dare*

The Attorney-General advised Lord Mansfield that proceedings should be taken to prosecute *Junius*. But Lord Mansfield said 'No.' He would 'confide in the good sense of the public and the internal evidence of his own conscience.'

5 Proceedings in Parliament

i *Lord Mansfield is severely censured*

Salvo after salvo rained upon Lord Mansfield. The climax came on 6 December 1770. A motion was made in the Commons for 'a Committee to inquire into the proceedings of the judges in Westminster Hall, particularly in cases relating to the liberty of the press.' In the debate, the conduct of Lord Mansfield was severely censured. In the House of Lords Lord Chatham and Lord Camden condemned him. In answer, Lord Mansfield retorted:

. . . The scurrility of a newspaper may be good information for a coffee-house politician; but a peer of parliament should always speak from higher authority.

ii *He says nothing*

He then intimated that he had something of importance to bring to the notice of the House. Lord Campbell tells us:[1]

On the appointed day there was an unusually large attendance of Peers. It was generally believed that the Lord Chief Justice was going to move a vote of censure on Lord Chatham and Lord Camden for calumniating the Judges, and the coming passage of arms between them was expected to be more dazzling than any ever before witnessed. But, oh! miserable disappointment! After a long pause, during which all eyes were fixed upon Lord Mansfield, he at last rose and said, – 'My Lords, I have left a paper with the clerk-assistant of this House, containing the judgment of the Court of King's Bench in the case of *The King against Woodfall*, and any of your Lordships who may be so inclined may read it and take copies of it.' To the astonishment of the audience, he resumed his seat without making any motion or uttering a syllable more.

iii *Lord Camden's six questions*

Next day, Lord Camden rose and said:

My Lords, I consider the paper delivered in by the noble and learned Lord on the woolsack as a challenge directed personally to me, and I accept it; he has thrown down the gauntlet, and I take it up. In direct contradiction to him I maintain that his doctrine is not the law of England. . . .

Lord Camden then asked six questions which, he said, required categorical answers. Lord Mansfield, looking very unhappy, declined to answer them. Horace Walpole describes the scene:

The dismay and confusion of Lord Mansfield was obvious to the whole audience; nor did one peer interpose a syllable in his behalf.

iv *Lord Mansfield's cry of 'Craven!'*

Lord Campbell makes this comment on Lord Mansfield's conduct:[2]

His cry of *Craven!* when the lists had been stretched and the trumpet had sounded for a passage of arms on the Libel field, lowered his character,

[1] *Lives of the Chief Justices*, vol II, p 487.
[2] Ibid p. 576.

and must have been a source of painful remembrance for himself to his dying day.

6 Thirteen years later

i *The Dean of St Asaph*

But, despite his discomfiture, Lord Mansfield still retained his view of the law. The judges still summed up in the way Lord Mansfield had directed. This was brought home 13 years later in 1784 in a case brought against the Dean of St Asaph. It covers 106 printed pages in the report in 4 Douglas 73, and was closely analysed by Lord Blackburn in *Capital & Counties Bank v Henty*[1]. I have told you of the case of the Dean of St Asaph in *What Next in the Law*, pages 44–46. It affirmed the ruling that 'libel or no libel' was for the judge and not the jury.

ii *Fox brings in a Bill*

The ruling in that case caused much upset. The whole country protested against the attitude of the judges. Charles James Fox introduced a Bill in the House of Commons which condemned as illegal directions which the judges had been giving. The Bill was opposed in the Lords by the Lord Chancellor, Lord Thurlow. He summoned the judges and obtained from them a unanimous opinion that 'libel or no libel' was one of pure law for the court alone. But Lord Camden, in his eightieth year, in a two-day debate swayed the House so that they passed the second reading of the Bill by 57 to 32. Rising in his place slowly and with difficulty, and still leaning on his stick, Lord Camden said:

I thought never to have troubled your Lordships more. The hand of age is upon me. . . .

iii *Lord Camden's illustration*

His voice, which at first had been low and tremulous, grew firm and loud. He gave his favourite illustration of a trial for murder:

[1] (1882) 7 App Cas 741, 772–775.

292

A man may kill another in his own defence, or under various circumstances, which render the killing no murder. How are these things to be explained? – By the circumstances of the case. What is the ruling principle? – The intention of the party. Who decides on the intention of the party? The judge? No! the jury! So the jury are allowed to judge of the intention upon an indictment for murder, and not upon an indictment for a libel!!! . . .

I ask your Lordships to say, who shall have the care of the liberty of the press? the judges or the people of England? The jury are the people of England.

So Lord Camden got a majority for the Bill on second reading.

iv *'No, I thank you!!!'*

But Lord Thurlow tried to damage it in committee by a clause which would enable the judges, if dissatisfied with the jury's verdict of Not Guilty, to grant a new trial:

Lord Camden What! after a verdict of acquittal?

Lord Chancellor Yes!

Lord Camden No, I thank you!!!

Those were the last words Lord Camden ever uttered in public. The Lord Chancellor withdrew his amendment. The Bill was read a third time.

7 Fox's Libel Act 1792

i *It declares the law*

It was framed – not as an amendment of the law – but as a declaration of the law. It declared that the law always had been as Lord Camden (then Mr Pratt) had told the jury in *Owen's case* in 1752: and all the other judges had been wrong all the time. These are the words of the statute – Fox's Libel Act 1792:

It is hereby declared and enacted that on every trial for the making or publishing of any libel, the jury may give a general verdict of Guilty or Not Guilty, upon the whole matter put in issue; and shall not be required or directed, by the court or judge, to find the defendant or defendants Guilty, merely on the proof of the publication of the paper charged to be a libel, and of the sense ascribed to the same in the Indictment or Information.

ii *A great constitutional triumph*

So ended the Thirty Years' War for the freedom of the press. Lord Campbell's verdict on it was this:[1]

This great constitutional triumph is mainly to be ascribed to Lord Camden, who had been fighting in the cause for half a century, and uttered his last words in the House of Lords in its support: but without the invaluable assistance of Erskine, as counsel for the Dean of St Asaph, the Star Chamber might have been re-established in this country.

[1] *Lives of the Lord Chancellors*, vol VI, p 435.

2 Legal points

1 Obsolescence

i *Seditious libel*

The offence of seditious libel is now obsolescent. It used to be defined as words intended to stir up violence, that is, disorder, by promoting feelings of ill-will or hostility between different classes of His Majesty's subjects. But this definition was found to be too wide. It would restrict too much the full and free discussion of public affairs. Juries were very loath to convict. So it has fallen into disuse for nearly 150 years. The only case in this century was *R v Caunt* tried at the Liverpool Assizes in 1947 when a local paper published an article stirring up hatred against the Jews. The jury found the editor Not Guilty.[1]

2 Modern applications

i *The civil law*

The 1792 Act was concerned with criminal libel. Yet it has been held applicable also in civil cases of ordinary libel, see *Capital & Counties Bank & Henty*[2]. There is some amplification, however, necessary. If the words are *not* reasonably capable of a defamatory meaning, the judge can – and should – rule as matter of law in favour of the defendant.

---

[1] See note by Professor E C S Wade, 64 LQR 203.
[2] (1882) 7 App Cas 741, 775 per Lord Blackburn.

But if they are reasonably capable, he must leave the case to the jury. In short, the defendant is not liable unless both the judge and the jury are against him. Fox's Act was passed in favour of defendants – not of plaintiffs.

ii *The intention of the publisher*

You will notice from my quotations the difference between Lord Mansfield and Lord Camden. In *Woodfall's case* Lord Mansfield told the jury that so far as the *intention*, the malice, of the defendant were concerned, these were mere formal words with which the jury were not to concern themselves: whereas in *Owen's case* Mr Pratt told the jury that they were not to convict the defendant unless he *intended* to sow sedition; and his favourite illustration was on the *intent* of murder.

I am sorry to say that Lord Mansfield's view has prevailed in the civil law. In *Hulton v Jones*[1] the House of Lords decided (contrary to the view of Lord Justice Fletcher Moulton) that the intention of the writer or publisher is immaterial. His meaning does not matter. All that matters is the meaning put upon the words by the readers. I have criticised this view in my book, *What Next in the Law*, pages 212–213. It has led to many unjust decisions – against the press. I said in my book:

I would like to see the House of Lords take *Hulton v Jones* by the scruff of the neck and throw it out of the courts, and start afresh.

The House would do well to go back to Lord Camden – whose views on libel were so much better than Lord Mansfield's – and were upheld by Parliament.

Lord Mansfield's view has also prevailed in the criminal law. In the *Gay News case* (which I describe later) it was applied in the case of blasphemous libel.

iii *Trial by jury*

The conflict has its repercussions today. In *Rothermere v Times Newspapers* I summarised the history, and said:[2]

[1] [1910] AC 20.
[2] [1973] 1 WLR 448, 453.

Looking back on our history, I hold that, if a newspaper has criticised in its columns the great and the powerful on a matter of large public interest – and is then charged with libel – then its guilt or innocence should be tried with a jury, if the newspaper asks for it, even though it requires the prolonged examination of documents.

So the important case when the religious cult known as the Moonies sued the *Daily Mail* for libel was tried with a jury even though it did last six months.

iv *The identity of* Junius

The Government would have dearly loved to discover the identity of *Junius* – so as to prosecute him. But they never found out. The printer Woodfall knew who he was and corresponded with him. But wild horses would not drag it out of him. It would be the same today. I examined the principle in the *Granada case*.[1] No court will order a newspaper to disclose its source of information unless it is *necessary* in the interests of justice. The identity of *Junius* was not necessary. Suffice it to prosecute the printer and publisher.

v *Verdict of acquittal*

Lord Camden was outraged by the suggestion that there should be any appeal against a verdict of acquittal or any new trial. That is still the case. It is fundamental in our constitution that once a man is acquitted by a jury, he goes free. The prosecution cannot appeal against it. Nor can the prosecution get a new trial. Likewise, if a man is acquitted by magistrates the prosecution cannot appeal unless a case is stated on a point of law.

At one time, if a man appealed against sentence – and failed – the Court of Appeal could increase it. Lord Goddard used that power. But now he must not be more severely dealt with than in the court below.

---

[1] [1981] AC 1096.

3 Blasphemous libel

1 What is blasphemy?

i *The trial of Jesus*

In the *Shorter Oxford Dictionary* blasphemy is defined as 'profane speaking of God or sacred things.' But I take its meaning in the trial of Jesus as recorded in the *Gospel of St Mark*, chapter 14, 61–64:

Again the high priest asked him, and said unto him, Art thou the Christ, the Son of the Blessed? And Jesus said, I am: and ye shall see the Son of man sitting on the right hand of power, and coming in the clouds of heaven. Then the high priest rent his clothes, and saith, What need we any further witnesses? Ye have heard the blasphemy: what think ye? And they all condemned him to be guilty of death.

Christianity was part of the law of England for a thousand years. To deny it was an offence against the spiritual law. It was also an offence against the temporal law. To prove this, let me tell you of some cases.

ii *Taylor's case*[1]

At Guildford in 1678 Taylor uttered 'divers blasphemous expressions, horrible to hear,' to wit:

that Jesus Christ was a bastard, a whoremaster, religion was a cheat; and that he neither feared God, the devil, or man.

Chief Justice Hale said:

---

[1] 1 Vent 293.

... that such kind of wicked blasphemous words were not only an offence to God and religion, but a crime against the laws, State and Government, and therefore, punishable in this Court. For to say, religion is a cheat, is to dissolve all those obligations whereby the civil societies are preserved, and that Christianity is parcel of the laws of England; and therefore to reproach the Christian religion is to speak in subversion of the law.

Wherefore they gave judgment upon him, (viz) to stand in the pillory in three several places, and to pay one thousand marks fine, and to find sureties for his good behaviour during life.

iii *Woolston's case*[1]

In 1742 Woolston published several discourses in which he said:

... that the miracles of Christ ... are not to be taken in a literal sense, but that the whole relation of the life and miracles of our Lord Christ in the New Testament, is but an allegory.

He argued that, even if they did amount to a libel upon Christianity, yet the common law has not cognisance of such an offence.

Chief Justice Raymond said that:

Christianity in general is parcel of the common law of England, and therefore to be protected by it; now whatever strikes at the very root of Christianity, tends manifestly to a dissolution of the civil government, and so was the opinion of my Lord Hale in *Taylor's case*.

He was found guilty and punished accordingly.

iv *Gott's case*

In 1921 a man named Gott was convicted at the Old Bailey for publishing a pamphlet in which he had described Christ entering Jerusalem as 'like a clown on the back of two donkeys.' He appealed but his appeal was dismissed.

2 *The Secular Society*

Now I would take you to a famous case in 1917. It is *Bowman*

[1] Fitz–Gibbons 64.

v Secular Society Ltd.[1] Charles Bowman made a will in which he left his money upon trust for the Secular Society Ltd. That was a company which was deliberately and entirely anti-Christian. It had, among its objects:

To promote . . . the principle that human conduct should be based upon natural knowledge, and not upon super-natural belief.

Lord Finlay, the Lord Chancellor, a sincere Christian, held that the purposes of the company were illegal and that the bequest was invalid. But the other four law lords held it was not illegal. Lord Sumner gave the reasons in a famous passage:[2]

. . . Our courts of law, in the exercise of their own jurisdiction, do not, and never did that I can find, punish irreligious words as offences against God. As to them they held that *deorum injuriae dis curae* (injuries to the Gods must be dealt with by the courts of the Gods). They dealt with such words for their manner, their violence, or ribaldry, or, more fully stated, for their tendency to endanger the peace then and there, to deprave public morality generally, to shake the fabric of society, and to be a cause of civil strife. The words, as well as the acts, which tend to endanger society differ from time to time in proportion as society is stable or insecure in fact, or is believed by its reasonable members to be open to assault. In the present day meetings or processions are held lawful which a hundred and fifty years ago would have been deemed seditious, and this is not because the law is weaker or has changed, but because, the times having changed, society is stronger than before. In the present day reasonable men do not apprehend the dissolution or the downfall of society because religion is publicly assailed by methods not scandalous. Whether it is possible that in the future irreligious attacks, designed to undermine fundamental institutions of our society, may come to be criminal in themselves, as constituting a public danger, is a matter that does not arise. The fact that opinion grounded on experience has moved one way does not in law preclude the possibility of its moving on fresh experience in the other; nor does it bind succeeding generations, when conditions have again changed. After all, the question whether a given opinion is a danger to society is a question of the times and is a question of fact. I desire to say nothing that would limit the right of society to protect itself by process of law from the dangers of the moment, whatever that right may be, but only to say that, experience having proved dangers once thought real to be now negligible, and dangers once

[1] [1917] AC 406.
[2] Ibid 466–467.

very possibly imminent to have now passed away, there is nothing in the general rules as to blasphemy and irreligion, as known to the law, which prevents us from varying their application to the particular circumstances of our time in accordance with that experience.

3 *Gay News*

i *Blasphemy obsolescent*

After 1921 there was no case of blasphemy for over 50 years. We all thought it was obsolescent like seditious libel. But then in 1977 it was revived in a sensational case, *R v Gay News Ltd*,[1] which took the headlines. A periodical called *Gay News* contained matter which was highly irreligious. It was no danger to the state or to society. Yet it was held to be a blasphemous libel. The case was tried by a friend of mine, His Honour Alan King-Hamilton QC. He was one of the best of judges and has told the story of it in his book, *And Nothing But the Truth*. It was, he says, irresistibly absorbing.

ii *A shocking drawing*

Gay News is a newspaper for homosexuals. In 1976 it published a poem entitled 'The love that dares to speak its name.' Printed alongside it was a drawing. It is unnecessary to describe the poem or the drawing. Suffice it to say that it was shocking and horrifying. It portrayed Our Lord in the most revolting homosexual circumstances before and after the Crucifixion. It featured the body of Christ in the embrace of a Roman centurion.

The paper circulated mainly among homosexuals. It may or may not have been revolting to them. I suppose it was not, else it would not have been provided for them. But by chance a copy came into the hands of a senior probation officer. He only got it because the same issue contained an article about the probation service. Later, he saw this shocking piece about Jesus Christ and passed it to Mrs Mary Whitehouse.

[1] [1979] 1 QB 10.

iii *A prosecution is brought*

She took legal advice and instituted a private prosecution for blasphemous libel. That is important. It was, one would have thought, an obscene publication but it is difficult nowadays to get a conviction on that score. So the charge was only for blasphemous libel. The particulars charged the defendants with publishing

a blasphemous libel concerning the Christian religion, namely, an obscene poem and illustration vilifying Christ in his life and in his crucifixion.

4 The trial itself

i *The court is filled*

The court was filled and overflowing. The trial lasted seven days. It was widely reported at home and overseas. The facts were hardly in dispute. The contest was on the law. The main dispute was whether the jury were to inquire into the subjective intention of the publisher – into his state of mind – so as to see whether he *intended* to shock and horrify: or whether they were to inquire only into the objective effect of the publication – whether it was *such as* to shock and horrify.

Counsel cited to the judge books on either side. The argument on the law finished at about four o'clock. The judge only had overnight to prepare his decision on it.

ii *The ruling on the law*

Next morning he gave his ruling in favour of the objective test. It was in these terms:

The offence of blasphemous libel today occurs when there is published anything concerning God, Christ or the Christian religion in terms so scurrilous, abusive or offensive as to outrage the feelings of any member of or sympathizer with the Christian religion and would tend to lead to a breach of the peace.

I would be prepared to extend the definition to cover similar attacks on some other religion, as we have now become a multi-religion state, but it is not necessary for me to go so far for the purpose of the present case.

iii *A masterly summing-up*

After that ruling on the law, counsel made their speeches to the jury. The judge then summed up. He tells us in his book that he seemed to be inspired by divine impulse. This is what he says:

> From the time the trial began, I had an extraordinary feeling of unreality: that I was rather watching the trial, instead of presiding over it. I have never experienced a similar sensation before or since. As for the summing-up itself, I can confidently assert that it was the best, by far, that I have ever given. I can say this without blushing because, throughout its preparation, and also when delivering it, I was half-conscious of being guided by some superhuman inspiration.

(I would mention that later on, in the House of Lords, Lord Diplock said: 'The judge summed up to the jury in masterly fashion.' So did Lord Scarman.)

iv *Found Guilty*

At the end of the summing-up, the jury went out. After $4\frac{1}{2}$ hours they came back – not yet agreed. The judge told them that he would be prepared to accept a majority decision. After another half-hour they came back. By a majority of 10 to 2 they found the defendants Guilty.

The judge fined the company, Gay News Ltd, £1,000 and ordered it to pay four-fifths of the prosecution costs. The editor was fined £500 and ordered to pay one-fifth of the prosecution costs.

5 The appeal

i *The objective test*

The Court of Appeal, in a fully reasoned judgment by Lord Justice Roskill, upheld the conviction.[1] So did the House of

[1] *R v Lemon* [1979] AC 617.

Lords. But only by a majority of 3 to 2. The minority (Lord Diplock and Lord Edmund-Davies) held that it was necessary for the prosecution to prove a *wicked intent* by the publisher or the author in the sense that *subjectively* it was his *intention* to shock and arouse resentment among believing Christians: whereas the majority (Lord Dilhorne, Lord Russell of Killowen and Lord Scarman) held that his intention was not material. It was sufficient that he had published matter which, considered *objectively*, was likely in itself to shock and arouse resentment in any believing Christian, even though he did not intend it to do so. They applied the same test as Lord Mansfield had applied in the cases of seditious libel.

ii *Blasphemy defined*

Lord Scarman quoted with approval this passage:[1]

Every publication is said to be blasphemous which contains any contemptuous, reviling, scurrilous or ludicrous matter relating to God, Jesus Christ, or the Bible, or the formularies of the Church of England as by law established. It is not blasphemous to speak or publish opinions hostile to the Christian religion, or to deny the existence of God, if the publication is couched in decent and temperate language. The test to be applied is as to the manner in which the doctrines are advocated and not as to the substance of the doctrines themselves.

Everyone who publishes any blasphemous document is guilty of the [offence] of publishing a blasphemous libel.

Everyone who speaks blasphemous words is guilty of the [offence] of blasphemy.

6 The judge was a Jew

i *Able, learned and upright*

So the judge was held right. He was, as it happened, a Jew. He was the first Jewish judge to try a case of blasphemy in this country. He did it admirably. He quotes in his book a

---

[1] *Stephen's Digest of the Criminal Law* (1950), 9th edn, Article 214. (Quoted [1979] AC 617, 665–666.)

striking passage by Lord Macaulay in a debate in Parliament in 1833:

It has been said that it would be monstrous to see a Jew judge try a man for blasphemy. In my opinion it is monstrous to see any judge try a man for blasphemy under the present law. But, if the law on that subject were in a sound state, I do not see why a conscientious Jew might not try a blasphemer. Every man, I think, ought to be at liberty to discuss the evidence of religion; but no man ought to be at liberty to force on the unwilling ears and eyes of others sounds and sights which must cause annoyance and irritation . . .

These, Sir, are the principles on which I would frame the law of blasphemy; and if the law were so framed, I am at a loss to understand why a Jew might not enforce it as well as a Christian. I am not a Roman Catholic; but if I were a judge at Malta, I should have no scruple about punishing a bigoted Protestant who should burn the Pope in effigy before the eyes of thousands of Roman Catholics. I am not a Mussulman; but if I were a judge in India, I should have no scruple about punishing a Christian who should pollute a mosque. Why, then, should I doubt that a Jew, raised by his ability, learning, and integrity to the judicial bench, would deal properly with any person who, in a Christian country, should insult the Christian religion?

Alan King-Hamilton was all these – able, learned and upright. He dealt properly with *Gay News*.

ii *Were the majority right?*

After all is said and done, however, I am not sure that the majority of the House of Lords were right. If the minority view was accepted so that the intent of the publisher was to be considered subjectively – and the publisher had given evidence of it – I expect he would have said that *Gay News* was only for homosexuals but that he did not expect it to reach any Christian believers who were homosexuals. He would have added that, if it did, they would not be shocked or offended by it: or at any rate he did not intend them to be shocked or offended by it. On that evidence, the jury might have given him the benefit of the doubt and found him Not Guilty.

The newspapers, as you might expect, gave the decision a mixed reception. *The Times* said the verdict was right 'on the law as it stands,' but that the time had come for the law to be changed. *The Daily Telegraph* approved of both the verdict and the law. *The Guardian* disapproved of both. What do you think?

Part Eleven

Persecution

Introduction

Throughout the history of mankind there is one race that has been persecuted more than any other. It is the Jews. I speak of them as a 'race.' But in view of the Lords' decision in the *Sikh Boy's Turban case*[1] I might also say an 'ethnic group.' They have had an influence far outstripping their numbers. Why have they had this influence? Why have they been persecuted so greatly? Why have they been hated so much? I cannot tell. But I can tell you something of their story. I had occasion to look into it when I gave a lecture in March 1984 in memory of George Webber, a much beloved Jew, who was a Professor of Law at University College, London.

When I was at the Bar, I was asked this question: Have the Jews any right to be here in England? That was in the year 1938 just before the war. The solicitors wanted my opinion upon it. Their client was, no doubt, someone who was in favour of the Nazis. He wanted us to get rid of the Jews here altogether just as Hitler had done in Germany. Many Jews had fled from Germany and come to England. They sought refuge here and had been given it. Could they not be sent back whence they came? You may be surprised, but I have to tell you that there was some slight basis for the question. It was this. In the year 1290 one of the greatest of our Kings, Edward the First, banished all the Jews from England. That is undoubted. It is a historical fact – a landmark of the first importance. It was said that he did it by Act of Parliament

---

[1] *Mandla (Sewa Singh) v Dowell Lee* [1983] 2 WLR 620.

and that the Act had never been repealed. So it still held sway here. So ran the argument.

I had no difficulty in dealing with it. I did look into the history of it and found that ever since the days of Cromwell the Jews had been admitted here and eventually they have been given complete emancipation and equality with everyone else. That long history was enough to dispel any remains of Edward the First's order expelling them.

1 The Jews in legend and literature

1 In legend

i *The 'Wandering Jew'*

You know, of course, that throughout much of their long history, the Jews have been wandering across the face of the earth. Starting from Palestine – after the fall of Jerusalem in 70 AD – they have dispersed everywhere. The 'Wandering Jew' is a legend. It is said that when they were dragging Jesus from the judgment hall, the Jewish porter employed by Pontius Pilate struck Jesus on the back and said: 'Go faster, Jesus. Why dost thou linger?' To which Jesus replied: 'I indeed am going but thou shalt tarry till I come.' By those words the Jew was condemned to wander about the earth until Christ's second coming.

ii *He is converted*

There is a charming addition to this legend given by Matthew Paris, an English monk of St Albans. He died in 1259 AD. He tells us that the Jew who struck Christ was converted soon after and named Joseph. He lives for ever and is now a very grave and holy person. This was good propaganda for the conversion of the Jews. It may indeed have influenced the King of that time (Henry the Third) to found a charity for converted Jews.

iii *They retain their characteristics*

Despite their wanderings, the Jews have kept some characteristics which are distinctive of them, especially their features and their mental ability. This is largely because of their strong family ties and traditions. Most countries have settlements of them. They form distinct communities within the larger wholes. Only since 1947 have the Jews had a state of their own – the state of Israel. The brotherhood of Jews is world-wide.

iv *They are persecuted*

Yet the strange thing is that the Jews everywhere have been treated differently from other communities. They have been hated in country after country. In century after century. They have been despised. They have been rejected. They have been persecuted. They have been massacred. From the terrible persecution of the Jews in Spain by the Inquisition to the extermination of the German Jews in the twentieth century in the gas chambers.

v *Anti-Semitic*

So persistent has feeling been against the Jews that we have a word to describe it. It is 'anti-Semitic.' 'Sem' is the same as 'Shem.' Shem was one of the three sons of Noah (Shem and Ham and Japheth) who went forth out of the ark. You will all know the fable of Noah and the ark, of the flood of waters that covered the earth, and of the animals going in two by two. I call it a fable because I do not believe in the verbal inspiration of the Bible any more than most of you. In the book of *Genesis* it is said:

And God blessed Noah and his sons, and said unto them, Be fruitful, and multiply, and replenish the earth (*Genesis* 9:1) . . . These are the three sons of Noah: and of them was the whole earth overspread (*Genesis* 9:19).

The word 'Semite' may have some wider racial meaning,

but anti-Semitism today means simply 'opposed to the Jews.'

2 In literature

Another remarkable thing is the immense influence of the literature of the Jews. The *Old Testament* was originally in Hebrew. It was translated into Greek. The Greek was translated into English by William Tyndale. It takes up three-quarters of the *Authorised Version* of the *Bible*. I would beg your leave to give you instances of its influence.

i *Adam and Eve*

The story of Adam and Eve in the Garden of Eden (in *Genesis*) is known everywhere:

Who told thee that thou wast naked? Hast thou eaten of the tree, whereof I commanded thee that thou shouldest not eat? And the man said, The woman whom thou gavest to be with me, she gave me of the tree, and I did eat. And the Lord God said unto the woman, What is this that thou hast done? And the woman said, The serpent beguiled me, and I did eat. (*Genesis* 3:11–13).

ii *The Ten Commandments*

The Ten Commandments which Moses carried down from the mount gave to the people of Israel a code of conduct which was accepted as authoritative by all (*Deuteronomy 5:1–21*):

And Moses called all Israel, and said unto them, Hear, O Israel, the statutes and judgments which I speak in your ears this day, that ye may learn them, and keep, and do them. . . .

The Commandments are repeated in the *Book of Common Prayer* of 1662 of the Church of England, headed by the rubric:

Then shall the Priest, turning to the people, rehearse distinctly all the TEN COMMANDMENTS; and the people still kneeling shall, after every Commandment, ask God mercy for their transgression thereof for the time past, and grace to keep the same for the time to come, as followeth.

313

iii *David and Goliath*

The triumph of David over Goliath is known to every child:

And David put his hand in his bag, and took thence a stone, and slang it, and smote the Philistine in his forehead, that the stone sunk into his forehead; and he fell upon his face to the earth (I *Samuel* 17:49).

iv The Psalms

The Psalms of David were the hymn-book of the Jewish Church. They are repeated in the *Book of Common Prayer*. They are one of our greatest literary inheritances. They are said daily in our churches. *Psalm* 15 is usually sung at the beginning of the legal year in Westminster Abbey:

Lord, who shall dwell in thy tabernacle: or who shall rest upon thy holy hill? Even he, that leadeth an uncorrupt life: and doeth the thing which is right, and speaketh the truth from his heart. . . .

v '*Remember thy Creator*'

The words of the Preacher are put to music in the loveliest of anthems. I remember how they impressed me, as an undergraduate, when they were sung by the choir in my own college chapel at Magdalen:

Remember now thy Creator in the days of thy youth, while the evil days come not, nor the years draw nigh, when thou shalt say, I have no pleasure in them; . . . Or ever the silver cord be loosed, or the golden bowl be broken, or the pitcher be broken at the fountain, or the wheel broken at the cistern. Then shall the dust return to the earth as it was: and the spirit shall return unto God who gave it (*Ecclesiastes* 12:1, 6–7).

vi The New Testament

The New Testament is not accepted by the Jews. It is rejected by them. It has had even greater influence than the *Old Testament*. It contains the life and teaching of Our Lord Jesus Christ who was a Jew – and of all the twelve apostles who were Jews – and the letters of Paul who was a Jew. It contains the Sermon on the Mount which should be of comfort to the Jews, especially these two verses:

314

Blessed are ye, when men shall revile you, and persecute you, and shall say all manner of evil against you falsely, for my sake. Rejoice, and be exceeding glad: for great is your reward in heaven: for so persecuted they the prophets which were before you (*Matthew* 5:11–12).

2 The Jews in England

1 They come and go

i *Their 'coming' here*

The Jews came in numbers to England after the Norman conquest. They had no stake in the land. They were housed in separate quarters in the chief cities and towns of England. Winchester still has its 'Jewry Street.' Lincoln still has its 'Jew's House.' The Jews were vassals of the King. He treated them as his private property. They financed him. They were, however, most unpopular with the rest of the people. It was because they lent out money on usury. But the King protected them – because he needed them. He allowed them to have their own services in their own synagogues, provided they held them in 'low voice' so that the Christians did not hear. Professor G M Trevelyan puts this early period of the Norman Kings graphically in his *History of England:*[1]

The Jews were the King's sponges. They sucked up his subjects' money by putting their own out on usury, and were protected from the rage of their debtors solely by the strong arm of the King, who in his turn drew what he wanted from their ever-accumulating wealth. They stood to the King as the villein to his lord; all they had was, theoretically, his. His 'exchequer of the Jews' aided them to collect their debts. They were utterly at his mercy, for he was their only friend in a hostile land. Their unpopularity was twofold, for were they not the arch-creditors when no one else had money to lend on usury, and the arch-infidels when everyone else, of course, believed?

[1] (1945, 3rd edn), p 187.

316

ii *The House of Converts*

Then Henry III had an idea. He thought it would be a good thing to persuade the Jews – as many as he could – to abandon their Hebrew religion and to convert them to Christianity. In 1232 AD he actually formed a charity in aid of converted Jews. He provided a house for them and money to endow it. It was called 'the House of Converts.' It was in London, just off Chançery Lane.

iii *The deacon's apostasy*

But the reverse sometimes happened. A Christian might be converted to the Jewish faith. There is a well-authenticated case in 1222 AD. A deacon was converted for the sake of a Jewess. He was charged before the Archbishop, Stephen Langton, with apostasy. It is a strange word for us. It means renouncing his religious vows. He was convicted and deprived of his holy orders. This is the story as told by Matthew Paris, and retold by Frederick Maitland, the great legal historian, in the *Law Quarterly Review* (April 1886):

An English deacon loved a Jewess with unlawful love, and ardently desired her embraces. 'I will do what you ask,' said she, 'if you will turn apostate, be circumcised, and hold fast the Jewish faith.' When he had done what she bade him, he gained her unlawful love. But this could not long be concealed, and was reported to Stephen of Canterbury. Before him the deacon was accused; the evidence was consistent and weighty; he was convicted and then confessed to these matters . . . And when it was seen that the deacon was circumcised, and that no argument would bring him to his senses, he solemnly apostatised before the archbishop and the assembled prelates in this manner: – a cross with the Crucified was brought before him, and he defiled the cross, saying, 'I renounce the new-fangled law and the comments of Jesus the false prophet,' and he reviled and slandered Mary the mother of Jesus, and made against her a charge not to be repeated. Thereupon the archbishop, weeping bitterly at hearing such blasphemies, deprived him of his orders. And when he had been cast out of the church, Fawkes, who was ever swift to shed blood, at once carried him off and swore, 'By the throat of God! I will cut the throat that uttered such words,' and dragged him away to a secret spot and cut off his head. The poor wretch was born at Coventry. But the

Jewess managed to escape, which grieved Fawkes, who said, 'I am sorry that this fellow goes to hell alone.'

iv *Edward I expels the Jews*

The next King, Edward I, took different measures. By this time, according to the old historians, the Jews had become 'generally disagreeable to the people:' so, as I have told you, in the year 1290 AD he banished them from the kingdom. In the long run this was no bad thing. Professor Trevelyan in his *English Social History* tell us:[1]

In 1290 Edward I had expelled the Jews from England, so putting an end to the older method of raising royal loans. This expulsion of the Jews is one cause why anti-Semitism is today less strong in England than in many countries of Europe: our forefathers were compelled by the action of Edward I to undertake their own financial and intellectual life unaided by Jewry, so that when in Cromwell's time the Jews were allowed to return, the English had learnt to stand alone, and could meet without jealousy that gifted race on equal terms.

v *The profane villain*

You may be interested in an incident in the expulsion which is given by Dr Tovey in his *Anglia Judaica*:

The richest of the Jews having embarked themselves, with their treasure, in a tall ship of great Burthen; when it was under sail, and gotten down the Thames, toward the mouth of the river, beyond Queenborough, the Master of it, confederating with some of the mariners, invented a strategem to destroy them. And to bring the same to pass, commanded to cast anchor, and rode at the same, till the ship, at low water, lay upon the sands: and then pretending to walk on shore for his health and diversion, invited the Jews to go along with him; which they, nothing suspecting, readily consented to; and continued there till the tide began to come in again; which as soon as the Master perceived, he privily stole away, and was again drawn up into the ship, as had been before concerted.

But the Jews, not knowing the danger, continued to amuse themselves as before. Till at length, observing how fast the tide came in upon them, they crowded all to the ship's side, and called out for help. When he, like a profane villain, instead of giving them assistance, scoffingly made answer that they ought rather to call upon Moses, by whose conduct

[1] (1946, 2nd edn), p 32.

their fathers passed through the Red Sea, and who was still able to deliver them out of those raging floods which came in upon them: and so, without saying any more, leaving them to the mercy of the waves, they all miserably perished.

But the fact coming, somehow or other, to be known, the miscreants were afterwards tryed for it, by the Justices Itinerent in Kent, convicted of murder and hanged.

2 Rolls House

i *Granted to the Master of the Rolls*

By banishing the Jews, Edward I reduced the number of residents in the house for converted Jews. As there were to be no more Jews in England, there were none to be converted. The King saw this coming. He appointed the Master of the Rolls to be the keeper of the house for converted Jews. By letters patent he granted to him the house, the chapel and all the estate. The old name of 'the House of Converts' was no longer appropriate. It was changed. The house became Rolls House, the chapel became Rolls Chapel, the whole became the Rolls Estate.

ii *A high and profitable office*

Over the years the Master of the Rolls took full advantage of this grant to him. He became a property developer. He built houses all along Fetter Lane and Chancery Lane. He let them to tenants and received much rent from them. Many of them were burnt down in the Great Fire of London and replaced to the profit of the Master of the Rolls.

His office was one of the most profitable in the land and the least onerous. The King used to sell it – or the reversion of it – to the highest bidder.

iii *Smallpox seized him*

In proof of his wealth, there is a true account given by Edward Foss in his *Judges of England*.[1] It tells how Sir Charles

[1] (1870 London).

Caesar bought the office of Master of the Rolls. His father, Sir Julius Caesar, had been the Master of the Rolls. In 1639 Sir Charles paid

for that 'high and profitable place' no less than £15,000, 'broad pieces of gold,' with a loan of £2,000 more when the King went to meet his rebellious Scottish army. It is difficult to regret that he did not live long enough to profit by this iniquitous traffic of the judicial seat, as disgraceful to one party as the other. In November 1642 the smallpox seized the family,

and they all died including the Master of the Rolls himself.

iv *The end of the Rolls Estate*

The Master of the Rolls remained the owner until 1837. Then, as I briefly told you in *The Family Story*, Lord Langdale, the then Master, was very keen on preserving the records of the realm. At his instance, the Rolls Estate was by statute transferred to the Crown. Rolls House and Rolls Chapel were pulled down. The Public Record Office stands on their site in Chancery Lane – a fine purpose-built Victorian edifice.

3 In the time of Elizabeth I

i *The Jews trickle back*

The banishment of the Jews was never fully complete. Even in 1290. Some were converted to Christianity. They stayed. Others changed their names or went underground. So they were not found out. Over the next 200–300 years there was a trickle of Jews from Europe. By the time of Elizabeth I there were many Jews scattered throughout England. Even the Queen's physician, Roderigo Lopez, was a converted Jew.

ii *A plot to poison the Queen*

Roderigo Lopez was born a Jew in Portugal. He came to England and was a house physician at St Bartholomew's

Hospital. He became converted to Christianity. The historian, Harvey, tells us that Lopez

> by a kind of Jewish practis hath growen to much wealth and sum reputation as well with ye Queen herself as with sum of ye greatest Lordes and Ladyes.

Lopez engaged in a plot to poison the Queen. He accepted from the King of Spain 'a very good jewel garnished with sundry stones of good .value.' He was charged and tried at Guildhall. The prosecution was conducted by Sir Edward Coke. Addressing the jury, Coke said that Lopez was 'a perjured and murdering villain and Jewish doctor, worse than Judas himself.' He was convicted and sentenced to death. He was hanged and quartered on 7 June 1594. On the scaffold he said: 'I love the Queen as well as I love Jesus Christ.' William Camden, a historian of that time, tells us that this saying 'from a man of the Jewish profession moved no small laughter among the standers-by.'[1]

iii *The prototype of Shylock*

Lopez was taken by Shakespeare as the prototype of Shylock. You will remember *The Merchant of Venice*. It appeared a year or two after the execution of Lopez. It exemplified the public feeling of the time against the Jews. There was a famous actor, Richard Burbage, who played the part of Shylock. He died in 1618. His funeral elegy spoke of his playing the part of 'the red-haired Jew who sought the bankrupt merchant's pound of flesh.'

iv *'This cruel devil'*

I know well that play, *The Merchant of Venice*. I have quoted lines from it a thousand times. You will remember Shylock's demand for his pound of flesh:

> My deeds upon my head! I crave the law,
> The penalty and forfeit of my bond.[2]

[1] For this account, see *Dictionary of National Biography*.
[2] Act IV, sc 1.

And then Bassanio's plea to Portia:

> And I beseech you,
> Wrest once the law to your authority:
> To do a great right, do a little wrong,
> And curb this cruel devil of his will.

Note the words, 'this cruel devil.' So Shakespeare portrayed the Jew.

v *The doctrine of precedent*

This was followed by Portia's eloquent support of the doctrine of precedent, of which I have told you before:

> It must not be; there is no power in Venice
> Can alter a decree established:
> 'Twill be recorded for a precedent,
> And many an error, by the same example,
> Will rush into the state: it cannot be.

She received Shylock's celebrated commendation:

> A Daniel come to judgment! yea, a Daniel!
> O wise young judge, how I do honour thee!

You know the sequel. You know how Portia got round the doctrine of precedent – by requiring the cutting of the pound of flesh without shedding 'one drop of Christian blood.'

vi *'A Daniel come to judgment!'*

I used often to wonder why Shylock spoke of Daniel as being a wise judge. I knew from the book of *Daniel* in the *Old Testament* of his dreams and of his being cast into the den of lions. But that book told me nothing of his judicial qualities. Those are to be found in the *Apocrypha*. They are in the book of *Daniel and Susanna*.

vii *This was his judgment*

Susanna was a beautiful and devout woman. Two Jewish elders cast lustful eyes on her. When she refused them, they

322

gave evidence against her. They said she had been guilty of adultery with a young man. She was condemned to death. Then Daniel came forward. He urged that there be a new trial. (It is only in very recent times that the Court of Appeal here has been able to order a new trial.) The story in the *New English Bible* proceeds:

The Lord heard her cry. Just as she was being led off to execution, God inspired a devout young man named Daniel to protest, and he shouted out, 'I will not have this woman's blood on my head.' All the people turned and asked him, 'What do you mean by that?' He came forward and said: 'Are you such fools, you Israelites, as to condemn a woman of Israel, without making careful inquiry and finding out the truth? Re-open the trial; the evidence these men have brought against her is false.'

The trial was re-opened. Daniel examined the two elders separately. They told inconsistent stories. One said the two were together under a clove tree. The other said it was under a yew tree. They were disbelieved. The story goes on:

Then the whole assembly gave a great shout and praised God, the saviour of those who trust in him. They turned on the two elders, for out of their own mouths Daniel had convicted them of giving false evidence; they dealt with them according to the law of Moses, and put them to death, as they in their wickedness had tried to do to their neighbour. . . .

And then the end of the story is given:

And from that day forward Daniel was a great man among his people.

4 Cromwell allows them in

i *He consults the judges*

I have told you how the Jews were disliked in the reign of Elizabeth I. Fifty years later, at the time of Oliver Cromwell, the feeling against them had died down. A deputation made a petition for leave for them to return. Cromwell referred it to a Commission of Merchants and Divines. They recommended that the Jews be refused entry. Cromwell consulted the judges. They said they knew of no law against it. So the

Jews began to return. They lived here openly. Over the next 100 years, Jews from Central and East Europe came over in great numbers. By the end of the eighteenth century there were 20,000 in London, most of them very poor. By the end of the nineteenth century there were 67,000 in London.

ii *Pride of race*

Many of the Jews were proud of their Jewish race and Jewish faith. They retained their Hebrew names and their belief in the *Old Testament*. They married only Jews and so kept the purity of their race and faith. But some were converted to Christianity and believed in the *New Testament*. Yet others intermarried with Christians.

But still our courts did not recognise the Jewish faith. Thus in 1754 a Portuguese Jew who had come here made his will directing that £1,200 should be invested in government securities and the income applied for 'daily reading of the Jewish law and for advancing and propagating their holy religion.' Lord Hardwicke held that the bequest was invalid because it was 'in contradiction to the Christian religion which is part of the law of the land: for the constitution and policy of this nation is founded thereon.'[1]

iii *Described by Trevelyan*

I am no historian, so I would cover this period by taking the description given by Professor Trevelyan in his *English Social History:*[2]

Between the time when the Jews were expelled by Edward I and the time when they were readmitted by Cromwell, the English had learnt to manage their own financial and business affairs. There was therefore no danger of Hebrew domination and of the answering reaction of anti-Semitism. By Hanoverian times, England was strong enough to digest a moderate influx of Jews and, as the prosperity of Holland declined, many of them moved from Amsterdam to London and became prominent there in stockbroking. The Jew helped the development of 'the City.' 'He was ubiquitous and enterprising, persistent but not pugnacious; he

[1] *De Costa v De Paz* (1754) 2 Swan 487.
[2] (1946, 2nd edn), pp 394–395.

324

ran after customers without regard to his dignity, and made a profit out of articles and transactions which other people rejected or despised. For international finance the Jews had a special bent, overcoming by their tribal bonds the boundaries of nations, and yet as individuals retaining that mental detachment which is so necessary to financial analysis.'[1] During the Seven Years' War, Sampson Gideon was important in the City as a banker; in the next generation the Goldsmids came to the front; and in 1805 Nathan Rothschild founded the most famous of all Jewish houses in London, usefully linked with the family's establishments in other European lands. But besides the great City Jews, there was also a low type of Hebrew moneylender now prominent, abhorred not without reason by his victims, the impecunious and unthrifty of all classes.

To this I would add a few lines in which Byron told of the influence of Nathan Rothschild in international affairs. He provided funds for Wellington throughout the Peninsular War. In *Don Juan* in 1823 Byron wrote:[2]

> Who hold the balance of the world? . . .
> Jew Rothschild, and his fellow Christian Baring.
>
> Those . . .
> Are the true lords of Europe. Every loan
> Is not a merely speculative hit,
> But seats a nation or upsets a throne.
> . . . and even thy silver soil, Peru,
> Must get itself discounted by a Jew.

[1] C R Fay *Great Britain from Adam Smith to the Present Day*, p 128.
[2] Byron *Don Juan*, c XII, st v, vi.

3 The Jews in modern times

Introduction

Now I come to modern times – that is to say, from the accession of Queen Victoria to the present day. In this period the Jews in England have been accepted. All civil disabilities have been removed. It is to England that they and their forefathers have come, sometimes as immigrants, sometimes as exiles, sometimes as refugees. It is in England that they have found a home. They have filled the highest positions.

Benjamin Disraeli, first Earl of Beaconsfield, became Prime Minister. In 1876 he made a great financial coup. He got Nathan's son, Lionel Rothschild, to find £3,700,000 for the Suez Canal shares. He wrote to the Queen:

It is just settled. You have it, Madam. The entire interest of the Khedive is yours, Madam.

The delighted Queen replied:

This is indeed a great and important event.

Sir George Jessel became Master of the Rolls. He was one of the greatest judges in English legal history.

Sir Rufus Isaacs became Lord Chief Justice of England, Ambassador in Washington, Viceroy of India and Marquess of Reading. Fame indeed!

But in some parts of Europe, particularly in Germany, it has been very different.

326

The holocaust

i *The massacre of the Jews*

Never before had they been so systematically massacred as they were in Germany during the war of 1939–1945. There was no excuse or justification for it whatsoever. The Jews in Germany had been guilty of no offence. They were decent, law-abiding citizens. They had contributed greatly to the welfare of the state. They were in the forefront in science, in law, and in music. Yet Hitler whipped up hatred against them. At the time, we ordinary people in England knew little of what was happening. At any rate, none of us in the forces knew of it. We were only concerned with beating the enemy. I take this from the *Encyclopaedia Britannica* under the title *Germany*:

The Jews were singled out for attack from the first day of Hitler's Chancellorship. A law of the 7 April 1933 decreed the dismissal of the Jews from government service and the universities; they were also debarred from entering the professions. Under the Nuremberg laws of 15 September 1935, marriages between Jews and persons of 'German blood' were forbidden and the Jews were virtually deprived of all their rights. Their persecution reached its climax in the pogrom of 9/10 November 1938 carried out under the directive of the SS. The greater part of all Jewish property was confiscated and the Jews were restricted to a ghetto-like existence until the war, when they were systematically put to death. Altogether in German-occupied Europe, out of a total of about 8,300,000 Jews, 6,000,000 were killed or died in extermination camps of starvation or disease.

They were herded into gas chambers and put to death. The horrors of it all haunt mankind still. The massacre was not because of their religion but because of their race. Christian Jews were exterminated alongside Jewish Jews.

ii *Another exodus*

This terrible persecution led to another exodus. Many Jews came to England. They were accepted without restrictions. Many proved themselves to be good citizens. Starting with nothing, they achieved success in commerce and industry and in property development. Others came to the fore in the professions – in science, in law, and in medicine.

327

4 Coming together

1 'Jesus was a Jew'

It is commonplace to speak of 'the Jews.' The very phrase has some racial significance. When we speak of the 'Jewish lobby' in the United States bringing its influence to bear on policy in favour of the state of Israel, the very phrase 'Jewish lobby' has a racial significance. Even today, many are inclined to disparage the Jews, again with racial overtones. It is time all that was done away with. Christians and Jews should come together in the search for truth. This was emphasised in a striking leading article in *The Times* on Easter Saturday 2 April 1983. The heading was 'Jesus was a Jew' and it declared:

The message and vision of Easter must surely be that the triumph of the Resurrection is a universal truth, not a sectarian one, to be experienced and shared by all mankind. The Christian, in embracing mankind, must necessarily start with the Jews. There is unfinished business here; a legacy to be unwound; old old wounds. Jesus was a Jew. The Christian Church was started by Jews. The Bible, written by Jews, provides all Christians with their basic knowledge of God, without which they would be deprived of the elementary theology and morality common to both persuasions. . . .

. . . There are many signs that Christians are rediscovering the Jewish roots of their faith. The spirit of renewal within Christian churches is alive at all levels. There is a hum of desire to overcome the unmentionable fact – on both sides – that Jesus was a Jew. It is echoed among Jews themselves, rediscovering Jesus after the enmities of the Diaspora. Since the state of Israel was founded more works on Jesus have been published by Jews than during the previous twenty centuries.

Thus Jesus, the Jew, may become a symbol of some ultimate unity in the quest for truth between Christian and Jew, just as He is between Christian and Christian . . .

It is a question of recognising the massive gift with which Jewry has endowed the Christian world, and of rejoicing in it. That too would be a resurrection.

2 The Lord Chancellor sums up

In his Hamlyn Lecture in 1983 the Lord Chancellor, Lord Hailsham of St Marylebone, summed up in these words:[1]

When I was a boy, anti-Semitism was even intellectually respectable, and often unconsciously assumed, as much by so-called Liberals as by others. Both Belloc and Chesterton were distinctly anti-Semitic in tone, as, at the other end of the political spectrum, were Kipling and, I think, Saki. Yet, as time has gone on, Anglo Jewry, without being absorbed into something non-Jewish, has become a valued, loyal, and respectable part of the British establishment, enriching cultural, economic and political life, and that without positive discrimination in its favour.

[1] *Hamlyn Revisited: The British Legal System Today* (1983) p 9.

Part Twelve

Murder

Introduction

Now for a subject in which everyone is interested. It is the law of murder. During my time the law of murder has changed greatly. This is partly because capital punishment has been abolished. But also because of judicial decisions. They are landmarks. They should be known to all students of criminal law.

The leading case is undoubtedly *Director of Public Prosecutions v Smith*.[1] I sat on it myself as a Lord of Appeal in the House of Lords. I have told a good deal about it in *The Family Story* (pages 195–197). But now I wish to put it into context. So I will tell of cases before it: and cases after it.

[1] [1961] AC 290.

1 Cases before Smith's case

1 The question

i *Murder or manslaughter?*

You will know that until 1969 there was only one sentence for murder. It was capital punishment. So in nearly every case the accused sought to reduce it to manslaughter because then the judge had a discretion. He could make the sentence light or heavy if he chose.

ii *State of mind*

You will also find that in nearly every case the accused had done some act which caused the death. The controversy which raged was about his state of mind. What was his intention? If he struck or shot a man, intending to kill him, of course it was murder. But if he hit him on the head with a hammer, not meaning to kill him, but only to hurt him – and yet he died – was it murder or manslaughter? And then take this very point in *Smith's case*:

If he drove his car straight at a man in the road, not meaning to kill him, but to frighten him and make him jump out of the way – and the man did not and was killed – Was it murder or manslaughter?

I will tell you of the landmark cases on the subject.

2 The Fenian conspirators

i *Who were they?*

The case was in 1868. At that time the Fenians were very

334

troublesome. They were an association of Irish people who sought to overthrow the English Government in Ireland. They conspired to release a man who was in Clerkenwell Prison. They did not intend to kill anyone or even to injure anyone. They only intended to blow down a wall with explosives. Yet they were held guilty of murder.

The case was not reported in the Law Reports, but only in *The Times* newspaper for 28 April 1868.

ii *They blow down a wall*

The Fenian conspirators desired to get a man named Burke out of Clerkenwell Prison. So they planned to blow down the wall of the prison with gunpowder just at the time when the prisoners were taking their exercise. They set a keg of gunpowder next the wall and a man named Barrett lit the fuse. His *purpose* was to blow down the wall. His *desire* was for Burke to escape. He achieved his *purpose* – the wall was blown down – but he did not get what he *desired*. Burke did not escape. The Governor of the prison had been forewarned of the plot and had changed the hour when the prisoners took their exercise. But now comes the point. The charge of gunpowder was so large that it not only blew down the wall but destroyed houses near to it. A woman sitting in her home was cut by flying glass in the throat and so injured that she died. Barrett was held guilty of murder. And this was not because it was his purpose to kill or to inflict grievous bodily harm. His purpose was to blow down the wall. And it was not because of constructive malice. It was because he must, as a responsible man, have been aware that his act in exploding this large keg of gunpowder, so near to houses, was likely to cause death or grievous bodily harm to someone or other: and, as it did cause death, he ws guilty of murder. No one in England at the time doubted that it was murder. The only complaint made by *The Times* newspaper in its leading article was that the other conspirators were not found guilty as well as Barrett. And no one, so far as I know, has doubted it since.

iii *The summing-up*

The case was tried by two of the best of our English judges, the Lord Chief Justice, Sir Alexander Cockburn, and Baron Bramwell. The Chief Justice, summing-up to the jury, told them:

If a man did an act, more especially if that were an illegal act, although its immediate purpose might not be to take life, yet if it were such that life was necessarily endangered by it, – if a man did such an act, not with the purpose of taking life but with the *knowledge or belief that life was likely to be sacrificed by it*, that was not only murder by the law of England, but by the law of probably every other country. *If the jury were of opinion that those who blew up that prison wall with gunpowder must have been aware that in so doing they would necessarily occasion* danger, disaster, and *probably* destruction of life, *they were morally as well as legally guilty of the crime of murder.*

3 The Somerset milkman

i *A presumption of guilt*

Now I turn to the famous case of *Woolmington v DPP*[1]. For two centuries, at least, the judges had held that if a man killed another, it was presumed against him that he was guilty of murder. It was for him to prove his innocence or, at any rate, to prove that there were mitigating circumstances which could reduce it from murder to manslaughter.

That doctrine was overruled by the House of Lords in 1935. I was still a junior at the Bar. I remember well the stir it made.

ii *His wife left him*

It is a sad story about a man and his girl, Reg and Vi. Reg was a milkman on a farm. He was 21. Vi was 17 and lived with her mother in a village nearby. They fell in love. She became pregnant. Her baby was expected in October 1934. They got married two months before it was due. They went to live in a tied cottage on the farm. But in November 1934,

[1] [1935] AC 462.

when the baby was only one month old, Vi left Reg and went back with the baby to live with her mother. Reg was very distressed. Time after time he implored her to come back, but she would not.

iii *He got a gun*

Then came 2 December 1934. Reg had had a sleepless night worrying over the loss of Vi. He got up early and went to milk the cows. After milking, he went to the barn. He took the farmer's gun off the rack. It had been used for shooting rooks. He sawed off the barrel and loaded it with two cartridges. He got a piece of paper and then, or later, wrote this on it:

> Good bye all.
> It is agonies to carry on any longer. I have kept true hoping she would return this is the only way out. They ruined me and I'll have my revenge. May God forgive me for doing this but it is the Best thing. Ask Jess to call for the money paid on motor bike (Wed.). Her mother is no good on this earth but have no more cartridges only 2 one for her and one for me. I am of a sound mind now. Forgive me for all trouble caused.

> Good bye
ALL
I love Violet with all my heart
Reg

iv *He shoots her dead*

He then took the gun, got on his bicycle, and rode to Vi's mother's house. Next door there lived Vi's aunt, her mother's sister. She told the court her story. She was hanging out her washing. She heard Reg say to Vi:

Are you going to come back home?

Vi did not reply or, at any rate, the aunt did not hear it. Reg said:

Where's your mother?

Still no reply.

The aunt heard the door slammed. The gun went off. Reg came out, got on his bicycle and rode off. The aunt went into the house. She found Vi lying on the mat. She had been shot through the heart.

v *Sentenced to death*

That evening Reg was charged with murder. He said:

I want to say nothing, except I done it, and they can do what they like with me. It was jealousy I suppose. Her mother enticed her away from me. I done all I could to get her back. That's all.

Six weeks later he was tried at Taunton Assizes. The jury disagreed. Three weeks later he was tried at Bristol Assizes. The jury found him guilty of murder. He was sentenced to death.

vi *The golden thread*

At the trial the defence was that it was an accident. Reg said that he had intended to commit suicide, and show Vi the gun: but as he was doing so, it went off accidentally. The judge directed the jury that the burden was on Reg to prove that it was an accident. The Court of Criminal Appeal followed all the earlier cases and affirmed the conviction. The House of Lords quashed the conviction. Lord Sankey, the Lord Chancellor went back to first principles:

Throughout the web of the English Criminal Law one golden thread is always to be seen, that it is the duty of the prosecution to prove the prisoner's guilt subject to what I have already said as to the defence of insanity and subject also to any statutory exception. If, at the end of and on the whole of the case, there is a reasonable doubt, created by the evidence given by either the prosecution or the prisoner, as to whether the prisoner killed the deceased with a malicious intention, the prosecution has not made out the case and the prisoner is entitled to an acquittal. No matter what the charge or where the trial, the principle that the prosecution must prove the guilt of the prisoner is part of the common law of England and no attempt to whittle it down can be entertained.

4 A Hampshire jury

I turn to a case which added nothing to the law. I only tell it because it is a good example of the ways of juries. When we had capital punishment, they used to find manslaughter rather than murder.

It was when I was a young Queen's Counsel. I defended a sailor at the Assizes at Winchester. He had strangled a girl on Southampton Common. I urged the jury to find manslaughter. The judge summed up for murder. It was a Hampshire jury and I am a Hampshire man. The jury found manslaughter. The judge was furious. He reproached the jury in these strong words:

Get out of the box. You've been false to your oaths. You're not fit to be there.

But he had to accept the verdict. He could not sentence the sailor to death. He sentenced him to thirteen years' imprisonment.

It was one of my most dramatic cases. If you would like to read the full story, you can find it in *The Family Story* (page 132).

2 Smith's case itself

I now come to *Smith's case* itself. And first I would remind you of the facts of which I have told you before.

1 The Facts

i *The policeman on point duty*

A police constable was on point duty in Woolwich. He stopped a car driven by Smith. He told the driver to pull into the side. There were sacks in the back of the car containing scaffolding chips which had just been stolen. Suddenly the driver accelerated to get away. The policeman jumped on to the bonnet of the car to stop him. The driver zig-zagged trying to shake the policeman off. He did not succeed.

ii *So what did Smith do?*

The policeman had too firm a grip for that. He was stretched across the bonnet and banging on the window to tell Smith to stop. So what did Smith do? He drove his car his car right up close to the approaching traffic so that the policeman's body was struck up against the oncoming cars. Each of the drivers of those cars gave evidence. No one of them spoke of any zig-zagging at the time he was hitting them. They spoke of the car coming at them and swerving towards them. The policeman's body was struck against one car after another. A slight bump on the first. A heavier bump on the second. And a violent blow on the third, so violent that the offside front mudguard was knocked right in by the policeman's body – no marks being left on Smith's car. After that violent blow, the policeman was hurled off and came underneath the fourth car. He suffered a crushed skull and other injuries, from which he died.

2 The trial

i *The judge*

The case was tried at the Central Criminal Court by Mr Justice Donovan, afterwards Lord Donovan. At the Bar he had specialised in tax cases, but on the bench he had proved himself an excellent criminal judge. He consulted Mr Clarke QC, counsel for the defence, about the direction he should give to the jury. He agreed that he should take the words of Lord Goddard in a recent case of *R v Ward*[1].

ii *The summing-up*

The judge did so and told the jury:

If you are satisfied that when he drove his car erratically up the street, *close* to the traffic on the other side, *he must as a reasonable man have contemplated* that grievous bodily harm was likely to result to that officer still clinging on, and that such harm did happen and the officer died in consequence, then the accused is guilty of capital murder . . . on the other hand, if you are not satisfied that *he* intended to inflict grievous bodily harm upon the officer – in other words, if you think *he* could not as a reasonable man have contemplated that grievous bodily harm would result to the officer – well then, the verdict would be manslaughter.

iii *Guilty of murder*

The jury found Smith guilty of murder, and he was sentenced to death. The Court of Criminal Appeal allowed the appeal. They substituted a verdict of manslaughter. The House of Lords restored the conviction for murder. He was not, however, executed. He was reprieved.

[1] [1956] 1 QB 351.

3 The decision is condemned

i *Mischievous and wrong*

The academics bitterly criticised the House. They described the speech of the Lord Chancellor as 'mischievous and wrong.' They alleged that by using the words 'reasonable man' the House had introduced an objective test; whereas in a criminal case the test had always been subjective. Soon afterwards I answered the criticisms. I went to Jerusalem to give the Lionel Cohen lecture at the Hebrew University. In it I tried to explain the misunderstanding, saying:

> Whence comes, then, all this criticism from some of the most respected figures in the academic world? It cannot all be entirely beside the mark. I agree. May it perhaps be that in stressing the test of the reasonable man, that is, the responsible man, the House did not sufficiently point out that it was only a test – a criterion – to help find the intention of the accused man himself, and that ultimately the question is: Did he intend to cause death or grievous bodily harm? That is the subjective proposition which underlies the whole discussion. It is still, as before, the essential element of which the jury must be satisfied before they convict the accused of murder.

ii *The courageous naval officer*

In support of the decision in *Smith's case*, I would mention the case of the courageous naval officer. It was not reported in the Law Reports, but in the newspapers. I remember it well. I referred to it in a later case, *Hardy v Motor Insurers' Bureau*:[1]

> Take the case where the driver of a motor car is determined to escape from lawful apprehension or detention; and, for this purpose, aims his vehicle at a lawful citizen who stands in the way. Like the case of the courageous naval officer in 1944, Captain Binney, who stood in the path of motor bandits calling on them to stop. They ran him down and killed him; and were held guilty of murder. In any such case the driver has one overall intent – to get away at all costs. He is undoubtedly guilty of manslaughter, but may it not also amount to murder? And how do you distinguish between them? Only by reason of his state of mind at the time. If the thought flashed through his mind: 'Get out of the way'; and in

[1] [1964] 2 QB 745, 759.

consequence the man is killed, the driver is guilty of murder. And how can you find out whether such a thought passed through his mind? Only by asking whether, as an ordinary responsible person, he must have been aware that grievous bodily harm was likely to result. Such a state of mind, if death results, makes him guilty of murder.

Surely that is right. As an ordinary responsible person, *he* must have been aware. *He* is the subjective test.

iii *An Act of Parliament*

But the critics were still not satisfied. They were so vociferous that they got Parliament to restate the law as it always had been. By Section 8 of the Criminal Justice Act 1967 a court or jury

shall not be bound in law to infer that he intended or foresaw a result of his action, by reason only of it being a natural and proper consequence of those actions.

iv *Always the law*

That had always been the law. As far back as 1950 in *Hosegood v Hosegood*[1] I said:

When people say that a man must be taken to *intend* the natural consequences of his *acts*, they fall into error: there is no *must* about it: it is only *may*.

And in 1975 in *Hyam v DPP*[2] Lord Hailsham of St Marylebone, Lord Chancellor, said that if my interpretation of *Smith's case* had been adopted

there is little or nothing to over-rule, or indeed to require the intervention of Parliament in 1967.

[1] (1950) 66 TLR (Part 1) 735, 738.
[2] [1975] AC 55 at 72.

3 Later cases

I am comforted to find that two later cases have cleared up any misunderstanding.

1 The house on fire

i *A jealous mistress*

Mrs Hyam was separated from her husband. She met Mr Jones and became his mistress. He afterwards took up with a Mrs Booth, who was separated from her husband. Mrs Hyam was very jealous. She got to know that Mrs Booth was getting a divorce. Mr Jones and Mrs Booth were planning to get married and go on a holiday together. Mrs Hyam was so incensed that she became an incendiary herself.

ii *Petrol through the letterbox*

At two o'clock on a July morning Mrs Hyam drove in a van to Mrs Booth's house. On the way she passed Mr Jones's house. The lights were on. So he was at home. She passed him by. She did not want to hurt him. She went on further a little beyond Mrs Booth's house. She parked her van there.

She took a gallon can of petrol from the van and poured petrol through the letterbox of Mrs Booth's front door. She then put newspaper in the letterbox. She struck a match and lit the paper. There was a tremendous blaze. She then went home, saying nothing to anyone.

Mrs Booth was in the house with her two daughters. She escaped with her son from a window, but her two young daughters, Vivienne and Kim, were overcome by the fumes and died.

iii *Only meant to frighten*

Mrs Hyam was charged with murder of the two girls. Her defence was that she had only intended to frighten Mrs Booth. She asserted that she had not intended to kill or cause bodily harm to anyone. She admitted that she had been reckless. She pleaded guilty to manslaughter.

iv *The summing-up*

The case was tried by Ackner J at the Warwick Crown Court. He directed the jury in words which were much the same as Donovan J in *Smith's case*:

> The prosecution must prove, beyond all reasonable doubt, that the accused intended to (kill or) do serious bodily harm to Mrs Booth, the mother of the deceased girls. If you are satisfied that when the accused set fire to the house she knew that it was highly probable that this would cause (death or) serious bodily harm, then the prosecution will have established the necessary intent. It matters not if her motive was, as she says, to frighten Mrs Booth.

The jury found Mrs Hyam guilty of murder. She was sentenced to life imprisonment.

The Court of Appeal affirmed the conviction. So did the House of Lords, but only by a majority of three to two.

v *Like Smith's case*

If you compare the directions to the jury in *Smith's case* and *Hyam's case* you will see there is precious little difference. The crucial words in Smith's case were:

> If he must as a reasonable man have contemplated that grievous bodily harm was likely to result.

In *Hyam's case* they were:

If she knew that it was highly probable that this would cause serious bodily harm.

So the difference is only between 'what she must have known' and what 'she knew.' Those are the same: because the jury could only find what she 'knew' by saying to themselves 'she must have known.'

The facts were in all essentials identical. In each case the accused must have known that his act was likely to cause grievous bodily harm. In each case his defence was: 'I only meant to frighten.'

2 A row in a public house

i *Grievous bodily harm*

It was surprising that there should have been two Law Lords dissenting in *Hyam's case*. The reason was on a point which had never been challenged in *Smith's case*. In murder, was it enough to show that the accused had intended to inflict 'grievous bodily harm'? or had it to be shown that he intended to 'kill or endanger life'?

ii *Picked up a chair*

It came to a head in the Albin Public House in Margate. Mr Cunningham had a mistress whom he intended to marry. He suspected that a man called Kim was associating sexually with her. Out of jealousy, Cunningham picked up a chair and hit Kim with it. Kim fell to the ground. Cunningham hit him again with the chair as he lay defenceless on the ground. His skull was fractured. He died later.

Cunningham was charged with murder. He contended that it was only manslaughter. He was tried before Lawson J and a jury at the Kent Crown Court. He was found guilty of murder.

iii *The summing-up*

The appeal was only brought because in *Hyam's case* Lord

Diplock and Lord Edmund Davies had said that to constitute murder there must be an intent to 'kill or to endanger life,' whereas everyone had for many years said it was sufficient if there was an intent to do 'grievous bodily harm.'

The trial judge directed the jury in accordance with all the previous authorities. He said to them:

> As a matter of law, the question of fact on which your verdict depends is solely this . . . 'At the time when the defendant inflicted the injuries on Kim . . . did he intend to do him really serious harm?' If the answer to that question is 'yes,' you find him guilty of murder. If the answer to the question is 'no,' then you find him not guilty of murder, but guilty of manslaughter.

The House of Lords unanimously held that the authorities show that it was sufficient to intend 'grievous bodily harm.'

iv *Conclusion*

Looking back at it after those twenty-four years, I think that in *Smith's case* there were some passages of *obiter dicta* which were capable of being misunderstood – and were misunderstood – but fairly considered they were correct. And that the conviction was right, I have no doubt.

Part Thirteen

My Most Important Case

Introduction

I have often been asked: Which of your cases was the most important? Beyond doubt, the Profumo Inquiry. It was a landmark. It was not a law case. But it had a great deal in common with it. For it was an inquiry to find out the truth.

In June 1963 the Government of Mr Harold Macmillan was in jeopardy. Not so much because of the indiscretion of Mr Profumo. But because of the rumours to which it gave rise. First one minister was named. Next another. Up to a dozen names were being bandied about. Each of the rumours spoke of immorality or perversion in high places. If true, they opened the door to blackmail. They made the minister a security risk. He would have to resign. Others too. Each minister was asking himself, 'Will it be me next?' The morale of the Government itself was shaken. Of these rumours the words of Alexander Pope are most apt:[1]

> The flying rumours gather'd as they roll'd
> Scarce any tale was sooner heard than told;
> And all who told it added something new,
> And all who heard it made enlargements too.

So concerned were the Government and the ministers that they felt that the only way was to have an inquiry to see whether there was any truth in these rumours or not. I was asked to conduct it. The issue for me was in effect 'Let justice be done.' As I see it, 'Let justice be done between the ministers and the rumour-mongers.'

[1] *The Temple of Fame*, 1 468.

351

1 'Loud rumour speaks'

1 Two aspects

Besides the rumours, there was another aspect to my inquiry. It was the conduct of Mr Profumo himself. Was there any security risk? I gave a full account of this in the Report which I made in September 1963[1] and there are some extracts in *The Family Story* (pages 217–218) and *The Due Process of Law* (pages 67–73). I will not repeat it now. The affair was given so much publicity at the time that all my older readers will remember it. But for the younger readers, a distinction must be drawn between the security aspect and the moral aspect.

i *The security aspect*

The leading character in the story was Stephen Ward. He was utterly immoral. He picked up pretty girls and procured them to be mistresses to his influential friends. One of these girls was Christine Keeler. She had an affair with Mr John Profumo who was the Secretary of State for War. At the same time she was very friendly with a Russian diplomat, Captain Eugene Ivanov. It was said that she might have got confidential information from Mr Profumo and passed it on to Captain Ivanov.

ii *The moral aspect*

Next there was the moral aspect. This was because Mr

[1] Cmnd 2152.

352

Profumo told the House of Commons, 'There was no impropriety whatsoever in my acquaintanceship with Miss Keeler:' but later he had to admit that this was not true. In consequence, he resigned. This was followed by a spate of rumours to the effect that many ministers of the Crown had been guilty of immorality of one kind or another. I will take some instances.

2 The rumours

i '*The man in the mask*'

One rumour was that another minister was 'the man in the mask.' He took part in a dinner party which was nothing more nor less than a bestial sexual orgy. The men and women were all naked and indulged in indiscriminate sexual intercourse. The minister was said to have worn a mask to disguise his identity. He had a small waitress's apron round his middle: and nothing else.

ii '*The man without a head*'

Another rumour was that another minister was 'the man without a head.' This was because, in a divorce suit, a photograph was produced of improper conduct between a woman and a man: but the man's head had been cut off in the photograph. The minister was said to be the man and that his head had been cut off to conceal his identity. It was said that he had paid money not to be cited as a co-respondent.

iii '*The frequenters of the swimming pool*'

In addition, a French newspaper published a long article purporting to be from London, headed *Tous les familiers de la Piscine du Docteur Ward ne sont pas encore dans le bain* (All frequenters of Dr Ward's swimming pool have not yet been ducked in the water.) In the article the newspaper set out, with added spice, many of the rumours then current. It actually gave the names of some of the ministers.

iv The biggest liar in England

So serious were the rumours that everywhere people compared them with those spread by Titus Oates. In case you do not know your history, I will tell you about him. It was in 1678. Titus Oates was at one time a clergyman of the Church of England. But he became the biggest liar that England has ever known. He made out that the Papists were plotting to take over England. There was no evidence to support it. But he asserted that they had a scheme to set fire to the shipping in the Thames. The Papists were to rise at a signal and massacre all their Protestant neighbours. Three or four schemes had been formed for assassinating the King. He was to be stabbed. He was to be poisoned in his medicine. He was to be shot with silver bullets. Macaulay tells us that 'the public mind was so sore and excitable that these lies readily found credit with the vulgar.'[1] The excitement turned into popular frenzy when a London magistrate was found in a field dead with a sword run through his heart. The people believed that he had been murdered by Roman Catholics.

This frenzy led to most extreme measures being taken against all Roman Catholics. No citizen thought himself safe unless he carried under his coat a small flail loaded with lead to brain the Popish assassins.

The end of it all was that Parliament was dissolved and a new Parliament elected. Something of the kind happened after the Profumo rumours.

v Scandalous rumours

The rumours which followed the Profumo affair were different. They were not of plots to murder. But of misconduct in sexual relations. They were scandalous. People love scandals. They repeat them to everyone they meet, saying, 'Do you know what I have just heard?' Always under a pledge of confidence. 'Don't tell anyone.' The hearer promptly repeats them to the next man who comes along. They spread like wild-fire.

[1] *History of England*, vol I, chap II.

vi *Shakespeare's elegance*

Shakespeare describes scandals in such elegant words that I would remind you of them. He brings in a character called Rumour in the second part of *King Henry IV*. At the very beginning, the first actor comes on to the stage:

> Enter Rumour, painted full of Tongues.

Then this character Rumour speaks to the audience, telling them how much they like to hear rumour:

> Open your ears; For which of you will stop
> The vent of hearing, when loud Rumour speaks?

He goes on to show that rumours thrive upon scandal:

> Upon my tongues continual slanders ride;
> The which in every language I pronounce,
> Stuffing the ears of men with false reports.

He compares rumour to a musical pipe upon which many thoughtless people can easily play a tune:

> Rumour is a pipe
> Blown by surmises, jealousies, conjectures;
> And of so easy and so plain a stop,
> That the blunt monster with uncounted heads,
> The still discordant wavering multitude,
> Can play upon it.

In the story which I tell you, the people of England were 'the blunt monster with uncounted heads.'

vii *'But for the grace of God'*

To return to London in 1963. The leaders of the Labour party were at pains to stress the security aspect of the Profumo affair. They said they were not concerned with the moral aspect. Maybe they were not. Perhaps there were some who were perfectly innocent of any wrongdoing but who said to themselves, on hearing the rumours, 'There but for the grace of God, go I.'

2 A moral issue

1 It is raised

i *A clap of thunder*

It was left to *The Times* to stress the moral aspect. It was nicknamed *The Thunderer* in the 1830s because of the style of criticism used by Edward Sterling. It has thundered since on appropriate occasions. On 11 June 1963 it came out with a great clap of thunder. Its leading article was headed, IT IS A MORAL ISSUE.' IS was in italics. Whilst each of the political parties was playing down the moral issue, *The Times* was playing it up. This is what it said:

Mr Harold Wilson also is a shrewd politician and his immediate reaction was to stress that Labour's concern was about security, not about morals. . . . Everyone has been so busy assuring the public that the affair is not one of morals, that it is time to assert that it is. Morals have been discounted too long. A judge may be justified in reminding a jury, 'This is not a court of morals.' The same exemption cannot be allowed public opinion, without rot setting in and all standards suffering in the long run . . .

No one would wish the security aspects of the matter to be ignored. There is no danger of this . . . For the Conservative Party – and, it is to be hoped, for the nation – things can never be quite the same again . . .

Whether in the next few days some heads fall or none, damage has been done. It may be a caricature for the *Washington Post* to say that 'a picture of widespread decadence beneath the glitter of a large segment of stiff-lipped society is emerging.' But the essence of caricature is to exaggerate real traits. There are plenty of earnest and serious men in the Conservative Party who know that all is not well.

ii *Other ministers come in*

The next day *The Times* brought in other ministers too.

On ministerial morality, all that may be said for the present is that in the middle and lower rungs of the Administration there are now to be heard voices asserting the need for high moral standards in all those who rise to leadership, and insisting that next Monday Mr Macmillan and his principal lieutenants must wipe the slate absolutely clean.

iii *Another clap of thunder*

Then on the next day, 13 June, *The Times* came out with another clap of thunder. In a leading article headed 'A MATTER OF CONSCIENCE' it said:

Throughout the past two days *The Times* has been receiving messages from readers of all kinds. Rarely on any public issue have the letters and telephone calls been so largely one way . . .

This sorry business has passed from being one of politics to one of conscience. Many high-minded men in the Government must be deeply troubled.

iv *Lord Hailsham thunders*

That same evening on the television Lord Hailsham thundered too. According to *The Times* of 17 June he went to the heart of the matter at the outset:

'It's a crisis about national morality, public and private morality, and about the integrity of public life.' Once the matter is accepted on that plane the work of redemption can begin.

2 Political expediency

i *A still small voice*

There came from the side-lines a hint of political ineptitude. It was the still small voice of a Queen's Counsel. *The Times* published a letter on 15 June from Mr Ralph Kilner Brown QC (now a judge of the High Court):

Sir, – Is there not a duty on the Labour Party as the official Opposition to challenge the Government on the moral issue? The reported decision to limit criticism to the security aspect appears to many like me to be a deliberate subordination of moral obligation to political expediency.

The electorate may well ask whether anyone in Parliament cares to speak for them or to represent their notions of what is right and what is wrong.

ii *Is there a decline?*

Although the leaders of the Labour Party asserted vigorously that they were only concerned with the security aspect, they must have noticed the way in which the moral issue was developing in their favour. Nearly every rumour implicated a member of the higher ranks of the Conservative Party. Later on, a member of Lincoln's Inn, writing to *The Times*, gave vent to a surmise which had been current:

The profusion of rumours must surely have arisen in part from political motives and not solely from the desire for financial reward . . .

If the press is in part to blame for the spreading of rumours, so also are professional and amateur politicians for seeking political capital out of them. It may well be that the true decline in standards is in our political rather than private morality.

iii *'A great shock'*

Meanwhile the Prime Minister asked the Lord Chancellor (Lord Dilhorne) to inquire into the security aspect. He did so and reported on it. The Commons debated it. The Prime Minister (Mr Harold Macmillan) declared:

A great shock has been given to Parliament and indeed to the whole country.

3 Morale at a low ebb

i *The moral issue*

The morale of the Government was by this time at a low ebb. Something had to be done. It was done. The Prime Minister invited me to conduct an inquiry: into the security aspect. He made it clear that I could also inquire into the truth or falsehood of rumours. He told the House of Commons on 21 June:

I have heard these terrible things being said about all sorts of people which, if allowed to go on, will destroy not only this side of the House of Commons but the other side of the House of Commons.

. . . I think the course of sending for Lord Denning, and asking anyone who feels himself aggrieved to ask for an inquiry into the rumours about him – apart from the technical side – is the best and, indeed, the only efficient way of getting the matter handled.

The course thus proposed proved right. I started my inquiry at once and finished it in three months. I cleared the ministers. The rumours were dead and buried. But even today people raise new points.

ii *The record of the evidence*

In December 1982 I gave evidence before a select Committee of the House of Commons. It was concerned with the keeping of public records. I was asked:

You yourself were in charge of a very famous inquiry 20-odd years ago . . . Would it be appropriate for many of those papers to be kept back for longer than 30 or 50 years?

I replied:

. . . They ought to be kept closed for more than 30 years, but I would not say for 100 . . . I should have thought . . . 50 years would be ample.

All the evidence of the inquiry was taken down in shorthand. The transcripts were kept secure in a special cabinet. I was told afterwards that they were destroyed. But Mr Callaghan when he was Prime Minister assured the House that they had not been. So they may be available to future generations of historians. But I do not think they would add anything to my Report except to give the names. Disclosure of the names might be hurtful to those concerned or their families. They should not be disclosed until 50 years have elapsed.

But I would add a word in vindication of some of those concerned or out of sympathy with them.

4 Some of the witnesses

i *Sir Roger Hollis*

In the last two or three years investigative journalists have been investigating the Security Service. They have had considerable success in disclosing past lapses. They have cast aspersions on the loyalty of Sir Roger Hollis. He was the Head of the Security Service at the time of the Profumo affair. They say that he was an agent of the Russians. He is now dead and unable to answer for himself. In fairness to his memory I would like to say that I do not believe the allegations. I trusted him completely. He was supported by his deputy. They knew all that was going on. One of their officers had reported that

If a scandal results from Mr Profumo's association with Christine Keeler, there is likely to be a considerable political rumpus. . . .

but they thought that that was essentially a political matter which was then in the hands of the politicians and not the concern of the Security Service. They were governed by a Directive issued by Sir David Maxwell Fyfe in 1952 which said that

It is essential that the Security Service should be kept absolutely free from any political bias or influence. . . .

Since I wrote those words, there has been a fresh development. On 16 July 1984 Mr Peter Wright – who had served in MI5 under Sir Roger Hollis – appeared on Granada Television's *World in Action* claiming that

intelligence-wise, it was 99 per cent certain that Sir Roger Hollis had worked for the other side.

This amazed everyone. Lord Trend had sifted through all the evidence and acquitted Sir Roger. I find myself in agreement with Sir William Hayter who wrote to *The Times:*

I naturally watched last night's programme about him [Sir Roger Hollis] with interest. I found it entirely unconvincing. If this is the best the critics of Sir Roger can do, they had better shut up.

Probably any unprejudiced person asked to choose between judgments by Lord Trend and by Mr Peter Wright would choose the former.

ii *Stephen Ward*

Likewise the investigative journalists publicised Stephen Ward again. They got information from officials in the Security Service. In consequence, in *The Sunday Times* of 28 November 1982 they said that Ward 'was in fact working for the security services' and that 'if the security services had spoken up for him, he might never have been driven to his death.'

I do not accept this for one moment. I was in a position to know all about him. He was the villain of the piece. It is quite ridiculous to suggest that he was working for MI5.

iii *Christine Keeler*

She was the leading lady. I saw her twice. I felt sorry for her. She was not the bright and beautiful creature who had held the centre of the stage. When she came before me she was tired and pale. She talked in a soft voice. She recounted her experiences in a matter-of-fact way. People should sympathise with her and not condemn her.

iv *Marilyn Rice-Davies*

She stole the show – so far as the newspapers were concerned. She was called by everyone Mandy. She has described her feelings in July 1963 (in the midst of my inquiry) in this entertaining passage:

The only certainty in my life on that summer afternoon was the fact that my place in history was already assured as a central figure in the biggest sex scandal of the century. Mandy Rice-Davies, or was it Randy Mice-Davies? Have you heard the one about? . . . Already a stream of Randy Mandy jokes was in circulation, record shops were selling a Mandy-inspired satirical album and cartoonists were stimulated at finding a new character to replace the tired politicians.

Everybody knew me. The girl with the bouffant blonde hair, expensive clothes, audacious hats and enough jewellery to keep the wolf from the door for a few years yet. Invariably they saw me getting out of an expensive car, or arriving at Heathrow. Mandy – always smiling. That was my public image.

When she came to see me, she was quietly dressed, quietly spoken, and to me quite an ordinary little girl; nervous, but I tried to put her at her ease.

On one occasion she was asked by an American for her name:

'Call me Lady Hamilton,' she said.

Some years later a television interviewer asked her:

'Do you still think of yourself as Lady Hamilton?'

'No, Nell Gwynne!' she replied.

One of her remarks has actually achieved a place in the *Oxford Dictionary of Quotations*[1]. It was on 29 June 1963 at the trial of Stephen Ward. When told that Lord Astor had denied her allegations, she said, 'He would, wouldn't he?'

v *A prostitute*

There was one woman who was a prostitute. She told a story about a minister who is now dead. She said that he used to visit her in her apartment and there indulged in acts of sexual perversion. He used to get satisfaction by whipping her. She gave a lot of corroborative detail. She had, during my inquiry, gone so far as to enter into a conditional contract with a newspaper and get a payment on account.

I put her story to the minister. I told him I was concerned about it. He asked if I would see his solicitor. I did so. I gave the result in my Report:

I was satisfied that much of what I was told was untrue. If in what remained there were any evidence of a security risk, I would of course, report it. But after the fullest investigation I am satisfied that in each case there is no evidence that national security has been or may be affected.

There I must leave it, without setting out the details, for I am quite satisfied that if I were to do so I would be playing into the hands of these

[1] (1979, 3rd edn).

362

informers. They would, I am sure, go back to the newspapers and sell their stories for a high price. And my inquiry would be turned by them, not only into a witch-hunt, but also into an instrument for their sordid gain. This would be so distasteful a result that I beg to be excused from lending any aid to it.

vi *A passport*

Even now, recollections still come in. In January 1983 I received a letter from Major J F E Clarke. He tells how my Report took the place of a passport. Here is what he says:

In September 1963 I was promoting British technology. I was flying from New York to Toronto. I discovered that I had left my passport in my hotel room in New York. The cabin staff told me I would not be allowed into Canada and would have to return. But I went to the immigration authorities at Toronto and explained my dilemma.

Gee, you just can't come in.'

'But I am British from London, England.'

'No. You can't come in.'

A sudden inspiration came to me. I opened my brief-case and took out a copy of the Profumo Report.

'Have you heard of the British Government's dilemma over the Profumo affair and the Lord Denning Report?'

'Gee, is that a copy of *The* Lord Denning's Report?'

'Yes, it is and it has only just been published in England. I will let you have it if you let me have a 24-hour permit.'

'Sir, just wait there while I see the Chief.'

I was taken to the Chief's office and given a certificate in exchange for the Denning Report. I got to my important meeting.

3 Mr Macmillan sums up

1 Previous instances

To end this discussion on rumour, I would give the summing-up by Mr Harold Macmillan in the House of Commons on 16 December 1963:

We all know that from time to time – it is nothing of which this age is particularly guilty; it has been true of all ages – there sweeps over the country or some part of it a strange sense of emotion in which the wildest rumours circulate and obtain, if not credence, at least a good deal of circulation.

I think of Titus Oates and the Gordon riots. I remember in my lifetime Mr Pemberton Billing, who created a great position and actually got himself elected to Parliament on what was nothing but the circulation of libellous rumours. He attracted at the time a certain emotion and a certain position. All we can now say is that the means of circulation of them are wider, but there is nothing new in this. What is difficult at such a time is for men to keep their heads and try to judge objectively and fairly and not allow themselves to be swayed either from one side or the other from what seems to them the honourable cause. At least, I am very glad, and I think that the House is glad, to feel that this is at an end.

2 The merit of the inquiry

Mr Macmillan concluded by saying that no political party should resort to the weapon of rumour. It should be put away and buried.

Great as may be the divisions of opinion, perhaps sometimes violent conflicts – and they should be so on high issues and great political questions – this weapon against members of our House, of whatever side, whether in or out of office, is one which should be spurned and which has been, happily – this is the great merit of this form of inquiry – put altogether away.

So by my inquiry the rumours were put away. The ministers were cleared. That was the great merit of it. Justice was done.

3 His letter to me

On my retirement Mr Macmillan wrote me this letter, which I treasure:

28 July 1982

Dear Lord Denning,

I feel impelled to write to you now that your long and distinguished career as a judge is coming to an end.

My reasons are twofold. First I owe you a great debt of gratitude for the kindness which you did to me nearly twenty years ago at a very difficult and delicate time in my life as Prime Minister. I never shall forget the trouble which you took, the goodness of heart which you showed and the understanding which you displayed. I do not know whether at the time I was able to express to you my real gratitude for I was very soon taken desperately ill. Anyway it all comes back to me now and I want you to know that I shall not forget your kindness.

Secondly I have always been interested in the law and made some attempt to study it at one time. It seems to me that there were two different streams in English law which sometimes meant that on the whole their waters did not mix. The first has become much more prevalent since the vast mass of legislation which has been passed in the last one hundred and fifty years tends to base itself on a somewhat pedantic or at any rate a very close interpretation of the words of an Act of Parliament. The second which goes back to the great periods of the 17th and 18th century tends to base itself more upon commonsense, equity (in the non-technical sense), fairplay and justice. Of these the greatest proponents were perhaps Lord Mansfield and Lord Camden. To them will be added the name of Lord Denning.

Yours very sincerely,
Harold Macmillan

On his 90th birthday Mr Macmillan was made an Earl. I was present when he was introduced in the Lords. He was frail in body but alert in mind as ever. A very great man.

365

Epilogue

You may wonder how I spend my time now that I have retired. I can get about reasonably well. I am very glad that I have a new hip. Otherwise I should be in a wheel-chair. I go to London once or twice a week for various things there. But for the most part I am at Whitchurch.

My library

Much of my time is spent in my library. It fills the shelves of two large rooms of our Regency house. It is, I believe, the best collection of law books in private hands. All the reported cases in England for four centuries. All the Common Market cases from its beginning. Thousands upon thousands of cases. The volumes increase year by year. I sometimes wonder whether our system of case law will stand the strain. The weight is not relieved by our modern research tools like 'Lexis' and 'Eurolex'. They only aggravate it. They tell you, not only of reported cases, but also of unreported cases. So there are more to look up.

I have also a goodly collection of the classics of English history and literature. They are the source of much of what I have written here.

Here, then, are my tools of trade. It is with them that I have worked all my life. As Mr Winston Churchill said in a radio message to President Roosevelt in 1941 when we were fighting alone:

Give us the tools, and we will finish the job.

Epilogue

Cricket

I take an interest in all that goes on in Whitchurch. Especially in our village cricket. Our club is nearly 200 years old. Almost as old as that at Hambledon where the game was first played. As I told you in *The Closing Chapter* (page 23) our ground is in a perfect setting. We can say with Edmund Blunden:[1]

> On the green they watch'd their sons
> Playing till too dark to see,
> As their fathers watch'd them once,
> As my father once watch'd me.

I was able to tell something of a like ground in the landmark case of *Miller v Jackson*.[2] You may like to read it:

In summertime village cricket is the delight of everyone. Nearly every village has its own cricket field where the young men play and the old men watch. In the village of Lintz in County Durham they have their own ground, where they have played these last 70 years. They tend it well. The wicket area is well rolled and mown. The outfield is kept short. It has a good club house for the players and seats for the onlookers. The village team play there on Saturdays and Sundays. They belong to a league, competing with the neighbouring villages. On other evenings after work they practise while the light lasts. Yet now after these 70 years a judge of the High Court has ordered that they must not play there any more. He has issued an injunction to stop them. He has done it at the instance of a newcomer who is no lover of cricket. This newcomer has built, or has had built for him, a house on the edge of the cricket ground which four years ago was a field where cattle grazed. The animals did not mind the cricket. But now this adjoining field has been turned into a housing estate. The newcomer bought one of the houses on the edge of the cricket ground. No doubt the open space was a selling point. Now he complains that when a batsman hits a six the ball has been known to land in his garden or on or near his house. His wife has got so upset about it that they always go out at weekends. They do not go into the garden when cricket is being played. They say that this is intolerable. So they asked the judge to stop the cricket being played. And the judge, much against his will, has felt that he must order the cricket to be stopped: with the consequence, I suppose, that the Lintz Cricket Club will disappear.

[1] *Forefathers.*
[2] [1977] QB 966.

370

The cricket ground will be turned to some other use. I expect for more houses or a factory. The young men will turn to other things instead of cricket. The whole village will be much the poorer. And all this because of a newcomer who has just bought a house there next to the cricket ground.

I came to this conclusion:

In a new situation like this, we have to think afresh as to how discretion should be exercised. On the one hand, Mrs Miller is a very sensitive lady who has worked herself up into such a state that she exclaimed to the judge: 'I just want to be allowed to live in peace . . . Have I got to wait until someone is killed before anything can be done?' If she feels like that about it, it is quite plain that, for peace in the future, one or other has to move. Either the cricket club has to move: but goodness knows where. I do not suppose for a moment there is any field in Lintz to which they could move. Or Mrs Miller must move elsewhere. As between their conflicting interests, I am of opinion that the public interest should prevail over the private interest. The cricket should not be driven out.

Our club at Whitchurch is in no such danger. We are well supported. On the first Sunday in August, Lincoln's Inn came down again to play Whitchurch. This year Lincoln's Inn won on the last ball but one. A thrilling finish.

A walk around

Come on a fine day and I will take you for a walk around our grounds here, telling you about them as we go. Let us go first through the 'water meadows.' They are given that name because, in the old days, twice a year they were flooded with water from the river, controlled by the hatches. They were so fertile that they yielded two crops a year. That system of agriculture has long been abandoned. In its place we have planted poplars in long straight rows. That was 20 years ago. At that time they were said to be useful to make matchsticks. But the market is now supplied from overseas. Look at them now. They are fine tall trees. As I walk through them in the evening, I repeat to myself the words of the song:

And sometimes in the evening time apart,
The tall trees whisper, whisper heart to heart;
From my fond lips the eager answers fall,
Thinking I hear thee, thinking I hear thee call.

Look on either side as we walk along. The undergrowth is thick. It gives shelter for the young pheasants. The wild flowers are springing up. The kingcups are just over. The yellow flags begin to show their heads. There is the meadowsweet – as lovely as its name. Rabbits dig holes all about. They are a nuisance. Charlie with a ferret drives them from their burrows and gets rid of them.

You will notice these pathways where we walk. They have to be kept clear. We call them 'rides' because they used to be for horses. Now Charlie drives his tractor along them. He has to cross three wooden bridges over the streams to get here. He cuts a long swath through the trees to make these ways.

We are now getting out of the poplar plantation. Look ahead. There is the lush meadow bright with buttercups. See that little barn on its staddle stones. That is the one we moved brick by brick and rebuilt here. Now let us turn on our way back. Here is a broad avenue between the poplars. Further on we come to a hazel coppice. We pass through it and reach the footbridge. Here we are at the river again. We are nearing home.

Pause a moment. There is always something moving on the river. If you are quick enough, you may see a flash of blue like lightning. It is a kingfisher. As Faber put it:[1]

There came
Swift as a meteor's shining flame,
A kingfisher from out the brake,
And almost seemed to leave a wake
Of brilliant hues behind.

Look at those wagtails. We have both pied and grey here. Scores of them. Flitting at great pace above the water, feeding on the fly. As you pass, the ducks take to the water,

[1] *The Cherwell.*

372

with their broods of tiny ducklings. The coots have their
nests in midstream. The swans sail majestically by. Water
rats – they are really voles – bore holes in the banks.

Stop! There's a heron. Be quiet. Don't move. He stands
stock still in the water, ready to strike at a fish with his long
saw-like beak. He can see you 100 yards away. If you move a
muscle or blink an eyelid, he will see you and be off.

The best dry fly fishing anywhere in the world is on our
river. It rises four miles up. It is only 18 inches deep here. The
weed grows profusely below the water. Charlie cuts it at the
times agreed with others on the river. Our friends come to
fish. Last year Sir Max Williams, when he was President of
the Law Society, came with his son-in-law. They caught five
brace on the midday rise. It was a record. Look a little
downstream. As it happens, another friend of ours has come
to fish today, Sir Peter Bristow. He is a judge of the High
Court. He is fishing from the bank. He sees a fine trout above
the gravel bed. He casts a fly to tempt him. The fish is wise.
He ignores it. Time after time it happens. It would try the
patience of Job. But there! At last the fish has risen to the fly.
He takes it. Quick! A sharp jerk with the line. He is hooked.
He tries to get away. He turns and twists, upstream,
downstream, across stream. Let out the line, pull it in, keep it
taut. Gradually nearing the bank. Get out the net. He is
caught. He is landed. A knock on the head. He is dead. A
two-pounder. A beautiful brown trout. He is native. Not
like the rainbow. Now you know why fishermen love the
sport. And why I like Tennyson:[1]

> I come from haunts of coot and hern,
> I make a sudden sally
> And sparkle out among the fern,
> To bicker down a valley.

Now over the bridge and into the garden. I told you about it
last year. Like today, it was a glorious day in June.
Everything growing apace in the bright sunshine.

[1] *The Brook.*

The family

We still carry on. My brother Reg has just had his 90th birthday this June. We went over to Kent to join him and Eileen. They are in good form. All their family were there too.

At home here, my son Robert often brings his two small boys, Mark and Paul – aged 10 and 8 – to play in the garden. They leap on the swing across the river. They paddle fast in the canoe. They fall in and squeal. They rush round the paths on their little bicycles. They practice with bat and ball on the lawn. They are shaping well. Our greatest joy is the happiness of family life.

'Think on these things'

There it is. I have written these six books for you. In them I hope you will find material for the thoughts expressed by St Paul long years ago:[1]

> Whatsoever things are true,
> whatsoever things are honest,
> whatsoever things are just,
> whatsoever things are pure,
> whatsoever things are lovely,
> whatsoever things are of good report;
> if there be any virtue,
> and if there be any praise,
> think on these things.

[1] *Philippians* 4:8.

Index

Fox, Charles James
Bill on judges' directions, 292
Foxe, John
More's whipping of heretics, on, 74
trial of Ridley and Latimer, on, 92 *et seq.*
Frampton, Mr
action over Tolpuddle Martyrs, 106–107, 109
Francis, Sir Philip. *See* Junius
Freedom of assembly
Law Commission's proposal, 168–169
Universal Declaration of Human Rights on, 133
unlawful assembly,
Chartists, 165
common law, 139
Garden House Hotel, at, 166–167
Law Commission report, 164, 169
meaning, 163–164
nuclear protesters, 168
radical reformers, 154 *et seq.*
Salvation Army found not guilty of, 165–166
violent miners, 168–169
See also Demonstrations; Hunt, Henry; Mead, William; Penn, William
Freedom of individual
detention under Regulation 18B, 229–230, 231–233
exclusion, power of, 234
habeas corpus. *See* Habeas Corpus
misprision. *See* Misprision
secondary to security of state, 228, 234–235
slavery. *See* Slavery
Freedom of press
blasphemy. *See* Blasphemy
letters of *Junius*, 284–290
proceedings in Parliament, 290–292
See also Libel

Gaddafi, Colonel, 246
Garden House Hotel
unlawful assembly at, 166–167

Gardiner, Lord
terrorism in Northern Ireland, on, 228–229, 236
Gay News
appeal in case of, 303–304
blasphemous material in, 301
private prosecution of, 302
trial,
argument on law, 302
opinions on verdict, 305–306
ruling on law, 302, 303
summing-up, 303
verdict, 303
General warrant
authors, printers and publishers of *The North Briton*, issued against, 262–264
illegality of, 267–268, 277
Lord Camden's judgment on, 271
right to issue, 259
test case on, 270–271
George III
death of, 178
delight at marriage of George, Prince of Wales, 178
George IV
affair with Mrs Fitzherbert, 177–178
directs alteration of *Book of Common Prayer*, 178
wants divorce from Queen Caroline, 177, 179
See also Caroline, Queen
Gifts
acceptance by judge, 79–80
Glynn, Serjeant
appears for John Wilkes, 274
request for writ of habeas corpus, 264, 266
Goddard, Lord
appeal in case of *Sykes v DPP*, 240
knowledge of trial of *Bardell v Pickwick*, 194
misprision of felony, on, 241–242
Goodhart, Arthur
advice to Lord Denning, 173
Government Communications Headquarters
trade unions barred from, 124–125, 236